Banksters

and

Prairie Boys

Monier M. Rahall

©Monier Rahall 1997

First Edition

Canadian Cataloguing in Publication Data

Rahall, Monier, 1960 -

Banksters and Prairie Boys

Includes index
ISBN 0-9681810-0-7

1. Alberta - Politics and government   2. Alberta Treasury Branches   3. Banking scandal
4. Ralph. Klein

1. Title

332.12'24

Printed and bound in Canada by Hignell Printing Ltd.

Published by: Monopoly
                Suite 1044
                11444 - 119 Street
                Edmonton AB T5G 2Y6

Visit the World Wide Web page at: http://www.duban.com/banksters

To Mohana and Ahsan for their love and support and especially to my daughter, Monet, who made the future very important and worth fighting for.

ACKNOWLEDGMENT

I have many people to thank for their aid and input in the writing of this book. Without them, it would not have been possible. It is customary for the author to list the names of those who have contributed to the writing of a book in one way or another. However, I shall break from custom in this instance and not name names. Because of the nature of the material contained in the book, their anonymity is to protect their security and their livelihoods, not because of lack of appreciation. To all those who assisted me with information, time, and expertise, I thank you. You know who you are. Some will recognize veiled tips of the hat within the text. Any errors or omissions are mine and mine alone. Oh, and thanks to singer, Connie Francis. You'll see why in a moment.

TABLE OF CONTENTS

PART ONE: EVERYBODY'S SOMEBODY'S FOOL
Things don't always turn out the way you expect. A sick economy, government policies, and unethical professionals come together at one time to trigger my demise.

In which the economic policies of the provincial government contribute to the downfall of the City of Edmonton and in which I seek the assistance of the Alberta Treasury Branches, discovering instead, rampant corruption throughout the organization.

In which Coopers & Lybrand, one of the six largest accounting firms in the world, sells its integrity and in which I discover they were financial whores, the only question being whether they were for sale or rent.

In which I discover how to start a financial Armageddon from the ATB and how I became radioactive.

In which I find out that the higher I climbed and examined the rungs of ATB's corporate ladder, the greater and more devious the corruption became.

In which I learn that the Law Society of Alberta truly protects its own regardless of whether its members are innocent or guilty and pays lip service to the humble client.

PART TWO: WHERE THE BOYS ARE

PART THREE: WHO'S SORRY NOW?

I battle the legal system and the backroom boys of politics in Alberta and discover how they control government policy and certain legal decisions. The spin doctors then attempt damage control, but a sow's ear will always remain a sow's ear no matter the amount of make-up or magic.

"It is not the critic who counts; not the man who points out how the strong man stumbles, or where the doer of deeds could have done them better. The credit belongs to the man who is actually in the arena, whose face is marred by dust and sweat and blood; who strives valiantly; who errs, and comes short again and again; because there is not effort without error and shortcoming; but who does actually strives to do the deeds; who knows the great enthusiasms, the great devotions; who spends himself in a worthy cause, who at the best knows in the end the triumphs of high achievement and who at the worst, if he fails, at least fails while daring greatly, so that his place shall never be with those cold and timid souls who know neither victory nor defeat."

- THEODORE ROOSEVELT

INTRODUCTION

"Sometimes truth comes riding into history on the back of error."

-Reinhold Niebuhr

While researching this book, I came across a commemorative history of the Alberta Treasury Branches entitled "Treasured Memories - A Celebration of Alberta Treasury Branches 50th Anniversary" published in 1988. Mike Byfield of Alberta Report Magazine wrote in his introduction: "The reliance on personal integrity is valid grounds for concern. Nevertheless virtually no scandal has attached itself to the Treasury Branches in 50 years." Mr. Byfield obviously spoke too soon. He may want to reconsider his words.

The periods of consecutive Progressive Conservative governments have helped to forge a culture for the ethically-challenged and the degree of willful blindness that is demanded of both the Alberta Treasury Branches and the Alberta Government employees. What has offended me the most is their sense of infallibility in this massive cover up, thinking that they would never be exposed. Premier Ralph Klein, the current captain of the team, has shown himself to be the Attila The Hun of political corruption. Contrary to the vaunted arm's length description, this book will confirm that the relationship between the Government of Alberta and the Alberta Treasury Branches is more messed up than Ralph Klein during Calgary Stampede Week. An election day win by the Progressive Conservatives has become known in Alberta Treasury Branches' circles as "loan day." This book will prove to you, dear reader, that politics is indeed the art of the possible.

I will also bring to light the Alberta business versions of Rasputin, the controlling influences of the Alberta Government and the Alberta Treasury Branches, éminences grises such as the Ghermezians (West Edmonton Mall) and Mr. Pocklington (Gainers and the Edmonton Oilers) to mention just a few.

I suppose that like most projects, what follows in these pages is quite different from the project I had envisioned at the outset. I had originally planned to deal with the evolution of the Canadian banking system as a whole and its inequities and injustices. I had planned to incorporate a couple of brief chapters concerning my own travails with the Alberta Treasury Branches as a part of the larger work. But, the more research I did for those chapters, the more I realized the depth of corruption and mismanagement within the Alberta Treasury Branches and, in fact, the Government of Alberta itself. The cry for the subject to be dealt with in detail on its own and the fact that the individuals involved tasked me with their abuse became an overpowering impetus to bring this corruption to light. Because I dared to expose it, I was subject to unthinkable abuse of the process, all funded by the Alberta Treasury Branches. The result is what follows.

This story is told from a decidedly personal perspective and relates some of my experiences battling through a Company Creditors Arrangement Act and subsequent insolvency proceedings. You will learn, as I did, that the system does not always work as we suspect or expect; and in fact, it is highly dependent upon the credibility and integrity of all the parties involved--the professionals, the bank officials, the judiciary, the politicians and of course in this case, the bureaucrats. Due process and integrity have been sacrificed on the altar of financial expedience. It may appear to you that this tale might be one of Shakespearean complexity, but fear not. All shall be revealed.

These are the symptoms and examples of the system as it now exists in Alberta; but it is not enough to merely list these failures and shortcomings. There must exist a state or a pre-condition that allows the system or culture to evolve as it has. What really becomes important is the process that brings about that end result. In essence, the actual result can sometimes be moot. The Bolsheviks existed in Russia before the First World War, but the pre-conditions as a result of World War I caused the failure of the provisional government after the Czar's abdication and the opportunity for them to take power in the Russian Revolution. In the space of a few months, Lenin went from virtual obscurity in exile to the leader of a Soviet government. Consider also the Great Depression of the 1930s. Would it have been as severe without the banks exercising a tight money policy? To ponder another example, would Hitler have been able to gain power in Germany leading to the Second World War without the punitive conditions of the Versailles Treaty? Every period in history has a set of pre-conditions which determine the way events unfold.

Canadian history has always had connections between the banks and politicians; but in the case of Alberta, this relationship has been refined and perfected. The Alberta Treasury Branches, a so-called near bank, did not even have a board, as was traditional with the established national banks. It was supposedly run in an arm's length relationship with the government of the Province of Alberta; but as we shall see, this was a convenient fiction to promote. Banks have always had the political influence to lobby governments and win favourable financial legislation. Yet Alberta goes a little farther in that the government actually approves some loans directly, especially when those loans are for the party faithful and the political friends of the government. A clear example of this was the notorious West Edmonton Mall refinancing that I shall revisit in detail later.

The censure that befalls an individual who goes up against this established system reminds me of St. Augustine's story of Alexander the Great and the pirate. When Alexander captured the pirate and had him brought before him, he asked how dare the pirate molest the sea. "How dare you molest the World?"

answered the pirate. Because he was an individual capturing ships and pillaging the countryside, Alexander's prisoner was considered to be a pirate. When Alexander did the same thing at the head of a massive army, he was considered a great emperor. In this story, I guess I might be considered the pirate (at least in the symbolic sense). Many of my friends and associates never understood why I refused to give up and concede to the demands and threats of the Government of Alberta and the Alberta Treasury Branches--why I continued to dare to beard the lion in his own den. The simple answer is that it is not my nature to give up, and quitting was not an option. In the words of a famous Civil War General when asked to surrender, "I would rather die a thousand deaths," he replied. In a business sense, I sometimes felt that I did die a thousand times. If anyone does not believe that politics and the business of banking have not become intertwined blood sports in Alberta, then it is quite obvious that they have never stepped into that financial arena.

It has been said that real understanding comes from those who live within a particular situation. I truly believe that. Various books have examined the financial system and bankruptcy laws from a coldly analytical perspective. Their authors are either outside observers or banking industry apologists. In contrast, my point of view comes from within and as I lived it.

It has also been said that winners usually write history and that nobody cares for the bloodied soldier when the battle is over. Yes, the economic and political winners do write financial history, with the result that some of the questionable ethics and the tactics of the Alberta Treasury Branches and the Alberta Government get ignored or covered up. As Shakespeare said, "The devil can quote Scripture for his own purpose", a technique seized upon by the Auditor General of the Province of Alberta to rewrite history.

This is a memoir of a sometimes heart-rending, soul-destroying experience with the Alberta Treasury Branches, the government and judiciary. It's a warts-and-all description of what it's like to challenge the system and the accepted means of bankruptcy proceedings as practiced in Alberta. After my experience, I think that I can appreciate what it might be like to wrestle a herd of rhinoceros. I take no delight in what happened. I made mistakes, but this is not an apology. If it could have been done differently, by all means, I would have preferred it.

The value in this dubious experience is that I saw the corruption, the expediency, and the inequities of the system first hand. Most people in Alberta, I think, view the banking industry as some gray, faceless entity, that if they spend any time thinking about it all (aside from a place to cash a pay cheque or arrange a mortgage), would characterize it as benign. Perhaps this book will act as a wake-up call for some or a touchstone for others in their own battles. If even a modicum of increased fairness, honesty, and ethics are insinuated into the system, I will feel vindicated.

There is one additional note to help you get the sense of what you will discover in the following pages. As I edit this in the winter of 1996, events continue to unfold. I do not yet know what the final outcome of my particular case will be, but what will become evident is that the Alberta Treasury Branches have already been changed. Voltaire's assertion, nearly three hundred years ago that the pen is indeed mightier than the sword, rings true today. I am still in the eye of the financial hurricane. For that reason, I think that the points and observations contained in this book become even more valid. They have not yet been subject to the rationalization and erosion of time. This might strike some of you as self-serving. Perhaps. I believe that the sense of immediacy, of the ongoing struggle, contributes its own legitimacy. That struggle gives the feel of the predicament that businessmen/entrepreneurs can find themselves in. However, the final verdict rests with you, the reader. In my opinion, the true value of this manuscript will be judged by the ability to expose the inadequacies and injustices of the way in which the Alberta Treasury Branches and the Government of Alberta handled my particular case and the "Catch-22" trap of the bankruptcy system. I fervently hope that it inspires, encourages, and awakens the Yossarian in all of us.

Because of the practices exposed in this book and the description of the ethics of certain individuals well-known in the professional community of Alberta, this book is bound to be controversial. So be it. In their time, Jesus, Galileo, Martin Luther, and even Wilbur and Orville Wright were all controversial. While I certainly do not try to compare myself to them, I believe controversy is sometimes a necessary and cathartic element to expose the truth in its purest form. There is no politically correct way to accomplish this. Unlike Martin Luther, however, I rejected the idea of nailing my 95 complaints to the door of the Legislature. I wrote this book instead.

If there is one sustaining thought or rationale for struggling against the system with this book, I would sum it up best with St. Barton's Ode: "I am hurt but I am not slain! I will lie me down and bleed awhile--then I'll rise and fight again."

PART ONE

EVERYBODY'S SOMEBODY'S FOOL

CHAPTER 1
THE TENOR GETS STABBED

"It's like the ancient story of Milo of Croton, who is supposed to have lifted a calf every day until he was lifting a full-grown bull."

- Isaac Asimov

The essence of an opera (aside from the music) is the outlandish story-lines or libretti with their larger-than-life occurrences and descriptions of great tragedies. When the leading man, the tenor, gets stabbed, he does not bleed. Rather, he bursts into a plaintive aria. This book, Banksters and Prairie Boys, is my aria. As you will see, every other avenue was closed or taken away from me. All that was left after the stabbing was to embrace the drama's absurdity and sing. "Pity me not but lend thy serious hearing to what I shall unfold."

A dispute that started with one branch of the Alberta Treasury Branches (ATB), a dispute that should have been easily resolved, escalated out of all proportion to the amount of the loan involved. Soon I was fighting with the entire organization of ATB and then the Government of Alberta as well. I began to feel like Milo in Isaac Asimov's observation in this chapter's epigraph. The corruption of ATB employees and the continued cover up of that corruption meant that the escalation took on a life of its own. What started out as a problem over a simple bank loan became one of the most serious of banking scandals in Canada. I would not hesitate to say *even* in North America.

Let me first clarify one thing. I am the son of immigrants, not an immigrant myself. I was born and raised in the City of Edmonton, Alberta, and I was spawned from the humblest beginnings. I am a capitalist and fiscally conservative. Now that the ideological parameters have been identified and established, you can, perhaps, view the world through my prism for the following pages since some background is necessary to understand the paradigm in which I lived and functioned.

My business and real estate beginnings were in the mid-1980s. At the peak of my holdings in the early 1990s, I had acquired nearly 100 million dollars in real estate, as well as several diverse operating companies including office furniture retail, an international car rental agency, a new car dealership, automotive service and brake centres, an auto wrecker, and a day-care. These assets and operating companies were controlled by nearly fifty Alberta corporations. What went wrong? The majority of my assets were based in the City of Edmonton, which suffered the majority of the Klein government cuts to the public service. The effect was devastating.

The City of Edmonton ranked 103 out of 103 surveyed cities around the world in rental rates for commercial office space, which translates into the lowest values. To give you an idea how ghostly the downtown core of Edmonton appears now, City Council, it was rumoured, was considering changing the name of the main downtown artery from Jasper Avenue to Casper Avenue. Residential vacancy rates went from three to four percent in the late 1980's to double-digit vacancy rates in 1993 and continuing through to 1995. All of this occurred in a so-called "have" province. Out of all the major centres in Canada, Edmonton, by far, had the highest residential vacancy rate even surpassing that of St. John's, Newfoundland. According to an article in The Edmonton Sun, June 26, 1996, job losses, not personal debt, was the cause of record high bankruptcy rates. In fact, Edmonton had registered its thirty-first straight month of record business and consumer failures.

Notice how closely this period dovetails with the Klein government's term of office. World economists view two negative quarters as a recession. What would they think of eight negative quarters? The term is depression. These record failures coincided with the downsizing of public service employees, comprising a significantly higher percentage of the workforce in Edmonton than in Calgary. Edmonton Councilor, Allan Bolstad, filed a report in Edmonton City Council which showed that between July 1994 and July 1995, Edmonton lost 9,700 public administrator jobs and 1,100 salaried employees while Calgary lost barely 100 positions.[1] The trend to favour Calgary over Edmonton continued apace. By ripping the heart out of the public service sector of Edmonton's economy so quickly, the Progressive Conservatives' medicine in this instance killed the patient. In the case of Edmonton, the Klein Government gave no consideration to the effects on the city. These severe cuts had a multiplier effect on the balance of the

Edmonton economy, much like the pebble dropped into the glassy water of a large pond, the ripples touched every shore, near and far. These cuts reached each and every business owner. There was no one who could check this slash-and-burn mentality of the Klein government effectively. Mr. Klein, a former mayor of the City of Calgary, finished the job that was started by Mr. Peter Lougheed in making Calgary Alberta's Premier city, if you will pardon the pun. Mr. Lougheed attracted corporate head offices to Calgary by giving loan guarantees (Canadian Airlines International, for example) and other considerations which instilled a strong private sector for that city which would long out-live Mr. Lougheed's tenure as Premier of Alberta.

Mr. Lougheed's timing was perfect when he stepped down as the leader of the Progressive Conservatives (PCs). The effects of the National Energy Program had begun to take its toll on the Alberta economy. Unfortunately for his successor, Don Getty, the oil revenues were drastically reduced by the time he was in full control. His legacy to the Progressive Conservative Party would be a series of failed loan guarantees from which too many of the government's friends benefited and too few questions were asked. Mr. Getty did not have the talent to keep the backroom deals under wraps. Fortunately for Mr. Klein, the oil revenues bounced back and enhanced his public profile. Does time make the man or does the man make the time? I have heard that some oil executives (primarily located in Calgary) do not want Premier Klein's

---

[1] The Edmonton Sun. "Bolstad Blasts Klein Cuts." Wednesday, June 26, 1996.

22

reputation damaged by this book, as they consider him good for their bottom line. However, in the same breath, they candidly admit that he is not someone whom people envisage as the Premier of Alberta. His popularity has been solidified by rising oil revenues.

One of the duties of a government is to ensure that there is a conducive environment in which business can thrive. Unfortunately, the government did not understand this concept when it came to Edmonton. Edmonton has now been so disadvantaged that even a rising economic tide would not lift the boat.

In early December 1996, the Klein government admitted that it slashed and burned health care without having a real plan or without understanding the ramifications of their actions fully-- what many suspected from the beginning. Mr. Klein no more understood the effects of cuts to the health care system than he could perform an aria from "La Bohème." And, as with the health care system, the approach taken with the City of Edmonton was quite similar. Once again, Edmonton received the brunt of those health care cuts in comparison with Calgary. "Then Edmonton's four-year budget target is a 19.9 percent reduction compared to just 14.9 percent in Calgary."[2] The only difference is that the Klein government has not yet admitted its error in this regard, proving that any jackass can kick down a barn.

---

[2] The Edmonton Journal. "Health Cuts Deepest in Edmonton." Saturday, June 8, 1996.

Mr. Klein knew that he would not receive any opposition to his plans. First, his caucus did not include anybody from the City of Edmonton and second, the Liberal opposition was incapable of protecting its Edmonton constituents. As Mr. Klein himself alluded to in the <u>Edmonton Journal</u> on Friday, April 19, 1996, the Government would be able to serve the City of Edmonton if it had more Conservative representatives. "That is the political reality. You're always served better by the Government than the Opposition." This is an admission that the City of Edmonton has been treated as the poor cousin in order to send a message because the City voted against the status quo: Don't do it again since you have seen what can happen. The result was that the capital was severely punished for its audacity, so Mr. Klein's argument is very lame indeed. In a nutshell, Edmonton did not benefit by voting Tory for many years, and then it was even more severely disadvantaged for voting against the Tories. I daresay that nobody would question that Edmonton has borne the brunt of Mr. Klein's economic policies. Mr. Klein is not a businessman and he has never been in business. The fact is that Mr. Klein has been too swept up in his own euphoria to consider the inevitable economic fallout, if indeed he could recognize it. We may not ever see the full impact of such policies until several years hence.

As real estate values began to plummet in Edmonton, my natural inclination was to start restructuring debt. I thought that I would begin with the wholly-owned bank of the Alberta Government, the Alberta Treasury Branches. This was for two reasons. First, that the policies of the Alberta government and their effects on Edmonton's economy would be best understood by the Alberta Treasury Branches, the government bank. (In fact, the ATB was set up in the 1930s by Social Credit Premier Bill Aberhart to accommodate and be more sensitive to Albertans' banking needs and to deflect the influence of the eastern-based Canadian Banking System.) Second, the perception in financial circles is that the ATB is a "soft" lender. In other words, a bank with which loan agreements and debt restructuring might be more easily negotiated in comparison with other financial institutions; but in my case, there was a boomerang effect. The financial community of Edmonton thought that if I could not make a deal with ATB, then I could not make a deal with anyone. I felt that if I had the blessing of the Alberta Treasury Branches, I would be assured of a successful completion and restructuring under the Company Creditors Arrangement Act (CCAA).

Unfortunately, that was not to be how it turned out. I was seriously misled by the legal and insolvency professionals on whom I had counted to carry out the restructuring. As you will see throughout this book, time and time again Coopers & Lybrand was willing to sell its integrity in my case as well as others. Their questionable ethics and outright conflict of interest assured that the CCAA was doomed to fail, with the result being that I was petitioned into bankruptcy. The gory details of the deception and the failed CCAA will be discussed fully later; but for now, it is enough to know none of the damage done to both sides over the last two years had to happen. What makes this story so tragic for all parties involved, not only me, is that all of the damage could have been avoided so very easily. Had the Alberta Treasury Branches and its employees and agents done their jobs ethically and competently, the outcome would have been entirely different and, in fact, you would not be reading these words.

Does the flapping of a butterfly's wings in China cause a hurricane in Florida? In my case, the answer is definitely yes! I was expected to lay down and accept the abuse and be dispatched quickly. However, that is not my style. I could not begin to have my life nor my family's life, as well as the lives of many of my associates destroyed and disrupted and no one be held accountable. The book is a chronicle of my struggle and the forced reclamation of the Alberta Treasury Branches and the Alberta Government from their culture of willful blindness and political corruption. It consists, in part, of letters that I wrote to various Alberta Treasury Branch officials, Provincial Government Ministers, and bureaucrats. While some of the letters actually appear here, most of the information about the wilful blindness and political corruption was contained in letters sent to these Government officials to answer and verify, which they refused to do. In these letters, I focused on a number of areas in which the ATB and its employees, with full knowledge of the government (including the supposed watchdog guarding the Alberta taxpayers money, the Auditor General) acted unethically. I wrote these letters to ask a series of questions as research material for this book, seeking reaction initially, but also hoping for validation and confirmation. Some of the most revealing responses shine light on the personality and motivation of the individuals involved. Some chapters primarily consist of this correspondence because in those particular instances, the story was told first and best in those letters. The letters were written so that only a few details of each issue raised were revealed in any particular letter. I preferred to gently peel the onion rather than rudely slice into it. As you will see, the damage control evolved with each layer and letter.

CHAPTER 2
"LET'S HAVE A LITTLE LOOK-SEE!"

"Trust in Allah, but tie up your camel."

- Turkish Proverb

The title of this chapter comes from a euphemism used by the practitioners of insolvency. In an effort to see the manner in which the creditors can proceed, the creditors ask the debtor to have someone such as Coopers & Lybrand come in and review the debtor's financial situation. That is, "have a little look-see." This is one of the gravest illusions in insolvency that only a Las Vegas act like Siegfried and Roy might appreciate. The debtor mistakenly assumes that the professionals are there to help. Actually, I take that back. They *are* there to help--to help themselves, not the debtor. What follows is a comedy of errors by one of the largest accounting firms in the world. Most works like mine include the disclaimer, "the names have been changed to protect the innocent." Since most of the individuals involved in this story were not innocent, it saved me a lot of work.

In order to understand this, one must view it through the standard operating procedures of these insolvency practitioners and it's worth its weight in beans. A corporation such as Coopers & Lybrand goes out to a company's site to review all records and operations of the debtor. This is usually paid for by the creditor. Now, the insolvency practitioner has to report back to the creditor, while always protecting themselves to the detriment of both the creditor and the debtor. They do this using the following methodology of reporting. First, if there are no assets in the debtor's corporation, the insolvency practitioner will report back with the assessment that the situation is severe with no hope of saving it. In this case, which is the debtor's best protection, the creditor cannot justify paying fees to the insolvency practitioners without recovering any of its losses.

In a second scenario, if the debtor does have substantial assets left, the insolvency practitioners usually report back that the company should be put into receivership, as they do not see restructuring as a viable alternative. Let me explain why. In a corporate restructuring proceeding, the practitioners of insolvency must work with the debtor hand-in-hand with a no better than a 50/50 chance that such restructuring will be successful. The final outcome is this: If a company has no assets, the practitioners of insolvency are at risk with very little reward. If the corporation has assets, by putting it into receivership or bankruptcy, they can earn a substantial fee without risk. According to a study of commercial bankruptcies in 1995, trustees and legal experts benefit the most in a bankruptcy. Fifty percent of the assets liquidated were devoured by administrative costs.[3] They do not like to recommend restructuring because the fees are not as lucrative, and they will most certainly take the blame for any failed restructuring. This failure can affect

---

[3] The Globe and Mail. Wednesday, October 11, 1995. "Trustees, Lawyers Benefit from Bankruptcies."

their relationship in regards to future work and income from the creditor. Therefore, this situation has a high risk factor and is the least likely alternative to be chosen.

If anyone thinks that there is any integrity in the system, especially bankruptcy and insolvency work, then they have been misguided. In this case, Coopers & Lybrand, one of the Big Six accounting firms, sold its integrity time and time again to the Alberta Treasury Branches. The question is not whether they were insolvency whores, but rather if Coopers & Lybrand was for sale or just for rent.

At the writing of this book, the employees of Coopers & Lybrand, Edmonton, are currently under investigation by the disciplinary mechanism of the Canadian Institute of Chartered Accountants (CICA). (As a side note, the CICA has appointed a gentleman by the name of Ian Strang to investigate the matter and report to the Professional Conduct Committee. Mr. Strang's claim to fame was earned during his years with the firm of Ernst Young as the receiver who seized control of the Gainers operation from the infamous Peter Pocklington. Mr. Strang is also a well-known as one of the Tory faithfuls.) What can be seen in this book over and over again is that when the Alberta Treasury Branches had to do anything amoral, Coopers & Lybrand was hired. Senior management at ATB was assured that they could purchase the integrity of Coopers & Lybrand to protect their unethical practices.

I know what you must be asking. How did I get involved with Coopers & Lybrand? I'll give you one guess. The Alberta Treasury

Branches recommended Coopers & Lybrand as the best for the type of restructuring I needed. My current law firm checked around and found that yes, indeed, Coopers & Lybrand did do a lot of ATB work and logic would dictate that this would make for a smoother restructuring. In my initial meeting with them, I had my regular lawyer with me and we met with Senior Vice President, Don McLean. He informed me that it was not necessary to have my lawyer present at future meetings. Next, I met with Mr. McLean and Mr. MacNutt, also a Senior Vice President. (MacNutt is his real name; I didn't change it for comic relief!) You will recall that in the introduction, I portrayed myself as a kind of pirate. The reason I used the pirate description was because Mr. MacNutt was a swashbuckler himself, sort of a poor man's Errol Flynn. I thought he was helping me rebuild the ship; but instead, he made me walk the plank. I provided them with a retainer which, in my mind, signified that they worked for me. Then, there were some strange occurrences. In this meeting, Mr. McLean and Mr. MacNutt had me sign documents basically absolving them of their professional responsibilities. Conveniently for them, they never provided me copies of those documents. As someone with no experience in these matters, I was in a room with two senior vice presidents of insolvency directing me to sign documents to my detriment without independent legal advice. Both assured me that this was not unusual and that they had restructured hundreds of debts for the ATB. Mr. McLean also mentioned that he had struck deals in the past with the

Alberta Treasury Branches to accept millions of dollars in write-offs and that my case would be a piece of cake. Some cake!

I began to feel like Dorothy from the Wizard of Oz, being led down the Yellow Brick Road by Coopers & Lybrand. In keeping with this Ozian theme, I not only met people with no heart, no brains, and no courage; but in my trip, I also encountered characters with no conscience. The first attempt at the Company Creditors Arrangement Act, Coopers & Lybrand hired counsel, Mr. Charles Russell of the firm Cruikshank Karvellas. Mr. Russell was well known for his ability to make over a situation--to take a set of circumstances, alter their appearance and make them out to be much different than they actually existed. He could give a legal facelift to enhance an otherwise sagging case. (One should keep in mind that during my trials and tribulation, Mr. Russell became a partner at McLennan Ross, who represented the Alberta Treasury Branches in a textbook conflict of interest.) Naively, again I thought that after paying a large retainer, one ordinarily assumes the accountant or lawyer works for you. However, what they produced amounted to little more than a liquidation order, not restructuring under the Company Creditors Arrangement Act. This order included more than thirty companies, a large percentage of which were not insolvent. Coopers & Lybrand advised me to swear to documents that said that I co-mingled funds when I did not, and to swear that corporations were insolvent, when they were not. In essence, the recommendation and direction from these professionals was to break the law.

The Alberta Treasury Branches continually pressured me, telling me that if I did not swear to the documents, they would call all my loans. These documents are still on file with my lawyer. They were prepared to exercise their rights under the loan guarantees and petition me into bankruptcy if I did not cooperate. The whole purpose of this exercise was not to restructure the loans, but rather to avoid a lengthy legal dispute. I originally set up my corporations to segregate assets in case one of the assets had a problem to avoid any domino effect on the others. The Alberta Treasury Branches' modus operandi was to neutralize my corporate structure.

Coopers & Lybrand and its counsel also continued to pressure me for several weeks to sign the fraudulent documents. The final straw came for me when, after several months of thinking that they were working for me, they wanted my regular law firm to come in at the eleventh hour and file documents prepared by them. Coopers & Lybrand and its counsel informed me only at 4:00 p.m. of the day before the documents were to be filed (after several months of their legal advice) that Coopers counsel was not representing me. Why didn't they prepare the documents with my lawyers from day one so that my regular law firm could understand what was happening? The reason, of course, was that they were taking direction from the Alberta Treasury Branches and undermining my attempts at restructuring. Any lawyer worth his salt would have recognized this immediately. They also knew that my regular counsel was not insolvency experts and sought to capitalize on that fact, hoping that this would absolve them of their actions by rubber-stamping the process.

Mr. Russell had private appointments scheduled for late August and early September with Associate Chief Justice Allan Wachowich whom he had lined up to sign and give Court approval to questionable documents. In fact, he had arranged the meeting a number of times invoking Justice Wachowich's name to pressure me, hoping I would be intimidated at the thought of meeting with such a senior Justice. Keep this little ingot of information in the back of your mind. The reason will become clear later, like an echo in the still air of an alpine meadow. Certainly, it is not normal practice to have one law firm file documents for another. Coopers & Lybrand and its counsel were intentionally acting in bad faith to the detriment of their colleagues in order to cleanse their unlawful actions and to win favour for future work with the Alberta Treasury Branches. Needless to say, I did not file the documents that were prepared by Coopers & Lybrand and its counsel.

After my experience with Coopers & Lybrand and its counsel, I came to the realization that I definitely had to seek a lawyer well versed in insolvency practice. I finally settled on Mr. Roy Henning, a lawyer with an enviable record in representing insolvency cases. After reviewing Coopers & Lybrand and its counsel's documents that they wanted me to swear, Mr. Henning informed me that it was nothing more than a liquidation order orchestrated by the Alberta Treasury Branches which gave full control of my corporations to Coopers & Lybrand which was de facto control for the ATB.

Because of the barrage of legal actions triggered by the failed first attempt at CCAA, the only option left according to Mr. Henning's advice was to attempt a second CCAA. The failed first attempt started my financial Armageddon as word began to leak out, seriously undermining the second attempt and began what was somewhat akin to a run on a bank, only in reverse. (Such a run on an otherwise stable bank can make it insolvent and the effect was the same on the balance of my corporations.) To characterize the panic in another way, I had the plague while everyone scrambled to have as little to do with me as possible and tried to get as far away as possible. I had become the financial equivalent of a leper. To compound problems, the lawyers that represented the Alberta Treasury Branches advised other lenders of my situation, further undermining the process. Because of the magnitude of the situation and the pending litigation, the only way to proceed was to file a second attempt under the CCAA to stop all legal actions until a plan for restructuring could be formulated just as the legislation was intended to do and should have done.

At this point, Coopers & Lybrand and its counsel demonstrated their true nature. Mr. Henning, my counsel, prepared a second attempt that included the insolvent companies only; but the problem was that Coopers & Lybrand and its counsel still held the bonds that were required to file the second attempt at the CCAA, and time had become a critical factor. In fact, we believed time had run out and that it may have been already too late. There was no other alternative. Coopers & Lybrand and its counsel extorted me into allowing them to be part of the second CCAA attempt saying they would only release the bonds required to file if they were included in the second attempt. This was a prime example of their integrity being sold and their attempt at damage control over what they had created. Why else would they acquiesce to the second attempt that did not resemble theirs in the least?

In early November 1994, we won a decision over the Alberta Treasury Branches at the Law Courts Building in Edmonton. Doug Goebel at ATB called me the next day to discuss and I quote, "strategy." Once again the Alberta Treasury Branches were prepared to accept the second attempt at CCAA as long as I allowed Coopers & Lybrand and its counsel to be a part of it. I naively believed that the first attempt had taught them a lesson and their intention was to correct their indiscretions. Essentially, the clock was ticking and we had no alternative.

It must be noted at this point, that after the filing of the second attempt, Mr. Charles Russell, Coopers & Lybrand's counsel, changed law firms, becoming a partner at McLennan Ross, the law firm that represented the Alberta Treasury Branches. Now surely a move of this magnitude in someone's career--a senior partner of one major firm moving to another--must have been contemplated for several weeks, perhaps even months, yet he never bothered to mention to us that this was his intent before becoming a part of the second attempt. His announcement came only a few weeks after the filing of the second attempt. He took the inside knowledge of my companies' affairs to his new firm. Surely his professional ethics should have been questioned on this point alone. What Coopers & Lybrand should have done as an officer of the Court was to remove Mr. Russell as counsel because he was now in a textbook conflict of interest. Instead, Coopers & Lybrand and Mr. Russell came to us and assured us that confidentiality would be maintained (a Chinese Wall) and that there would be no conversation or communication with the ATB nor its solicitors at McLennan Ross. The Alberta Treasury Branches approved of this conflict of interest. True to form, the Chinese Wall was breached and information began to leak almost immediately. I had sent a letter, to Coopers & Lybrand directly in December 1994 and copied no one. Within hours, Graham McLennan, the counsel for ATB, came to my solicitor and informed him that they did not appreciate my letters to Coopers & Lybrand. I wrote another letter to Coopers asking how this information got out. To cover their exposed backside, Coopers wrote me a letter and I quote, "Your most recent fax suggests that there has been a breakdown in the Chinese Wall." Note that it was not a denial, but rather a characterization of the breach as an aberration. They were caught red-handed. It was quite obvious that this and other confidential information were being freely exchanged to my detriment.

During the second CCAA attempt, Coopers & Lybrand was constantly trying to undermine the CCAA as well as solvent corporations. At the same time, Lorna Moore, an audit representative from Revenue Canada, conducted a complete audit of source deductions for income tax, Canada Pension Plan, and so forth. After the audit was complete, she left satisfied that there were no problems and gave her stamp of approval that reflected this. When Ms. Moore arrived back the following Monday and was asked why she had returned, she confessed to my staff (sworn affidavits support this) that Thomas Klaray, one of Mr. MacNutt's staff from Coopers & Lybrand, whom you will remember was supposedly working for me, had told Ms. Moore to take another look at shareholders' loans and perhaps they should be deemed salaries and income to various shareholders.

Ms. Moore re-audited with Coopers' suggestion all my corporations as well as returning with an assessment that was totally unsatisfactory. This created all sorts of problems, as now source deductions had to be calculated and an appeal launched. What was ironic, though, was that while Mr. Klaray and Coopers & Lybrand were co-managers of the companies under CCAA, they refused to pay the same source deductions. They knew I would be personally liable for these payments and washed their hands of the responsibility. It was absolute betrayal. Coopers and Lybrand never once discussed the shareholders loans with me nor my staff and certainly had no business creating doubt in the mind of the Revenue Canada auditor. The CCAA order clearly stated that Coopers & Lybrand were co-managers and that no information could be supplied nor action taken without my agreement. They constantly violated their position as an officer of the Court with malicious intent to undermine my corporations.

The following are examples that show that Coopers & Lybrand was responsible for undermining the second attempt at CCAA. Incompetent, they mismanaged the entire exercise. Funds were co-mingled among companies, employees were paid by companies they did not work for, and funds were shifted among companies to the detriment of certain creditors. Coopers & Lybrand then wrote letters to the ATB in December 1994 and North American Life in March 1995 blaming me for the irregularities saying that I had coerced Mr. MacNutt, Mr. Klaray, and their staffs into committing these irregularities. In truth, their ass was out a mile, and this was their attempt to cover it. It begs credulity that I was bending the will of one of the largest accounting firms in the world.

One of the most crucial items in a CCAA is that no information be released until a proper restructuring can be presented. In fact, my CCAA order made sure that no decision or information was to be released without the input or agreement of both parties. Yet, notwithstanding this requirement, Coopers took it upon themselves to provide information to the Alberta Treasury Branches that jeopardized my corporations' positions and proposals. To give an example, the Dollar Rent-A-Car franchise I owned prepared a restructuring proposal that even the Coopers & Lybrand staff believed would work, yet Mr. MacNutt, the Senior Vice President would not support the proposal in Court. Then on that fateful day of February 2, 1995, I found out why. It should be noted here that fourteen lawyers, most of whom were on ATB's payroll plus the upper echelon of ATB management, were all present. The counsel for the Alberta Treasury Branches made a statement in Court that no proposal in any way, shape or form would be acceptable to the Alberta Treasury Branches under any of the CCAA's provisions. Not only did Coopers & Lybrand not present the Dollar Rent-A-Car proposal, they did not object to anything including the Alberta Treasury Branches' attempt to sever the original Court Order that still had a few weeks to go before the restructuring was due.

The Coopers & Lybrand employees had informed me that the General Security Agreement of the Alberta Treasury Branches had with Dollar Rent-A-Car was faulty, but Coopers failed to report that fact to the Courts. An employee of the Alberta Treasury Branches, Mr. Blaine Kennedy, also dealt in used and rebuilt vehicles on the side and enjoyed a lucrative income from this activity. (He was manager of the Edmonton Strathcona branch where I dealt.) Another account at the same branch, R&S Autobody rebuilt the vehicles that Mr. Kennedy was selling. Mr. Kennedy coerced me into purchasing twenty automobiles from R&S for Dollar Rent-A-Car, sight unseen. The loan that financed these vehicles was less than $300,000, and I needed to protect a loan portfolio of over ten million dollars with the same individual. With Mr. Kennedy, it wasn't *if* I was buying these vehicles, but *when*. Dollar did not need these used, rebuilt cars. It had a large line of credit with Ford Credit Canada Ltd. which was not fully utilized. R&S Autobody's obligation to Dollar Rent-A-Car was to rent these cars back on a set agreement, which was never fulfilled. R&S actually falsified rental contracts so the cars were sent out at the discounted courtesy rate when in fact the majority of the rentals were for insurance replacement. (That is, vehicles for customers whose own autobobiles were being repaired under their insurance coverage). R&S then kept the difference between the insurance rate and their own courtesy rate, defrauding Dollar Rent-A-Car of substantial revenues. To compound matters, their account became one hundred twenty days in arrears. R&S also began to purchase their own vehicles for body shop replacement use, further undermining the agreement. Mr. Kennedy arranged 100% financing of the vehicles and was paid a substantial kickback for arranging this deal for R&S. Dollar was left with a fleet of cars which it overpaid for and did not need. It was the General Security Agreement on these cars that the Alberta Treasury Branches used to put Dollar Rent-A-Car into receivership. Coopers & Lybrand was well aware of this and did no further investigation, civilly nor criminally.

I then went to Mr. Goebel, the Executive General Manager of ATB, and explained to him what Mr. Kennedy had done. Unfortunately, Mr. Goebel was the wrong person to go to as he had been a friend and colleague of Mr. Kennedy's for nearly thirty years. This was where the whole dispute really started. Mr. Goebel believed him and, in fact, did not investigate until he was forced to by his supervisors six months later. From January to June 1995, Mr. Goebel released a barrage of legal and accounting people to ensure that I understood who was in control. Mr. Goebel informed me that it was *not* Mr. Kennedy who stepped over the line, but rather it was I, and he was going to spend whatever it took to ruin me. When it

41

came to ATB employees' unethical conduct, Coopers & Lybrand looked the other way. Mr. Goebel, at least here, was true to his word.

The following was a barrage of things that were done to me. Without explanation, the Alberta Treasury Branches' solicitors severed the CCAA that they originally agreed to. No proposal in any way, shape or form would be acceptable. This can be seen by their actions in the Court Room of February 2, 1995. Normally, bank executives do not show up in Court, but Mr. Goebel, Mr. Fossen, and Mr. Piquette from the ATB took time out of their busy schedules to be present that day. On this day, Coopers & Lybrand did not prepare proposals they were required to do under the Court Order; they were only too eager to throw in the towel. They became receivers and trustees in bankruptcy of many of my corporations. This was incredible. They were now in a classic, textbook conflict of interest; they had worked for the debtor and now they were working for the creditor. But, there was more to come. Coopers allowed an unsecured creditor, Ericksen Nissan, a prime customer of the ATB, to rank ahead of secured creditors. Coopers and its counsel were violating their duties as officers of the Court by not fulfilling their obligations of informing the Court that unsecured creditors should not rank ahead of secured creditors; that Coopers would be in a conflict if it worked for both the debtor and the creditor. The Alberta Treasury Branches' lawyers had already prepared the orders that arranged the conflicts of interest, and these were granted without proper notice or application. All the

42

professionals involved were supposedly experts in their field. They obviously understood and recognized the conflicts but chose to subvert this knowledge to their baser instincts, greed, and the fear of being exposed by their colleagues. So, they controlled the investigation. It was quite obvious from its actions that Coopers & Lybrand and its counsel once again sold their integrity with total disregard for their conscience.

For the months to follow, there were many highlights or lowlights, depending upon your perspective. Coopers began to sell my assets with total disregard for their value. For instance, they sold a lawsuit that Dollar Rent-A-Car had with the franchisor, Dollar Rent-A-Car Canada, for $37,500--a lawsuit that potentially was worth several million dollars. The Alberta Treasury Branches and its solicitors went out of their way to contact lenders to see if they would join in the petition for bankruptcy. While many did not want to have the cost attributed to them, they began calling their loans to protect their position. This included lenders such as Royal Trust, the Royal Bank, Sun Life Trust, the Bank of Nova Scotia and many more. Most were not a part of the CCAA but called all of my loans after being contacted by the Alberta Treasury Branches and its Counsel. By ravaging the good assets, the ATB's obvious intention was not to realize on their guarantees but rather to punish me.

I was a guarantor on a $200,000 line of credit for Auto Row Saturn, a General Motors dealership. When the original loan was set up, it was agreed that I would be a silent guarantor. Shortly after the ill-fated second attempt at CCAA, the ATB contacted General

Motors and divulged my involvement in the Saturn dealership despite being duly noted within the credit that this was to remain privileged information, a proviso which they agreed to. The Alberta Treasury Branches clearly had no qualms about divulging such information about me. To fest their consistency and conscience, I asked them later in the process what professional fees had been billed on my file; they refused to answer citing confidentiality, even after a Freedom of Information and Protection of Privacy Act request. This has to be one of the most incredible ironies in Alberta history. There must be different grades of confidentiality at ATB. General Motors then seized the dealership and changed the locks within a few days of that meeting. The $200,000 ATB line of credit was paid out by General Motors, and all other capital was lost.

Here's another example of Goebel's barrage. Ducky's Office Furniture operated out of a warehouse that had an ATB mortgage on it. The Alberta Treasury Branches began an absolute legal assault with the intent of severing its lease. The ATB was well aware that Ducky's was one of my operating companies; in fact, it had an operating account at ATB. Knowing this, they could have required me to seek their approval for any lease signed by Ducky's. They did not do this. The legal assault was in front of Madame Justice Bielby, the same person who granted orders allowing Coopers to work for the debtor as well as the creditor, and also issued an order that allowed an unsecured creditor to rank ahead of a secured creditor. Brian Summers, the lawyer for the Royal Bank, received a call from Graham McLennan suggesting that Royal should call its loans, as I was being petitioned into bankruptcy which he did obligingly. The writing was on the wall--the system was hijacked. They had forced us to shut down. Soon, more of my corporations followed a similar modus operandi. Their objective was to ruin me. It was not to realize monetarily ontheir guarantees.

While I do not pretend to get up every morning and adjust my halo, it was quite evident that the Alberta Treasury Branches and its agents conspired to undermine the stability of my businesses. Lucrative work for large financial institutions has corrupted the system. I naively trusted and believed in their integrity. In short, my trust was misplaced. One should not assume that lawyers and accountants are the guardians of justice and fairness. This was living testimony of what was happening to the insolvency practitioners and an admission that integrity can be purchased. In the infamous words of the well-known philosopher, George Lucas, the saga continues.

CHAPTER 3
RADIOACTIVE MAN

"I got a real dumb father. He worked for a bank for thirty years and got fired for stealing pens."

- Rodney Dangerfield

The various and nefarious doings of the numerous participants led me to become a radioactive man. These participants were the agents or what I like to call operatives, if you will, in a plan initiated by the now departed Doug Goebel of the Alberta Treasury Branches and the lovely and talented Mark Gunderson of McLennan Ross. These individuals launched me on a roller coaster ride that consisted of far more downs than ups, and I can truthfully say that both Mr. Gunderson and Mr. Goebel treated me like a king--Rodney King! While their motivations were different, their agendas were the same.

I first encountered the lovely and talented Mark Gunderson when he represented Penmore Investments, a pension fund that funded commercial mortgages. He was the lawyer processing these mortgages. How can I describe Mark Gunderson? He's the kind of guy who would have tripped Terry Fox. Penmore had given me a commitment on approximately 20 million dollars in financing. After a six-month financial review that ended in June 1994, I finally received approvals from the Canadian Mortgage and Housing Corporation (CMHC) for Undertakings to Insure or UTI. A UTI is really an insurance policy backed by the

Government of Canada essentially guaranteeing the loans and thus involves no risk to the lenders. The UTI assures that any financial institution in Canada would be prepared to fund such a mortgage. Because the loan is guaranteed, with the resultant lack of risk, they can offer a lower rate of interest. Penmore could not do anything less than a five year term mortgage. I informed Penmore that a five-year term was unacceptable under the conditions set out in the UTI. I then took my Undertakings to Insure to People's Trust and was given a commitment on a shorter term basis which fell within the guidelines.

This, of course, did not sit well with the executives of Penmore Investments who were quite bitter that they were losing such lucrative funding. Mr. Ron Kunciak, the representative of Penmore, called me and tried to blackmail me by saying at the end of July 1994 that he knew that I was going to file under the Company Creditors Arrangement Act and that if I did not allow him to keep over a hundred thousand dollars in loan commitment fees (or at least the major portion of it), he would inform CMHC of my plans and sabotage the new financing and UTI with People's Trust. Mr. Kunciak lived in Vancouver, and the ATB and I were both located in Alberta; so the question inevitably arises as to how he knew the details of my situation. The answer was so obvious that he could not deny that it was the lovely and talented Mark Gunderson. Mark Gunderson had violated a confidentiality. Mr. Gunderson was perhaps embittered because he was denied a substantial amount of legal work. The point here was that Mr.

Kunciak should never have been privy to this information in the first place, but he went out of his way to make sure that I knew that he knew about my situation.

Of course, Mr. Gunderson was not stupid, and he was most certainly aware of his conflict of interest position--representing both Penmore and being lead counsel for the Alberta Treasury Branches. If you asked a hundred lawyers about being in such a conflict of interest position, more than likely, one hundred would resign from one of the files, unless, of course, they had ulterior motives. The fact that the Alberta Treasury Branches did not require Mr. Gunderson to resign from one of the files only condoned his behaviour. This was made very clear in June 1994 when I broached the subject in a meeting with him and the ATB in which they refused to deal with the conflict. Mr. Gunderson clearly acted in bad faith with total disregard for his own professional conduct. Janice Hill of CMHC confirmed that transferring the UTI was a mere formality because I had already successfully completed a six-month financial review. After Penmore Investments, however, had gone to CMHC and slandered me to the point that before getting both sides of the story, CMHC pulled my undertakings to insure.

While it was true that I was filing under the Company Creditor's Arrangement Act, most of the properties involved in the CCAA were office buildings which were the worst performing part of the market. As pointed out earlier, in a world survey of major cities on office lease rates, Edmonton ranked 103 out of 103. In retrospect, I may well have been better off to allow Penmore to blackmail me, as I had lost the UTI and the deposits have yet to be returned; but I understand that Mr. Gunderson got his fee paid. In a nutshell, Mr. Gunderson stood in the middle of nearly 30 million dollars in financing, approximately 20 million from Penmore and 10 million from the Alberta Treasury Branches.

To show how damaging this was, if those projects had been allowed to fund, at one of the worst points in the downturn in the summer of 1994, the mortgages would have come up for renewal in the summer of 1996. Upon a renewal in 1996, the interest rate would have been nearly 3% less on 20 million dollars and would have created tremendous cash flow for these properties today. Even if all my other projects would have been non-viable, these projects alone would have given me the ability to repay creditors if they had not been undermined by the Alberta Treasury Branches and its agents. This is how I became radioactive within the financial community. The perception in the lending community was that if you can't make a deal with the Alberta Treasury Branches, then you can't make a deal with anybody. If the ATB was interested in monetary remuneration, their actions were to the contrary.

In negotiations with the ATB, Mr. Gunderson was usually present for the Alberta Treasury Branches. All the while, he was sabotaging the process by leaking information, and he knew that my position was weakening. He erected barriers and formulated conditions that made negotiations impossible. In October 1994,

49

Mr. Gunderson put a pre-condition on the negotiation of a settlement. I was to provide $500,000 before any negotiations could begin--a sum he knew was impossible for me to raise. We never got close to a satisfactory solution. The Alberta Treasury Branches and their counsel were always of the arrogant and smug view that if I did not do as they suggested, they would petition me into bankruptcy.

One must analyze Mark Gunderson's zeal in his efforts to destroy me. Besides the Penmore billing, he had most recently lost the West Edmonton Mall file as well. (It is interesting how many ways and times the West Edmonton Mall refinancing will reappear in this saga.) Mark Gunderson had to replace this lucrative work somehow; if he could fan the spark of my dispute with the ATB, perhaps a full inferno could be started and sustained. If I were to settle with the Alberta Treasury Branches, then a third lucrative billing would be snatched from his grasp. Thus, he could continue to bill for work, and masquerade as the ATB fire fighter all the while pouring fuel on the blaze. The ATB labour lawyers confirmed that Mr. Gunderson was billing the ATB approximately 120 thousand dollars per month. Mr. Gunderson knew that I was tenacious by nature and that this file could yield at least some or, if fortune smiled on him, all the replacement revenue for Penmore and West Edmonton Mall. He proceeded to ensure that such an outcome was likely, and his actions were premeditated.

Mr. Goebel, like Mr. Gunderson, was no saint either. He was the beneficiary of a number of trips to Phoenix, Arizona, and beautiful British Columbia. These little excursions came courtesy of those fine folks at Coopers & Lybrand Limited and some well-known local law firms, purveyors of gifts, golf, wine, and song for Mr. Goebel's pleasure and relaxation. Think of the effect on Mr. Goebel's integrity and objectivity when it came to allocating Alberta Treasury Branches' work to Coopers & Lybrand and law firms like McLennan Ross. A few customers also looked after Mr. Goebel. He received a 25 thousand dollar personal payment for a loan approved from Murray Sparrow, brother of Don Sparrow, the late Tory Cabinet minister (in addition to a trip to Las Vegas). Only a person of the most zealous moral rectitude could resist the temptations of the earthly delights being offered. Doug Goebel, to say the least, was not that person.

Mr. Goebel had an entirely different motive than did Mr. Gunderson for ruining me. In a private conversation in December 1994, I pointed out to Mr. Goebel that the employees of the Alberta Treasury Branches, including the ones I was associated with, were not above reproach. He was extremely bitter about the proof that I had that Blaine Kennedy, his protégé of more than thirty years, was guilty of unethical conduct on my file. You will recall, Mr. Kennedy as the architect of the demise of Dollar Rent-A-Car. Instead of investigating the matter properly, he tried to cover up Mr. Kennedy's conduct by forcing my senior accounts manager, Brian Jones, to resign. Ostensibly, this gentleman was let go for unethical behaviour; but in reality, he became the sacrificial lamb, the Judas goat, the appeasement to the Gods in order to prevent the taint of scandal from touching Mr. Goebel's friend, Blaine Kennedy, and others further up the corporate ladder--futilely as it turned out.

Coopers & Lybrand and its counsel were taking their direction from Mr. Goebel and Mr. Gunderson. They were the architects of the first failed attempt at the CCAA and the trail of bad decisions that followed. The irony in all this, of course, was that Mr. Russell, the counsel for Coopers & Lybrand who was in constant contact with Mr. Gunderson over several months beginning in June 1994, eventually became his law partner in December 1994 after our second attempt at filing under the Company Creditors Arrangement Act. (It's probably just a coincidence.) This was a case of the inmates taking over the asylum. It was the epitome of their arrogance in thinking they could do whatever they wanted to whomever they wanted, whenever they wanted.

One of my corporations was Dollar Rent-A-Car and it became the flashpoint that ignited the entire dispute. Dollar Rent-A-Car, just like other rental car agencies, operated new vehicles and really had no practical use for the used vehicle purchase arranged by Mr. Kennedy.

Mr. Kennedy was trying to protect his lucrative relationship with the owner of R&S Autobody, Rod Skinner, the previous owner of the cars. He realized that he could help himself and Mr. Skinner who had been on the verge of insolvency for years by arranging the sale of vehicles to Dollar Rent-A-Car and receive $10,000 in cash for doing it. Mr. Kennedy arranged for the 100%

financing of these vehicles in a matter of days. This type of funding was quite easy for Mr. Kennedy when compared with some of the other financing he had put in place.

Now I had offended the powers that be; Mr. Goebel was now going to go out of his way to ensure that Mr. Kennedy was protected. This was the beginning of the end. He was prepared to spend whatever was necessary to protect his friend and protégé. He unleashed a legal barrage that would have been the business equivalent of the Normandy invasion. He went out of his way to influence other lenders such as the Royal Bank, Royal Trust, and the Bank of Nova Scotia in an effort to get me to recant what I had said about the ATB employees. At this time, I took a defensive position still hoping that cooler heads would prevail and make a resolution possible, a variation of Mohammed Ali's "rope-a-dope" strategy.

This full legal onslaught began in January 1995 and continued mercilessly until a standstill agreement was called for in May of 1995. After the standstill agreement ended, Mr. Goebel was once again in charge of the file, along with Les Bellan, Vice Superintendent of the Alberta Treasury Branches. Mr. Goebel was able to allow Mr. Kennedy to retire in July 1995 with a severance package, and I refused to walk away based on the ridiculous offer they had made. Details on this offer appear in the next chapter. They decided to carry on with their strategy of a legal onslaught beginning with the date of petition, October 3, 1995. This strategy was to deny me the resources for my own defense and pursuit of my legal action against ATB. I was not to be allowed to invoke my rights and privileges. Mr. Goebel approved a 2.5 million dollar line of credit for me in January 1994, but I was not allowed to use it. I was told it would be increased to 4 million dollars to meet my real needs. The increase never happened. In taking an offensive position, I began writing letters after I was petitioned detailing not only what happened to me, but also how the ATB in general was riddled with corruption. Mr. Goebel's campaign against me reminded me of Napoleon. First, there was an obvious comparison of Mr. Goebel's and Napoleon's physical stature; the second was, like Napoleon, Mr. Goebel never gave his opposition a chance to regroup and mount a counter attack. The object was to pursue and annihilate the adversary and press a clear advantage so that the opponent would not return to fight again another day. Mr. Goebel made a small error in judgment, however, when he did not realize that when he was playing Napoleon, I was forced to assume the role of Wellington. This dispute became the Alberta Treasury Branches' Waterloo. The bottom line was that while Mr. Gunderson and Mr. Goebel may have acted for different reasons, the fact remains that their agendas were the same. While Mr. Gunderson's motivation was unlikely to have been anything but greed, Mr. Goebel's chief motivation was revenge and protection of his colleagues at the Alberta Treasury Branches through the use and abuse of the insolvency process. As Lady Macbeth said, "What need we fear who knows it, when none can call our power to account? Yet who would have thought the old man to have had so much blood in him?" It was time to call the Alberta Treasury Branches and the Government of Alberta to account. They originally thought that because of my younger age, they were simply going to steamroll over me with the petition into bankruptcy; but it actually had the reverse effect. The ATB had backed me into a corner and I no longer had anything to lose monetarily. The damage was done. I was radioactive. Since I could no longer make deals, I directed my full energies towards the fight.

CHAPTER 4
THE STANDSTILL AGREEMENT

"Oderint dum metuant"[4]

- Caligula

In May of 1995, I was presented with a petition into bankruptcy by the Alberta Treasury Branches for June 1, 1995. When this occurred, I felt it necessary to take the gloves off and go over Mr. Goebel's head to the Acting Superintendent of the ATB, Mr. Elmer Leahy. Mr. Goebel was in denial that the ATB employees had acted unethically on my file.

Mr. Henning, my counsel contacted Mr. Leahy in May 1995. They met within days of that telephone call to discuss Mr. Goebel's continued cover-up of the corrupt practices of ATB employees and his friends. Mr. Henning gave a detailed description of what had taken place to date including the fact that Mr. Goebel was well aware of the ATB employees' conduct. He presented Mr. Leahy with proof of what had gone on in the form of cancelled cheques with Blaine Kennedy's name on them. Upon hearing this, Mr. Leahy called for a standstill agreement so they could look into things further.

A few weeks later, the manager directly involved with my file, Mr. Kennedy, retired. It was the official word, yet under cross-examination under oath in September 1995, ATB management admitted that he was forced to resign for unethical behaviour. This

---

[4] "Let them hate provided that they fear."

was to set a precedent for the way in which they handled subsequent dismissals. Mr. Leahy then asked for another meeting with Mr. Henning. He informed Mr. Henning that Mr. Bellan, the Vice-Superintendent, and Mr. Goebel would try to negotiate a settlement. This was somewhat puzzling since Mr. Goebel had created the problem.

What happened was that Mr. Henning had a series of meetings in July and August 1995 with their counsel who was, as you will recall, the lovely and talented Mark Gunderson. Mr. Gunderson, who was part of the cover up and went out of his way to ensure the problem was not resolved, now offered to walk away from the loans on my operating companies as compensation. In return, I would release the properties to ATB. I was dumb-founded. Mr. Gunderson and his firm, McLennan Ross, had already destroyed all of my operating companies in conjunction with Coopers & Lybrand and ATB. They had also influenced lenders to my property corporations to call their loans because of their actions. Finally, they had ruined my credibility through a malicious assassination of my character by undermining my ability to obtain new loans which impaired my ability to do future business. The lending community was well aware that I was being petitioned and many had ex parte orders ready for the petition, as most mortgages have a clause that reads if the principal becomes insolvent, the mortgages become due and payable. The ATB had started a financial avalanche and was trying to give me back companies that they had already destroyed.

I told Mr. Henning this proposal was unacceptable. Mr. Gunderson informed Mr. Henning that it was our last chance to accept or they would continue with the petition into bankruptcy. Because the damage was done and I had nothing to lose, I refused to accept their offer. I am convinced they were betting that I had something to hide which they would find in a forensic audit. Their arrogance was showing that they controlled the system. They believed that I was hiding something; now they had to prove it irrespective of the truth. Finally, it must be remembered that on the day that I was served the petition, it was Mr. Gunderson who approached me after I was served. He made an uppercut motion with his arm, and smiling smugly said that it would be all over soon and everyone could move on. One could have characterized this episode as a lynching, and I was the party nominated to test the rope. He was beaming and glowing about their strategy to petition me into bankruptcy.

A new date was set for the granting of the receiving order, October 3, 1995. There is irony in that date. I was petitioned into bankruptcy on the same day that O. J. Simpson was acquitted. It was a dreadful day for justice. In the Courtroom that day, senior ATB officials (right in front of me and I suspect for effect) decided to return to the offices of McLennan Ross for a victory drink. One has to keep in mind that it was admitted by ATB officials, as well as ATB lawyers, that the purpose of the petition was to control my actions through a trustee that would make it easier to get my properties through foreclosure, as well as eliminate my lawsuits against the Alberta Treasury Branches by asking for security for costs. Security for costs is like a deposit for legal costs if the plaintiff should lose. My lawsuits were struck not based on their merits or lack thereof, but rather on the fact that the Alberta Treasury Branches were able to use the Bankruptcy and Insolvency Act as a way of covering up their corruption. I appealed the orders. They were going to take me apart forensically in an effort to discredit me. It was the biggest fishing expedition since Captain Ahab went looking for Moby Dick. Fait accompli.

The Trustee that was chosen by the Alberta Treasury Branches and its solicitors was Price Waterhouse Limited (the auditors for the PC Alberta Fund and Ralph Petersen, my Trustee, was one of the largest contributors to this Fund. It was probably just a coincidence.) The first act of good faith by Price Waterhouse as an Officer of the Court was to appoint counsel. This was when I knew the fix was in. They chose Douglas Tkachuk of the law firm Bryan & Company. Unbelievable! Mr. Tkachuk had acted against me for the Alberta Treasury Branches and Metropolitan Trust. To make matters worse, his partner at the firm, Eric Young, acted against me in nearly 10 million dollars in real estate foreclosures for Confederation Trust and Royal Trust. (Mr. Young is also President of the Progressive Conservative Party of Alberta. It's probably just another coincidence.) I objected to Price Waterhouse's choices, as I believed it was a conflict of interest.

All the professionals knew that Bryan & Company did a substantial amount of the work for the Alberta Treasury Branches.

The first thing on the agenda was the foreclosure of the properties. All the players were in place. The ATB no longer had to fight me, as the Trustee whom they were paying now spoke for the estate. The solicitors for the Alberta Treasury Branches brought a motion forward in Masters Chambers for the final foreclosure of all of my properties with ATB financing.

First let me give you some background. The Alberta Treasury Branches' appraisals they were relying on in the foreclosure proceedings were nearly nine months old. These were not presented to the Court until I was petitioned. On December 6, 1995, there had been one adjournment and now we were appearing in front of the Master. Between the appraisals that I had ordered and the appraisals that the ATB had ordered were discrepancies of nearly 2 million dollars. In the case of the higher values of my appraisal, there would be no shortfall to the Alberta Treasury Branches--if one took into consideration an insurance claim, there may have even been a surplus. I suggested a judicial sale to prove the real value of the property, as this would be fair to both sides. The counsel for the Trustee agreed with the counsel for the Alberta Treasury Branches that the property should be transferred immediately to the ATB at the lower value. What a surprise! It was quite obvious that the counsel for the Trustee did not want to expose the properties to the market because he had been instructed by the ATB to make sure that the deficiencies were suitably large.

It was crystal clear that the agenda for the ATB was to obtain the largest deficiency possible and to control my actions by keeping me in bankruptcy longer than was necessary. The need to show such a mammoth deficiency was to enable them to justify their excessive expenditures for the ATB's actions.

To his credit, Master Breitkreuz recognized that they were trying to shove it up a particularly sensitive portion of my anatomy. He ruled that the properties were to be exposed to the market until March 31, 1996. I did not appeal this order because I thought it was fair. As a side note, the counsel for the Trustee, Doug Tkachuk, was so sure his position was identical to the counsel for the Alberta Treasury Branches, he was able to catch up on some sleep in the Court Room. He was slipping in and out of consciousness repeatedly during the presentation. It was my understanding that this slumber was some of Mr. Tkachuk's finest work. It was quite obvious that the counsel for the Trustee got way too much ice time. The ATB was extremely upset over this, as they were paying an incredible amount of money and getting very little in results.

This was one of my first experiences with the Trustee, Price Waterhouse. It is difficult to explain the entire nature of my relationship with the Trustee. To chronicle the full story would require another book itself, but the following are some of the highlights that will give you the flavour of what I was subjected to. As you soon will realize, the comedy of errors continued.

The inspectors of the estate, the individuals chosen as representatives of the creditors to oversee and help direct the Trustee, deserve examination. One of the four inspectors was a gentleman by the name of Gil Ramsey who was employed by the Alberta Treasury Branches. Mr. Ramsey was an experienced insolvency practitioner. In fact, he was a retired senior partner at Coopers & Lybrand--sound familiar? He was also no stranger when it came to suckling on the teat of the ATB. At the Creditor's Meeting, Mr. Ramsey volunteered to be an inspector and then nominated Rory Gronberg, an ex-business associate of mine who did not have a judgment against me; he was not a personal creditor. Mr. Gronberg is, I shall say to be politically correct, somewhat intellectually-challenged. He is the type of guy that when you look into his eyes, you get the feeling someone else is driving. Mr. Gronberg hired Blaine Kennedy, the ATB employee who was forced to resign for unethical behaviour on my file. Mr. Gronberg had become very close to Mr. Goebel, who kindly doubled Mr. Gronberg's line of credit with the Alberta Treasury Branches from 2 million dollars to 4 million dollars. I pointed out all these conflicts of interest to the Trustee, but alas, I wasn't paying him.

To give a glimpse into the character of the Trustee, I should like to cite a specific example. Mr. Peterson had sent letters to the Law Society of Alberta, one on October 10, 1995, and one on December 8, 1995, in which he blatantly contradicted himself about my file. In the October 10 letter, he said, "This insolvency is not without its various complexities." And yet on December 8, he wrote, "It is certainly not what we would view as complex." Which was it? The burden of proof to the Trustee's character was displayed by his two letters in which he revealed his professional dishonesty.

The Counsel for the Trustee also deserves a close examination. Mr. Tkachuk was guilty of dereliction of duty for failing to investigate the merits of the Dollar Rent-A-Car lawsuit and his failure to exercise his obligation to the creditors instead of taking direction from the Alberta Treasury Branches. He never disagreed with the ATB's lawyers' position in Court and never asked for an adjournment to study the merits of their actions. He never once disagreed with their position. It was obvious he was in awe of their legal prowess. The Dollar Rent-A-Car lawsuit, which had the potential to realize millions for the estate, was allowed to be sold for $37,500. He brought civil contempt motions against me on orders proposed by Mr. Russell, the Counsel for Coopers & Lybrand. When I would appeal an order, the Trustee's Counsel would write me a letter questioning me about the cost of such an appeal, normally $200 to $300. This was ridiculous. I am sure that the Trustee and Counsel would discuss this matter, both billing the ATB, then the Counsel would write a letter concerning it. This had to be a minimum of a thousand dollar legal billing in order to question my expenditure of $200 for an appeal. This 5 to 1 ratio for every dollar recovered was ludicrous! In the letter, Mr. Tkachuk's warning me about expenses depleting the estate was the burning point of hypocrisy. This was not about money. It was about ruining me through the abuse of the process at whatever price.

Allow me to inject another telling example of the Trustee's ill-disguised harassment over trivialities, his predilection to wrangle for an ass's shadow. Demosthenes told the story about a man who hired an ass for a long journey. At midday, he dismounted to sit and rest in the animal's shadow. The ass's owner happened by and claimed the right to sit in the shady spot by saying he hired out only the ass, not his shadow. The two men began to wrangle over the issue and while they were fighting, the animal bolted, leaving both men in the noon sun's glare. The Trustee concentrated on such trivial issues to the detriment of the creditors. The overwhelming desire on the part of the Trustee to find anything at all that would serve to hang me, coloured his judgment. As an example, there were a few hundred dollars that were accidentally charged on a credit card after the bankruptcy petition, although *not* by me. I never charged anything after the bankruptcy, and the Trustee confirmed that it was not my signature on the charge slips. The few hundred dollars that were charged were paid back. In an estate that was, at its peak, worth nearly $100 million in assets and operating companies, the Trustee forwarded to the RCMP for investigation this credit card matter.

Do you remember the story of the dissident during the Stalinist era of the Soviet Union? He ran through the streets and alleyways of Moscow, shouting at everyone that Stalin was corrupt.

Predictably at the time, he was arrested and brought before the Soviet judge. When asked how he would plead, he replied, "Not guilty." The judge then summarily sentenced him to twenty-five years in the Gulag. The dissident was stunned and asked how he could be sentenced so quickly for a crime he pleaded not guilty to. After all, he said, I told the truth; Stalin is corrupt and a criminal. The judge froze him with a withering look. "That is not the crime you are charged with comrade; you have been charged and found guilty of revealing a state secret!" I had become a legal pinata to the lawyers being paid by the ATB.

During this period, I began a letter-writing campaign. The battle was on. They were taking me apart forensically in an effort to discredit me. In this case, it was not enough to kill your enemy, you must first dishonour him. Something strange began to happen. People saw that even after what they had done, I refused to give in; and I began to receive information about the rampant corruption within the Alberta Treasury Branches and the Alberta Government. Many wrote or called me feeling that I may be the one to finally expose it. In essence, they were vicariously living their morality through me without repercussions to them personally.

I previously made mention of Mr. Gunderson's zeal in his efforts to destroy me. It was obvious that he had never read Romans 10:2 which warns against zeal without understanding.

Shortly after my letter campaign began, my counsel received a call from the lovely and talented Mark Gunderson to ask if anything could be done to stop the letters for the sake of the Government and the institution of the Alberta Treasury Branches. My counsel informed him that the damage had been done and the ATB had acted in bad faith; therefore, they could not be trusted to ensure a good faith resolution. I wrote more letters and Mr. Gunderson made an appointment to see my counsel in early November 1995, reiterating the same remarks. My counsel informed him that a negotiation would be possible, but that he was unacceptable as the negotiator.

I did not trust nor believe anything that Mr. Gunderson had to say so I continued to write my letters. Then, my counsel was contacted in mid-November 1995 by two separate parties, Mr. Jake Superstein and Mr. Larry Rollingher, both Tory faithful; but there was something more to this. They had a great deal at stake. First, the gravy train at the Alberta Treasury Branches could end for them and their friends; second, their own sordid practices may be exposed; and third, if they could resolve the problem, ATB employees and Government officials would be beholden to them.

These individuals informed my counsel that the Acting Superintendent, Mr. Leahy, could not address my abuse and that if the letters continued, he would not survive and may not survive anyway in his position. Mr. Leahy admitted to the above and was prepared to resolve it as soon as his corporate position was stabilized. Their fear initiated a number of clandestine meetings between them and Mr. Henning, my Counsel, in various meeting locales in Edmonton later in November. Mr. Superstein's and Mr.

Rollingher's preference was the Hilton in downtown Edmonton. It was a cloak-and-dagger operation worthy of the worst Hollywood "B" movies. The parties would arrive separately and leave separately to try to ensure the meetings would not be discovered.

Note that I had negotiated a buy-back of one of my former properties, the Liberty Building mortgage in early 1995. Because of what was happening to me, one of my associates exercised the right to purchase the first mortgage on the Liberty Building. His option ran out, and he could not replace the funds. Mr. Rollingher lent Mr. Henning the funds to purchase the option as legal action commenced. I was allowed to remain in my office but knew very well that I could not be a part of any of this, as the Trustee would find a way to use it against me. This was one of many deals that I could have done if the ATB had not petitioned me into bankruptcy. As of the writing of this book, the building was lost to the City of Edmonton for taxes.

On February 28, 1996, I wrote a letter to the counsel of the Alberta Treasury Branches stating that I had interested parties to purchase the properties and asked him if I should present the offers in Court or submit them directly to his office. These were the same properties that Master Breitkreaz had given me until March 31, 1996, to dispose of. For reasons that were to become evident, the ATB's counsel chose not to respond. On March 22, 1996, having received no response to my letter, I wrote directly to the Court asking how to proceed. The Court informed me that I should bring a motion to present the offers to purchase in

Chambers. I gave a Notice of Motion for March 28, 1996, and ensured that all documentation for the Notice of Motion was sent to the counsel for the Alberta Treasury Branches well in advance.

That morning, ATB's counsel presented an affidavit signed by his secretary and a letter dated March 28, 1996, from James Cox, the legal representative for the purchaser withdrawing the offer. (I also understand that he was one of the partners in the venture.) If an offer to purchase was to be withdrawn, surely the letter would be directed to me rather than the ATB's counsel, Graham McLennan. This was peculiar. I had presented in Court an offer to purchase that was substantially higher than the values of the ATB appraisals and a 25 thousand dollar deposit in trust. The purchaser had full knowledge of the values of both sets of appraisals to ensure that he had a full picture beforehand. The only purpose behind the deal was to eliminate or reduce as much as possible the shortfall to the creditor, ATB. The purchaser and his counsel were well aware of my antagonistic relationship with the Alberta Treasury Branches.

I was extremely curious as to why Mr. Mercier, the purchaser, had so suddenly withdrawn the offer. The purchaser on more than one occasion since then had informed me that his counsel had a discussion with Roderick McLennan, a member of the same firm and father of the counsel of the Alberta Treasury Branches, Graham McLennan. Mr. Roderick McLennan informed them that if they followed through with their offer to purchase, they would be blackballed within the business community. The reason that the offers could not be allowed to proceed is that there would be little justification for their malicious actions against me, and secondly, the Alberta Treasury Branches would not be able to justify the amount of time and money spent chasing a file with no shortfall. Mr. Roderick McLennan's actions were a desperate attempt to save the rapidly dwindling integrity of his firm. Judging from the methodology of his actions, one would believe that Mr. McLennan thought that William Aberhart was still Premier of Alberta. He had the arrogance to assume that others in his law firm had some judicial immunity that allowed them unlawful interference in a legitimately presented offer. While their conspiratorial nature was not new, their intentional inducement to breach of contract was.

After the foreclosures, the Alberta Treasury Branches and its Counsel sold some of these properties to my ex-associates who had provided them with information about my assets for far less than the offers I presented. The ATB was a part of this farce because they accepted lower offers, verifying what I had said all along. They were not interested in the realization on their loans; only the largest deficiency possible. Mr. McLennan was the living epitome that justice was not based on equal treatment before the law, but rather based on lawyers who know lawyers and lawyers who know Justices creating the arrogance that they are above the law.

In February 1996, when he was supposedly not involved as solicitor of record, Mr. William Kenny asked my counsel, Mr. Henning, if the ATB would step aside from funding the Trustee, would I walk away. The answer was no. However, on May 3 at 6:30 p.m., Roy Henning met with Elmer Leahy, the Acting Superintendent, and Russ Douglas, the Vice-Superintendent. During the course of this meeting, several things were discussed: their grave concern about my book; that the letters had a devastating effect; and that both Mr. Leahy and Mr. Douglas agreed that the ATB had been abusive to me. They admitted to controlling the Trustee and its Counsel. In the meeting they also suggested a new thirty day standstill agreement, as they wanted me to prepare a wish list of things that I wanted to resolve the situation. Finally, they wanted to know if I could be trusted.

At 11:00 a.m. on May 20, 1996, my counsel met again with Mr. Douglas and Mr. Leahy. Mr. Douglas confirmed that he had removed Graham McLennan as lead counsel and installed William Kenny as his replacement. Sound familiar? They agreed to "call all the dogs off" and enter into the standstill agreement. The interesting thing to note was Mr. Kenny's involvement--whether or not he was solicitor of record. In a letter to Mr. Kenny, I included a story about an Irishman that Mr. Kenny professed to like very much. There were two Irishmen embroiled in a shouting, kicking, scratching donnybrook when a third Irishman strolled by. His eyes lit up, a smile animated his face and all the while, he was rubbing his hands together in gleeful anticipation. Finally, he could contain himself no longer and shouted above the din of the now furious scrap, "Is this a private fight or can anyone join in?" I mentioned to Mr. Kenny that he now appeared to be the third

70

Irishman at the scene of the brawl. As you will see, Mr. Kenny was brought in on the West Edmnton Mall and Stewart Green files just as he was on my case.

On May 31, 1996, Mr. Douglas called my counsel (while Jake Superstein, backroom dealer extraordinaire whom you will remember from the earlier clandestine meetings was in Mr. Douglas' office) to inform him that the ATB had instructed Mr. Kenny to stop funding the Trustee. Mr. Superstein was present because he was promoting Mr. Douglas as the next Superintendent of ATB, for reasons that will become obvious.

My counsel had a discussion with Mr. Kenny on June 4, 1996. In that discussion, Mr. Kenny undertook once again to stop the funding of the Trustee. Being the sly fox that he is, Mr. Kenny waited until October 31, 1996, to do so. He knew that had he done so immediately, it would have incriminated him and his client. Mr. Kenny understood that time creates uncertainty. Mr. Douglas never became the Superintendent of the ATB and is likely to be removed (or resign or retire) shortly.

Since I have mentioned Russ Douglas, let me continue his vignette. I began a series of meetings with Mr. Douglas and Mr. McBean, Manager of Security, that started on September 24, 1996. After several meetings, Mr. Douglas decided that the ATB should make restitution for what had taken place. He never defended the ATB's position nor did he ever take issue with the chain of events that I pointed out to him. He said that he would come back to me with a specific amount with accommodating interest rates and a

71

line of credit to help me get back on my feet again. On October 9, 1996, we met and after promising me he would come back with a resolution, he informed me he was unable to offer me such a resolution at this time. Once again, the ATB was willing to admit guilt, but unwilling to resolve this issue. In the end, it appeared to be nothing more than an attempt to stall the publication of my book. I made every attempt to resolve it in as business-like manner that I possibly could, but the effort turned out to be wasted. For the second time, negotiations went nowhere.

CHAPTER 5
THE "ALBERT SCHWEITZER SOCIETY FOR THE PRESERVATION OF LAWYERS" AKA: THE LAW SOCIETY OF ALBERTA

The Law Society of Alberta is a very difficult institution to take on. I don't mean procedurally, but in the sense that it is frustrating. Picture someone trying to push a rope or throw a tissue across a room. The intention and the physical effort are both there, but the results are negligible. That about sums up my experience with the investigative abilities of the Law Society of Alberta. There is really no adequate form of checks and balances on the conduct of their members nor on the Law Society itself. The Law Society is run by lawyers. If you do not believe that the Law Society is doing its job, you can launch a lawsuit; but try to find a lawyer who will take the case. No matter what avenue you turn to, the final authority always rests with someone who is or has been a member of the Law Society. I decided to do it myself.

To grasp this, one must keep in mind the words of the Law Society's own legislation on the conduct of lawyers.

Rule 85(2): if a complaint or other information is brought to the attention of the Secretary under subrule (1) is not then in writing, the Secretary shall (a) in the case of a complaint, attempt to obtain the complaint in writing and, if the attempt fails, prepare a memorandum summarizing the complaint as accurately as possible on the basis of the complaint's oral statements and any records submitted by the complainant.

The information brochure states, "it may take up to six weeks to obtain the information we need to make a decision about your complaint." As you will see, the Law Society of Alberta's own words will come back to haunt them. I made my first complaint to the Law Society on October 4, 1995. I had several conversations with a complaints officer, and in these conversations different stall tactics were used on me repeatedly. After the writing of my first complaint, I was told that my letters needed to be more specific, so I rewrote the letters, putting in more detail. Then, I was told that there was too much detail and could I re-submit my complaint in point form. Again, I followed instructions and submitted my complaint once again. Still, the Law Society did nothing. Because of their ineptness during this period, other lawyers began to take their liberties thinking they were immune from being reprimanded by the Law Society.

I was quite dismayed by their lack of diligence and stall tactics directed to my complaint. To deflect attention from their dithering, they continually directed and redirected me for months. Under the spirit of their own legislation, I did not feel it was my responsibility or duty to do their investigation for them. Finally, after pleading with them for nearly eleven months (well beyond their information brochure's suggested six weeks), I had not even achieved the first step in their complaint procedure.

The first step was a review by the Deputy Secretary to either dismiss the complaint or send it to the appeal committee. They basically refused to do anything. Their decision was not to make a decision, hoping the courts would absolve them of their responsibilities. They left me no choice. In order to get their attention, I filed a lawsuit against Roderick and Graham McLennan of McLennan Ross. Still there was no response. I then filed a lawsuit against the Law Society. People who have lived in glass houses should clean their windows once in a while. The ludicrous part of this whole episode was that had the Law Society exercised its authority under its own legislation, they may have been able to stop the abuse of the process by its members. Instead, their silence encouraged it.

The various unethical practices of its members such as textbook conflicts of interest, the breaking of confidentialities, the continual violation of the Rules of Court, and the unprofessional conduct of its members were totally ignored by the Law Society of Alberta. The majority of these unethical practices were to be found at the hands of the various members of the law firm McLennan Ross. The old adage that large firms control the law societies appears to be true here. Large firms make up a large portion of the financial support required to operate the Law Society. He who pays the piper, calls the tune.

Let's first deal with the lawsuit against the McLennans. I brought the lawsuit after several motions and swearing of affidavits about Mr. Roderick McLennan inducing the breach of a contract. Not once did he swear or deny that he had done so. He had such an opportunity in a letter he sent me, but chose to childishly insult me instead. He traded honour for hubris. The fact that his letter resorted to the trivial and avoided the real issues spoke volumes about his guilt and impropriety. For someone who had been litigating for approximately forty years, he displayed no example of learned, dignified, and redeeming discourse as to his point of view. As a result, I felt that his partners must surely be thinking of returning the firm's name to Ross McLennan after this demonstration of Roderick McLennan's professionalism.

In a press report concerning the lawsuit, Mr. McLennan said, "His complaint is that we did far too good a job."[5] But, once again he did not deny his interference. The Law Society hired Mr. Paul Sharek from the firm Emery Jamieson to defend the McLennans. Their counsel filed a statement of defense. I then filed a notice to produce documents. Their counsel agreed to provide me with the documents but asked for extra time because of the volume of documents involved. I agreed to this.

When I next filed a lawsuit against the Law Society of Alberta, oh, what a surprise--they had hired the same counsel as for the McLennans, Mr. Sharek. No wonder they can't recognize a conflict of interest; they promote them. My lawsuit against the Law Society was basically that the Law Society acted negligently by violating its own rules governing the conduct of its members and that it was also negligent in protecting the public interest. Its actions had created a breeding ground where moral turpitude was allowed to thrive. Lo and behold, I finally got the Society's

---

[5] The Edmonton Sun. "Lawyers Deny Any Wrongdoing." Business Focus. July 17, 1996.

attention. As you will remember, the counsel for the McLennan's and the Law Society had agreed to provide me with the documentation. What I got instead was a Notice of Motion asking for the lawsuits to be struck, as I had no legal status as a bankrupt. Reality became a little distorted here. Associate Chief Justice Wachowich appointed Mr. Justice Belzil who heard the matter five days later. One must remember that this was happening at the same time I was trying to bring a motion to have Mr. Justice Lefsrud removed, which nearly four months later has yet to be heard for reasons which I shall detail fully in Chapter 7.

Not only is justice elusive, but access to justice is elusive. The Law Society was now using as its defense the same argument that was in my original complaint about the McLennans. The Law Society was now avoiding the truth through the same premise. This was not very good law, but it may make a pretty good episode for the X-Files. Normally in a lawsuit, the defendant files a defense denying the allegations. In this case, and I must say it was consistent; it did not even want to file the defense. It is quite obvious that if you take no stand, you cannot be held accountable. At this point, I feared that people would start calling me Yossarian. The bad news was that the lawsuits got struck, go figure! The good news was that I appealed the order. The basic argument was this: their counsel stuck to his guns saying that I had no status, instead of having his clients, the McLennans, swear affidavits saying my allegations were untrue.

My argument was that the Bankruptcy and Insolvency Act was oppressive and undermined the Canadian Bill of Rights. To give you an example, a normal appeal is $200 but in Bankruptcy and Insolvency Court, the appeal is $300. The Court says that the individual is either bankrupt or insolvent, then raises the cost of the appeal, thereby abrogating an individual's right to due process and the right of appeal. The Bankruptcy and Insolvency Act must be revised to ensure the individual's rights are not abrogated. The second part of my argument was that the Law Society had violated its own legislation. While Justice Belzil did rule against me, it must be pointed out that he conducted himself as an absolute gentleman. The problem with his thirty-page decision was that it curiously did not deal with the Law Society's own legislation, one of the cornerstones of my argument, more about that later, however. He then awarded the Law Society the legal costs. I pointed out to him that if the Law Society had adhered to their legislation (which I reiterate he failed to address in his thirty-page decision), then the actions would not have been necessary.

Finally, let's put this in context. I had offended Justice Belzil's brethren, and if you offend one, you offend them all. The Justices do protect each other and will be colleagues for years to come, as opposed to me who will probably be nothing more than a footnote in the Court ledger. Next, Justice Belzil was also once a member of the Law Society, and it is highly unlikely that he would rule against them. In my argument on transcript, I make an offer to discontinue my lawsuit against the Law Society on one condition:

that they either dismiss my complaints or proceed to a professional conduct committee. My offer was flatly denied and to date the Law Society has still not started the investigation, nearly fifteen months after the fact.

Lawyers complain about their reputations, but the inaction of the Law Society fosters the perception that the legal profession is a closed shop. It is not a coincidence that there are more jokes told about unethical lawyers than say unethical accountants. Lawyers have always been their own worst enemies in the public relations war. The legal profession has a reputation for looking after its own and, quite frankly, my experience with the Law Society to date only served to cement that belief.

I had always thought that legality and morality were synonymous. I would like to thank the Law Society of Alberta for clarifying they are not. In my pursuit of the McLennans and the Law Society, the only thing I was seeking was the truth about what had happened and, to use some boxing jargon, I could not even get close enough to lay a glove on them. This became the Canadian version of the Fifth Amendment in the United States. Under that Amendment, an individual can remain silent as his testimony may tend to incriminate him. The McLennans and the Law Society were allowed to invoke this privilege when no legislation exists for it. I am in awe of their masterful manipulation of the system. In Sir Thomas More's great work, Utopia, in which he sets forth the framework of what he envisioned as a perfect, pure, and just world (a world which conspicuously did not include lawyers), he made a comment which could just as easily have been written about McLennan Ross and the Law Society of Alberta. "They have no lawyers among them; for they consider them as a sort of people whose profession it is to disguise matters." Sir Thomas' comment is perhaps too genteel to describe the fiasco with the Law Society, but surely his sentiments are correct. What makes this statement even more powerful is that Sir Thomas trained as a lawyer himself.

CHAPTER 6
COURT OF QUEEN'S BENCH COLLECTIONS

"There is no cruder tyranny than that which is perpetuated under the shield of law and in the name of justice."

- Montesquieu

In Brobdingnag, the land of the giants in Jonathan Swift's Gulliver's Travels, written more than 200 years ago, the Queen asks Gulliver about his English homeland, in particular about the law and justice. Gulliver, dubiously answers and the Queen, much surprised, remarks that English style justice must be very expensive. If that is so, then she questioned him as to how poor people afford justice. To paraphrase Gulliver's answer, the poor people don't need justice, they are too busy working. Not much has changed in the Queen's Court. *Plus ça change, plus cést le même chose!*

When debtors are in court, they are facing an array of bank lawyers and banking representatives with their reserves of bank capital. Now, unless the debtor's lawyer is prepared to work on a contingency basis because he believes in the debtor's case, the debtor's legal representation is likely to fall far short of what the banks can afford to align against him. My own situation was a prime example. At one point, early on in the proceedings against the Dollar Rent-A-Car Edmonton franchise, my lawyer and I faced a phalanx of 13 lawyers, the majority for the Alberta Treasury Branches. I know from personal experience what really being out-manned feels like.

This financial and political influence perpetuates itself because of the structure of the system. Once the political influence is established, it can be used to influence governments to pass legislation favourable to the bank's position on any issue. The majority of politicians come from the ranks of guess who--lawyers, who can help ensure that the interest of their former colleagues, employers, and clients are well looked after.

So, what we have is somewhat of a classic Catch-22 situation. Banks can preserve the status quo and make sure that any future legislation is favourable to their position. The judiciary enforces and rules on laws in favour of banks which have influenced politicians to pass laws in the first place. It is a cycle of self-preservation and entrenchment.

To summarize this, the system perpetuates itself through its own incestuous structure. An outsider would find it extremely difficult to gain entry into this domain. In such a closed loop, the dispensing of justice, despite all public declarations of impartiality, is anything but. The justices and masters may rule against a plaintiff or defendant just because of past animosity. The phenomenon was observed first hand in my dealings with the system.

As an old proverb maintains, "The best laws leaves the least discretion to the judge." The abrogation of justice can always be identified when a justice continues to make decisions that do not lie within the law.

The relationship between the debtor and the creditor is never a fair one. When the original documents are drawn up, the equality of the parties in those documents never exists. The debtor is continually subjected to the will of the creditors even if there are extenuating circumstances. The bankruptcy and insolvency laws are written with the purpose of subtlely undermining the rights of the individual. It is my opinion that there is a growing danger that the Court of Queen's Bench will be renamed the Court of Queen's Bench Collections. The law has become a business and is not any longer about justice.

If one offends the system or questions the balance of the scales of justice, you not only offend the judge who you are questioning, but you also offend the entire brethren of that court system. The individual who fights back against the system is discredited and his character continually questioned. Some of the judges would have you believe that I should be fighting with Dorothy Joudrie for the bunk near the window at the Alberta Hospital. At the beginning of the entire process, professionals, politicians, and the judiciary believed that I was some kind of crank. Then, I went from crank to someone they took very seriously. The more you fight the judicial system, the more elusive justice becomes. Simply put, the system never loses.

The counsel for the Alberta Treasury Branches, Mr. Graham McLennan, sometimes referred to as Diogenes (the reason I like to call him Diogenes is because he liked to expose himself in public, in the symbolic sense, much the same as the famous philosopher did in the literal sense; Mr. McLennan's college major was also philosophy) insisted on the case management judge to avoid the normal rotation of justice assignments, or, in other words, the luck of the draw. Through Mr. McLennan's manipulation, he had made Madame Justice, Myra Bielby, the pseudo-case management judge without the approval of Associate Chief Justice Allan Wachowich by continuing to bring matters before her, regardless of the normal rotation.

After Mr. McLennan had petitioned me on October 3, 1995, I believed that Justice Bielby had heard far too much and that someone new should come on the scene as case management judge. I feared, too, that Madame Justice Bielby believed in the ancient Scottish legal maxim, guilty until proven innocent. Associate Chief Justice Wachowich appointed Mr. Justice John Agrios on October 13, 1995.

In late 1995, I wrote a letter to Jack Briscoe, then the Executive Manager of Public Affairs of the Alberta Treasury Branches and here, in part, is what I said:

Oh, by the way, here is another frightful 'coincidence.' The case management judge on my file in the dispute with ATB is none other than John Agrios, brother of the aforementioned Jack Agrios. Methinks this is not by accident and Elmer Leahy's ghastly work arises once again. Mr. Leahy must have a deep and abiding respect for fraternal relationships, since he uses them so often.

The excerpt describes two things: That Mr. Leahy had used his brother to front his sundry activities; secondly, Jack Agrios played a pivotal role in the West Edmonton Mall refinancing representing the Ghermezian family. It must be kept in mind that Justice Agrios was not privy to this communication. In fact, he is not even the main subject of the letter. Suddenly, in the New Year, Justice Agrios resigns. The following is the letter I received from Associate Chief Justice Wachowich that announced this development.

January 25, 1996

Wendy Badry

RE: Alberta Treasury Branch and Rahall - 9503-11327, 9503-02091, 9403-20415 & 9503-17052

> *On October 13, 1995, the above mentioned proceedings were assigned to Justice Agrios for the purposes of case management. In view of allegations that have been made by one of the parties against Justice Agrios, the case management of all of these actions is now being transferred to Justice Bielby. Please note this on your records and I will leave it to counsel to now contact Justice Bielby as to the scheduling of further meetings.*

Allan H. Wachowich

cc: Justice J. A. Agrios
Justice M. B. Bielby
McLennan Ross
ATTN: Mr. Graham McLennan
Weir Bowen
ATTN: Mr. C. Roy Henning. Q.C.
Bryan & Company
ATTN: Mr. Doug Tkachuk

This was novel. His extremely polite words were like Nutra Sweet--supposed to satisfy, but not the real thing. I did not criticize Mr. Justice Agrios at all, but I merely referred to him in another context as Jack Agrios' brother. I certainly did not ask for him to be replaced as case management judge. How did Mr. Justice Agrios know about my comment in the letter to ATB? More damningly, he obviously read enough importance into my comment to bring it to Associate Chief Justice Wachowich's attention and to realize the grave consequences for his brother and his role regarding the West Edmonton Mall refinancing. This line of communication which I maintained existed, and which all of the involved parties vehemently denied, was exposed in writing. I wrote the following letter on March 11, 1996, to Associate Chief Justice Wachowich.

11 March 1996

Dear Sir:

Re: Bankruptcy of Monier M. Rahall

I have received the copy of your correspondence to Ms. Badry, Civil Trial Coordinator. Thank you for your consideration of my position and the appointment of a new case management judge, but I still believe my statements were warranted.

However, kindly note that I did not ask to have Justice Agrios removed, he resigned. Actually I am curious as to why he stepped down since I only referred to him obliquely in a letter I sent to the Alberta Treasury Branches discussing his brother's connections to the upper echelon of ATB management. Justice Agrios should not have been privy to that so it appears he had acted with unseemly haste.

The reason that I remain so adamant about this is that I was petitioned into bankruptcy to take away my rights to due process. I believe that the second stage in Mr. McLennan's plan is to move towards having my lawsuits discontinued or at the very least require security for costs. While Mr. Henning is willing to litigate on a contingency basis, Mr. McLennan knows that a bankrupt would be unable to comply with security for costs, thus eliminating the lawsuits and due process. Alberta Treasury Branches petitioned me into bankruptcy but these practitioners of law are petitioning the bank of due process towards insolvency. Therefore, it is important to have a Justice who understands and who recognizes the ways in which the judicial system can be undermined by these practitioners of law.

I remain as always,

MONIER RAHALL P.Eng.

cc: Graham McLennan   C. Roy Henning Q.C.
    McLennan Ross   M. D. Fossen
    Doug Tkachuk   Alberta Treasury Branches
    Bryan & Company   (Strathcona)

After Mr. Justice Wachowich had received my letter, he confirmed my letter was indeed correct. He wrote as follows:

March 14, 1996

Dear Sir:

> *RE: Bankruptcy of Monier M. Rahall*

> *I acknowledge receipt of your letter of March 11th.*

> *Justice Agrios asked to be removed from this assignment and I granted his request.*

Yours truly,

Allan H. Wachowich

cc: McLennan Ross FAX 482-9100
    ATT: Graham McLennan
    Bryan & Company FAX 428-6324
    ATT: D. N. Tkachuk
    C. Roy Henning, Q.C. FAX 423-7076
    M. D. Fossen
    Alberta Treasury Branch FAX 433-4165

This reminded me of a bad episode of Columbo in which one of the suspects offers an answer before being questioned, thereby exposing his guilt. The dialogue would be something like this:

SUSPECT: "I never saw a woman in a red convertible leaving the West Edmonton Mall."

COLUMBO: "Who said anything about a woman in a red convertible leaving the West Edmonton Mall?"

Though his time as case management judge on my file was brief, Justice Agrios did leave an indelible impression. The issue was conflict of interest. Mr. Tkachuk, who was appointed as counsel for my Trustee, had already acted against me by representing Metropolitan Trust (the firm that was headed by the newly-appointed Superintendent of the ATB, Paul Haggis) and the Alberta Treasury Branches' Hy's Centre branch in a matter pertaining to Dollar Rent-A-Car. It was also well known by Justice Agrios and others that Mr. Tkachuk and his firm, Bryan & Company, did a substantial amount of work for the Alberta Treasury Branches. Additionally, one of Mr. Tkachuk's law partners, Eric Young, was in the process of doing 10 million dollars in foreclosures against my corporations. Justice Agrios, taking all this into consideration, allowed Mr. Tkachuk to remain as counsel for the Trustee, unable to recognize not only one, but several conflicts of interest. Several professionals came to me and expressed their disbelief that Justice Agrios would allow this to happen.

Justice Wachowich then landed a low blow. He allowed Madame Justice Bielby to re-hear matters by appointing her to the file. She was never my choice for case management judge and, in fact, I raised objections to her in the first place. This was like Montezuma's revenge. Madame Justice Bielby was Graham McLennan's choice, and with Justice Wachowich's assent to her re-hearing matters, a line of communication between Mr. McLennan and Justice Wachowich, one of his father's old friends, was indicated. I felt that it was very important to not let this go unchallenged and in order to set the record straight (and by the sheer fact that I thought it would make a hell of a chapter for this book), I wrote the following letter.

13 February 1996

Dear Sir:

Re: Concerns Regarding the Appointment of Madame Justice Bielby as Case Management Judge in Matters Pertaining to Monier M. Rahall.

I would like to draw your attention to some concerns I have with Madame Justice Bielby's renewed and continued involvement as the Judge presiding over matters pertaining to me. It is my feeling that Madame Justice Bielby has heard far too much from the lawyers acting for Alberta Treasury Branches including the continued assassination of my character by the likes of Mr. Russell, Mr. McLennan, and Mr. Tkachuk. All three of these individuals are being paid by the Alberta Treasury Branches while they continue to promote this character assassination, which is somewhat ironic considering that the Alberta Treasury Branches have admitted, formally in writing, that several of their employees have been let go for unethical behaviour. Some of those employees dealt directly with my file. Yet somehow, Madame Justice Bielby has seen fit to overlook this point.

I objected to Justice Bielby's continued involvement in matters concerning me because of this very reason and because I felt that a detectable bias against me and my position was materializing. It was you, Associate Chief

Justice Wachowich who had Justice Agrios appointed as case management Judge. Despite the fact that Mr. <u>Justice Agrios was the case management Judge, the three aforementioned practitioners of the law Mr. Russell, Mr. McLennan, and Mr. Tkachuk continued to bring matters before Madame Justice Bielby</u>. These actions beg the following questions:

1.   <u>If they perceived no legal advantage, why did these three lawyers continue to bring matters before Madame Justice Bielby</u>? All three of these practitioners of the law had full knowledge that Justice Agrios was now the case management Judge. It strains credulity to believe that this is mere coincidence.

2.   Why, knowing that Justice Agrios was the case management Judge, did Justice Bielby continue to make time available to hear motions against me even after I had made it known that this was unacceptable to me and the Justice Bielby had already heard far too much to continue to be objective?

3.   Why is Justice Agrios no longer the case management Judge and why, if Justice Bielby was not acceptable in October 1995, is she acceptable now?

This goes against the normal rotation of the case assignment of the Justices. I pointed this out in a letter dated December 14, 1995 sent to Mr. Maurice Dumont, Complaints Officer with the Law Society of Alberta. As I wrote at the time:
"Mr. Russell, mislead Justice Bielby as to the extent of the information available to him concerning the Dollar Rent-A-Car lawsuit and thus the case was not argued on its merits. Why else would he continue to insist that all proceedings be conducted before Justice Bielby unless he perceived that he had a clear legal advantage in doing so? Thus regarding the aforementioned Dollar Rent-A-Car (Canada) lawsuit, he made the appointment to appear before Justice Bielby which

took additional time to achieve. He was willing to trade this time for the increased comfort level he felt placing the matter before Justice Bielby and because he could not afford to continue the comedy of errors. Mr. Russell could not gamble on the normal rotation of the case assignments of justices with its built in system of checks and balances. This, of course, would not suit his purposes, but would allow an element of risk to affect the outcome of his carefully laid plans. His instructions from the Alberta Treasury Branches made it perfectly clear that he was to wrap up the file as expeditiously as possible, and thus with a justice made sympathetic to his point of view by means of a constant assassination of my character by the gang of three, he had no reason to worry about due process or my rights."

These practitioners of the law were so blatant about the continued use of Justice Bielby that even when I was at the Law Courts Building on other issues, some of their colleagues would joke that if I didn't cooperate or if I put up a fight in Masters' or Justices' Chambers, they would bring the matter before Madame Justice Bielby.

As a further example of this manipulation, Mr. McLennan brought a civil contempt motion on an order issued by Madame Justice Bielby eight months prior. I was ordered to appear when Mr. McLennan's motion did not even specify what the specific basis of the civil contempt was for. I was not found in civil contempt and satisfied the court that I had complied with Madame Justice Bielby's original order to the best of my ability. Now, I have been threatened with a second civil contempt motion on another of Madame Justice Bielby's orders initiated by Mr. Russell. However, this motion of civil contempt is being brought forward by Mr. Tkachuk (notice not by Mr. Russell) five months after the original order was issued.

I firmly believe that Madame Justice Bielby has heard far too much and that she cannot possibly be objective any longer. This attempt to bring this matter to your attention is only a brief synopsis of what has really transpired. If you so desire, I am more than willing to further elaborate on the details for you. I must reiterate that I strongly object to Madame Justice Bielby's renewed and continued involvement (however you choose to characterize it) in these matters and I feel that this prejudices my position and rights to due process.

MONIER RAHALL

cc: Chuck Russell   Doug Tkachuk
        McLennan Ross   Bryan & Company
        Graham McLennan   M. D. Fossen
        McLennan Ross   Alberta Treasury Branches
                                        (Strathcona)

The letter touched on many issues, but there are many more that I did not include. Justice Bielby signed orders that allowed Coopers & Lybrand to work for both the debtor and the creditor in a textbook conflict of interest. She also signed orders that allowed unsecured creditors to rank ahead of secured creditors. And finally, she constantly granted orders to Mr. McLennan without proper Notices of Motion or applications being made, an absolute violation of the Rules of Court. One can hardly defend themselves when no notice is given in order to deliberately undermine the process. Is it any wonder that Graham McLennan preferred to have Justice Bielby hear matters rather than another Justice? I complained further about this latest appointment, Madame Justice

Bielby subsequently resigned, and Associate Chief Justice Wachowich appointed the third case management judge, Mr. Justice Erik Lefsrud. Things then became truly bizarre and deserve a chapter unto themselves.

CHAPTER 7
THE HONOURABLE ERIK THE RED

"Once Law was sitting on the bench,
And mercy knelt a-weeping.
`Clear out!` he cried, `disordered wench!
Nor come before me creeping.
Upon your knees if you appear,
`Tis plain you have no standing here.`"[6]

I guess, for the benefit of those who are not of Nordic extraction, Mr. Justice Lefsrud's heritage, I should explain the concept of a Viking funeral. When a Viking warrior died, his community would lash the body to the mast of a long boat, set it aflame, and send it out to sea. Many times in Mr. Justice Lefsrud's Court, I was lashed to the mast.

Mr. Justice Lefsrud, as you will recall from the very end of the last chapter, was appointed as case management judge in March 1996. I was always brought up to believe "that men in high places should be like Caesar's wife, beyond suspicion." In fact, as time passed, I began to realize that the Associate Chief Justice, Allan H. Wachowich had a type of "cabinet" of judges that he relied on in difficult matters. A case in point, watch for Justice Lefsrud to appear in some very high profile cases involving the Alberta Treasury Branches.

---

[6] Devil's Dictionary. Ambrose Bierce. Page 69.

Justice Lefsrud was indeed consistent--consistently unfair each time I appeared before him. I am not sure, but I have watched a lot of episodes of Hogan's Heroes, and I am fairly certain that my treatment violated the Geneva Convention. In all the motions brought by me and against me, he never, ever, ruled in my favour; never, not once, granted an order that I was seeking. He was undermining the basics of legal reasoning which is concerned with the legitimacy of the process. Surely, even I, as a legal layman could be right one percent of the time. Justice Lefsrud was continually rude and patronizing at best and this was not merely my opinion. The various proceedings are all available on transcript for anyone to examine. Because the Justices were taking the matter quite seriously indeed, any appearance I made in the court room was now being recorded on transcript. Whenever I had a good point or excellent argument to make, Justice Lefsrud continually cut me off and made sure that my argument did not become part of the record. In addition, every time I made a good point that he could not answer, he would drag out some tired argument about the Rules of Court. It became obvious that he was unfamiliar with these Rules, as he was unable to apply them accurately or fairly. As the reader will see, it was evident that Justice Lefsrud had two different sets of rules in his court room.

At my first appearance before Justice Lefsrud in April 1996, he granted orders for Mr. Graham McLennan, Counsel for the Alberta Treasury Branches, to strike my lawsuits against the ATB. (My Counsel, Roy Henning, was basically run off by Justice

Lefsrud, so from this point on, I was representing myself.) I explained to the Justice that Mr. McLennan had admitted to me, my counsel, as well as others, that he petitioned me into bankruptcy in order to eliminate my lawsuits by asking for security for costs, which he knew the Trustee would never agree to because the Alberta Treasury Branches was paying the Trustee. It was fait accompli for Mr. McLennan and the Alberta Treasury Branches.

On July 9, 1996, there was no doubt from these proceedings that Justice Lefsrud discarded any pretense of fairness whatsoever. It was after that July 9 session that I wrote the following letter to him:

10 July 1996

Dear Sir:

I was extremely disheartened by the fact that in yesterday morning's proceedings (9 July 1996) I was denied the right to be heard fully before the Court. The Court refused to apply the Bankruptcy and Insolvency Act and I was not allowed to present the argument, that according to Sec 168.1(f) 168.4, and 169.1 of the Act, I was automatically and absolutely discharged as of 29 February 1996, or nine months after the making of the receiving order of 1 June 1995. I was not allowed to apply the law. This was not a frivolous argument; in addition, I had spent several days researching applicable case law for my arguments and to guard against misinterpretation, checked my position against information from Industry Canada in Ottawa, as well as other Trustees. Their information confirmed my reading of the Act. The Trustee failed to deliver the report within the prescribed period of nine months. The choice of Trustee and Counsel was not mine. If the Alberta Treasury Branches imprudently chose an inadequate Trustee and Counsel, then I can hardly be held responsible. <u>I was absolutely and automatically discharged; there was no court order required</u>. With all due respect sir, the decision regarding discharge is contained within the Act itself and does not require a judicial order. I quote the relevant sections here:

Section 168.1(f) where the Superintendent, the trustee or a creditor has not opposed the discharge of the bankrupt in the nine month period immediately following the bankruptcy, then, subject to subsection 157.1(3), (i) on the expiration of that nine month period, the bankrupt is automatically discharged.

Section 168.4   An automatic discharge by virtue of paragraph(1)(f) has, for all purposes, the same effect as an absolute and immediate order of discharge.

Section 169.1   Subject to Section 168.1, the making of a receiving order against, or an assignment by, any person except a corporation operates as an application for discharge, unless the bankrupt, by notice in writing, files in the court and serves on the trustee a waiver of application before being served by the trustee with a notice of the trustee's intention to apply to the court for an appointment for the hearing of the application as provided in this Section.

Consequently, I will be appealing your order in this situation. Since I was denied my fundamental rights and was refused my right to be heard fully and properly before the Court, I feel I was denied justice. I will be requesting a copy of the transcripts of the proceedings to study in detail and for the use of the appropriate parties.

Concerning my application to hold Mr. Peterson (the Trustee) in contempt, Mr. Tkachuk was allowed to go through every facet of his contempt motion. During the trial of Socrates, both sides were given equal time to speak to safeguard justice and due process. In my case, I was not even allowed to discuss the unanswered questions in my cross-examination of Mr. Peterson. Mr. Tkachuk had made Mr. Peterson and Mr. Edwards available in the courtroom, but <u>not only was I denied the right to ask them questions, I was denied that right before I even posed the question.</u>

Over the course of my three hour cross-examination, Mr. Peterson, on five affidavits that he refers to, uttered less than nine hundred words in response, refusing to answer questions directly pertaining to his civil contempt motion against me. Yet my family and associates are subject to bench warrants and civil contempt motions because they cannot answer undertakings which are not within their control.

As well, included in the civil contempt motions against me were sworn affidavits by Mr. Peterson. By refusing to answer the questions put to him that directly concerned those affidavits, Mr. Peterson was able to avoid confronting the validity of the issues contained therein. I have sworn additional affidavits in regard to this issue, and these affidavits have not been addressed. The Canadian Bill of Rights, Sec 2(e) established that:

Every law of Canada shall, unless it is expressly declared by an Act of the Parliament of Canada that it shall operate notwithstanding the *Canadian Bill of Rights*, be so construed and applied as not to abrogate, abridge or infringe or to authorize the abrogation, abridgement or infringement of any of the rights or freedoms herein recognized and declared, and in particular, no law of Canada shall be construed or applied so as to...

(e) deprive a person of the right to fair hearing in accordance with the principles of fundamental justice for the determination of his rights and obligations.

I was also reminded that an order which has not been appealed, stands. That may be so, but I have had to be selective as to the orders that were appealed. When one is petitioned into bankruptcy, the right of appeal becomes burdensome because of the cost. The fact that I did not appeal the order should not in any way construe my acquiescence in the matter but should be interpreted within the financial considerations only. I am being forced to swear an affidavit, which I believe further violates my rights

To further enhance my position, case law exists to show that the Canadian Bill of Rights "applies to the Bankruptcy Act and takes precedence over any provisions of the Bankruptcy Act..." as stated by Justice Berger J. of the Supreme Court of British Columbia re Bryden.

I will remain respectful of the Court, notwithstanding my recent experience, in that I will endeavour to gather the information which the Trustee seeks. However, this action will be without prejudice to my position that I am completely and absolutely discharged and all the actions of the Trustee and his counsel are done with the knowledge of my position in accordance with the law.

With all due respect, sir, one must examine the entire picture in order to get a full appreciation of it. It is not enough to destroy me financially. These professionals must also discredit me. All the individuals in attendance at yesterday's proceedings (Mr. Peterson, Mr. Edwards, Mr. Livingstone, Ms. Hurlburt, Mr. Tkachuk, and Mr. Kenny) have their services being paid for by the Alberta Treasury Branches and no other creditor. I find it amazing that no one seems to understand or recognize blatant conflict of interest. Ms. Hurlburt and Mr. Russell have been the counsel for the

Trustee of Subway Investments (that being Coopers & Lybrand Limited). Coopers & Lybrand Limited in this case worked for both the debtor (myself) and the creditor (the Alberta Treasury Branches). To further intertwine these relationships, both Mr. Russell and Ms. Hurlburt are with the firm McLennan Ross. Graham McLennan, and Stephen Livingstone of the same firm, represent the Alberta Treasury Branches. This is a text book case of conflict of interest and I offer this point to further validate my concerns as to the manner and method of how I have been treated. This has been an incredible abuse of the process. Any shortcuts to justice are indefensible.

MONIER M. RAHALL

cc: **Associate Chief Justice Wachowich**
   William J. Kenny
   Cook Duke Cox
   Doug Tkachuk
   Bryan & Company
   Katherine Hurlburt
   McLennan Ross
   Stephen Livingstone
   McLennan Ross

I finally received a copy of the transcript with a great deal of difficulty. The cold, hard facts of that transcript confirmed what I had said in my July 10 letter. Now, armed with these facts, I replied to Associate Chief Justice Wachowich's letter which was dated July 15, 1996. It struck me as a little strange that the Associate Chief Justice would not want to be kept informed of what was being done by the third case management judge appointed by him. In addition, my circumstances were made somewhat unique in that Court Reporters and full transcripts were part of the proceedings, a requirement that was out of the ordinary in such an instance. It was similar to a judge saying to you that you have to have capital punishment or how else are they going to learn the law. I chalked it up to the Associate Chief Justice having a bad day.

I wrote him once again on August 14, 1996, with excerpts of the transcript of the July 9 proceedings. The text of my letter follows:

14 August 1996

Dear Sir:

Re: Your Letter of 15 July 1996

Firstly, in your letter you say, and I quote "You serve no good purpose in providing me with copies of your correspondence." I had hoped that the Associate Chief Justice of the Court of Queen's Bench of Alberta would have an interest in the conduct of a Justice and, more particularly, a Justice who was appointed case management judge by yourself. This is now the third Justice to address these matters, a fact which in itself, says there is sensitivity to this case.

Secondly, in your letter, you say, and I quote again "...if you are not satisfied with the decisions handed down, your recourse is to proceed to the Court of Appeal." I am well aware of my right to appeal this matter, which I have already done. However, with all due respect, sir, you did not deal with the issues that were contained in my letters.

It is a necessary implication of the prescribed procedure that neither the Bankruptcy and Insolvency Act nor the Canadian Bill of Rights should be changed by judges. "In the absence of law, a judge is a functionary without a function."

I am now in receipt of the transcript of the proceedings before Mr. Justice Lefsrud on 9 July 1996 which clearly shows that I was deprived of my right to be heard fully and present arguments pertinent to the decision. For your enlightenment, I have enclosed a copy of the transcript.

My initial reaction to the events of that morning were reinforced by close examination of the transcript. <u>A clear abridgement of my rights is demonstrated in various instances,</u> some of which I shall highlight for you. For example, consider the following:

<u>"Well, the discharge isn't going today."</u> (pg. 4, ln. 21).

<u>Justice Lefsrud had already made up his mind before he had heard any of my arguments.</u> I fully believe, that under the provisions of the Bankruptcy and Insolvency Act, in particular Sec 168.1(f), I was automatically discharged and it was not Justice Lefsrud's decision to make. He further demonstrated that he was completely unfamiliar with those provisions. When I attempted to acquaint Justice Lefsrud with the relevant portions of the Act and thus the reason for my argument, he dismissed it out of hand. Consider the following portion of the transcript:

"MR. RAHALL: The receiving order for the bankruptcy was filed on June 1st, 1995. The bankruptcy starts on June 1st, 1995. I was automatically absolutely discharged on February 29th, 1996.

THE COURT: It's too bad you're the only one that knows, including me. Just to make sure we're talking about everything, this is Action Number 49096, I take it?

MR. RAHALL: Yes, Sir. Under the provisions of the Bankruptcy Act, it clearly states in 168.1(f).

THE COURT: 168?

MR. RAHALL: 168.1(f), Sir, automatic discharge after nine months if there's no opposition by the trustee. The trustee, Sir, as I pointed out to you on several occasions has been derelict in his duties in maintaining a balance in this thing. But when I called Mr. Peterson three weeks ago and I reaffirmed and gave him a chance to explain to me what had happened, he refused to do so, only confirming that the bankruptcy was October 3rd which was absolutely incorrect.

THE COURT: Well, Mr. Rahall, let us not bore each other." (pg. 6, ln. 19-27, pg. 7, ln. 1-13).

MR. RAHALL: Further,
    "Sir, if he wanted to bring an objection to this bankruptcy, he should have done it before February 29th of 1996. Pursuant also to the Act --

THE COURT: Mr. Rahall, we're not going to waste a lot of time on this. The discharge does not go today. And it is going to be put over for a year. That deals with that application.

MR. RAHALL: This is an act of parliament, Sir" (pg. 8, ln. 1-8).

When I attempt to continue to make myself heard and make a reasoned, researched argument, Justice Lefsrud cuts me off repeatedly and refuses to consider the arguments, and dismisses the application summarily.

104

"MR. RAHALL: <u>May--can I go back to the--I wasn't quite done, Sir, I'm sorry.</u>

THE COURT: <u>Well, you're done with the bankruptcy discharge application.</u>

MR. RAHALL: <u>I have cases here, Sir, that prove that</u> -

THE COURT: <u>You know, am I not making myself clear to you? The application is over. The discharge is not being granted. It is put over for a year.</u>" (pg. 8, ln. 25-27, pg. 9, ln. 1-6).

After that, Justice Lefsrud demonstrated his lack of impartiality by continually making sarcastic and condescending remarks. As an example of his tone consider the following:

"THE COURT: This conflict of interest thing, you've reported everybody to everybody to you can report them to and then probably more than once. " (pg. 50, ln. 13-15).

These type of comments are not expected and are certainly not becoming of a Justice of the Court of Queen's Bench of Alberta. What is more, I find it ironic that Justice Lefsrud continually harps on the Rules of Court, yet when I attempt to present an argument, he runs roughshod over the facts of the law.

Justice Lefsrud realized the seriousness of his denial of my right to be heard. When a transcript was requested, that request was denied and that individual was told that Justice Lefsrud wanted to speak to anyone making such a request and until he had spoken with them, no transcript could be ordered. I was under the impression that this was a public document, therefore, I do not see the need for jurisprudence. Please find enclosed an affidavit which documents this.

Since Justice Lefsrud is the third Justice on this case, I do not believe any of these Justices' brethren in the Court of Queen's Bench of Alberta could act in an impartial and unbiased manner concerning any matter to do with me. <u>Justice Lefsrud had demonstrated this by making comments regarding the departure of Justice Agrios, which can be found on earlier transcripts</u>. The actions of the previous Justices clearly indicated that I have become nothing more than an administrative process. The odds on getting a fair and impartial hearing are greatly reduced. The public entrusts the Justices within the judicial system to ensure the stewardship of neutral principles.

As I am sure you have deduced from my tone, the reason for this letter is to acquaint you with several complaints I have with the 9 July 1996 proceedings, but mainly as a result of those proceedings, I will be making a formal complaint to the Judicial Council. Because of this formal complaint, I no longer believe that it is possible or just for Justice Lefsrud to continue to hear these matters. Since my main difficulties were with the Alberta Treasury Branches and by extension, the Government of Alberta, ATB's owner, in order to receive a fair hearing I am requesting that a Justice from another province be appointed as case management judge to assure my rights to due process and impartiality. "A judicial system cannot simply come to a fair decision without regard to the means; it must do so through fair procedure, which over time has come to be known as due process!"

MONIER M. RAHALL
cc: **Justice E. S. Lefsrud**   **William J. Kenny**
    Law Courts   Cook Duke Cox
    Doug N. Tkachuk   **Graham McLennan**
    Bryan and Company   McLennan Ross

By this time, the Associated Chief Justice was becoming exasperated and I knew I had offended the powers that be. Note that

I had sent Associate Chief Justice Wachowich a large copy of the file of cases I was not allowed to present, the same file I had sent to Justice Lefsrud. His August 30 reply was a pretty good indication that nothing was going to come to me very easily.

August 30, 1996

Dear Sir:

I have your letter of August 29, 1996. Mr. Justice Lefsrud will remain as the case management judge in these proceedings. If you wish to apply to have him removed you are to do so by way of formal Notice of Motion returnable before him asking for this relief.

This court and no court in Canada has the authority to appoint another judge from another province to sit as a judge outside of the province to which he/she is appointed, nor does a judge have the authority to act as a case manager outside of the jurisdiction that he/she is appointed.

Yours truly,

Allan H. Wachowich

Well, I could see that I was up against it. I now had to bring a motion before Justice Lefsrud for his own removal from the case. This is something that only someone like Clarence Darrow would attempt and what choice did I have? You guessed it. Why couldn't Mr. Justice Lefsrud do the honourable thing and, like a disgraced general, fall on his own sword by resigning as case management judge? I had to write the Associate Chief Justice once again with the incredible chain of events:

19 September 1996

Dear Sir:

Re: Your Letter of 30 August 1996

In your letter to me you suggest that I seek the removal of Mr. Justice Lefsrud as case management judge by way of a formal Notice of Motion returnable before him. I did as you suggested and enclosed for your information is a copy of the Notice of Motion filed September 12th for September 17th.

Notwithstanding this, Mr. Justice Lefsrud refused to deal with it during my appearance Tuesday morning and wanted a new time set up for this particular motion. I had served Mr. Tkachuk so he was well aware of the motion as well as the July 9th, 1996 transcript that I relied on. In his refusal to hear the motion, he pointed out that all parties should be served properly but even Mr. Tkachuk commented that the parties that needed to be concerned were already in the Court room. Everyone involved was familiar with the material that I relied on for my motion. Therefore, it is logical that the motion of this sensitivity should take precedence over the others that were also to be heard.

Yet, what is highly ironic, is that while Justice Lefsrud refused to hear the motion, he did address the issue of the July 9th, 1996 proceedings for his own benefit on the record. He was well aware that I had written you and asked that he be removed as case management judge as I believe he would have a bias in future applications because of my complaint against him to the Canadian Judicial Council. In addition, he also referred to the Affidavit of Kerryanne Doyle and denied that it was his instructions that no transcript be released without discussion with him (although these instructions were confirmed on two separate occasions with different individuals in the Court Reporter's Office). Justice Lefsrud's denial of this fact proves beyond doubt that now this adversarial mess has reached the point where contradictory evidence is being given by a Justice and a third party. In this instance, Justice Lefsrud put a statement on the record regarding an issue he refused to hear. Had he treated the matter impartially, he would have made no further comment. Am I to assume by

Justice Lefsrud's actions, that the way to ensure that an individual's rights to be fully heard are not abridged or abrogated is by denying the motion being set forth in the first place? It appears that the logic here is that his previous conduct was indefensible, so why defend it at all and just move on.

I have now tried it your way. I am in total disbelief that Justice Lefsrud would proceed with the other applications without addressing this extremely sensitive matter first. To make matters worse, outside the Courtroom, Mr. Tkachuk asked me why I was wasting my time on the motion as he was sure Justice Lefsrud was not going to remove himself from this case. Did he have some sort of inside knowledge that I was not aware of?

Allow me to preface the description of the actual proceedings by saying that two very strange things happened. First, when the Notice of Motion to have Justice Lefsrud disqualified was filed, the filing Clerk called my office to ensure that the motion was indeed to have Justice Lefsrud disqualified. She was assured that it was. I found it highly unlikely that a Notice of Motion unusual enough to be questioned and checked twice by the Clerk on such a sensitive matter does not reach Mr. Justice Lefsrud. The Clerk filed the document and double checked it. If there was a problem with the motion, I should have been contacted by the Clerk of the Court or the Trial Coordinator and no such contact was ever made. In addition, Mr. Tkachuk has written me on several occasions informing me that it was improper for me to have contact with the Justice. For Justice Lefsrud to not hear the motion is unacceptable and defies credulity. Second, Mr. Justice Lefsrud's previous commitment at 10:00 a.m. was cancelled which he mentioned to me during the proceedings (which is on the record). At approximately 9:40 a.m., the proceedings were adjourned for a short break, until 10:00 a.m., and then the rest of the applications took about ten minutes. The point I wish to make is that had Mr. Justice Lefsrud the will to hear my motion, the Court Reporter and the other people were in place to do so. He was familiar with the material and the time was available to hear the motion as Courtroom 312 was available. Mr. Justice Lefsrud had already indicated that with his 10:00 a.m. session cancelled, time could not have been a factor in his decision not to hear my motion. Let me just reiterate. I filed a Notice of Motion on September 12th for the 17th of September; I relied on evidence that all the participants were familiar with; and finally, there was adequate time to hear the motion if so desired. Surely jurisprudence would dictate that the sensitivity of this motion would take precedence over the other applications as it affects the outcome of the others. For Justice Lefsrud not to hear this motion under these conditions only reaffirms his bias in trying to administer damage control in this matter.

In the applications that were heard, Mr. Mechan, my associate was out of the country. His counsel, Mr. Hamish Henderson, had informed Mr. Tkachuk and Justice Lefsrud that he was in a trial in Grande Prairie and was unable to attend. Notwithstanding these two factors combined, Mr. Henderson and Mr. Mechan were not given the courtesy of an adjournment. I delivered a letter to Mr. Justice Lefsrud that was faxed to me by Mr. Mechan (and which I have enclosed) indicating his inability to attend on the September 17th date as well as his discomfort at not having counsel available. Mr. Justice Lefsrud dismissed the letter out of hand.

After delivering the letter which clearly states that Mr. Mechan believes that he had fulfilled his commitment in answering the undertakings, and if they were not acceptable to Mr. Tkachuk, he had the right to re-examine Mr. Mechan on those undertakings. I was offended at what took place next. Justice Lefsrud did not even review the undertakings that Mr. Mechan had provided and accepted Mr. Tkachuk's thirty second argument that they were unacceptable. The entire application took less than five minutes. The result was one of the strongest orders issued to date. What makes this so high-handed is that a review of Mr. Mechan's undertakings, was not a factor in Justice Lefsrud's decision. Yet in my case, despite Mr. Tkachuk wanting to review only those matters with which he had questions, Justice Lefsrud insisted on reviewing all of the answers within the order, ninety percent of which, even in Mr. Tkachuk's opinion, I had complied with (which the transcript of September 17th will clearly show). Where is the consistency? The neutral principles of law have been absolutely violated here by the extreme application of jurisprudence. The Canadian Bill of Rights clearly states that Mr. Mechan has the right to counsel. Justice Lefsrud should have adjourned the matter until counsel was present for Mr. Mechan. Where the law, statutes, and the Canadian Bill of Rights stops, so must the Justice stop. I will be pointing out to Mr. Mechan that I believe his rights were violated under Sec 2(e)(ii) and Sec 2(d) of the Canadian Bill or Rights.

Let me refer you to the transcript of the July 9, 1996 proceedings, specifically page 5, line 8, and I quote:

"MR. RAHALL: May I ask in your presence, Sir, may I ask Mr. Peterson a couple of questions that I think are very prudent?
THE COURT: We're here making applications.
MR. RAHALL: All right.
THE COURT: We're not giving evidence today. You and I have discussed the Rules of Court from time to time. They apply to everybody. You have to comply with them just like everybody else."

Firstly, Mr. Tkachuk made the trustee Mr. Peterson available in the Courtroom that morning for the very reason to answer questions. In a three hour cross-examination on five affidavits, Mr. Peterson uttered barely 900 words. In addition, the cross-examination was not complete and Mr. Tkachuk refused to complete it saying that he would make the Trustee available in Court so that Justice Lefsrud could decide on whether or not to complete the examination as well as the questions that he refused to answer.   Justice Lefsrud refused to allow me to ask any questions on Mr. Peterson's cross-examination and other matters, before I even posed those questions. Yet, later in the transcript, Mr. Tkachuk is allowed to go through every facet of his questioning verbatim. Contrast this with the way I (and Mr. Mechan) have been treated. Not only are we to provide answers and undertakings which are subject to re-examination, my problem is that the re-examination is in front of Justice Lefsrud. In our case, we are not allowed to even pose a question; while in Mr. Tkachuk's case he is able to deal with the most minute details before Justice Lefsrud. The contrast is appalling. The problem that I have with all of this, when I have a valid point to make before the Court, rather than deal with the issue, Justice Lefsrud refers to the Rules of Court. It is my belief that two sets of rules exist, the Rules of Court that apply to me and the refusal to hear properly filed motions and the ability to pose questions are denied. In Mr. Tkachuk's case he is granted orders without application and motions and is allowed to ask whatever questions he cares to. The

111

only scrutiny that Justice Lefsrud is subject to are by professional colleagues as well as the Canadian Judicial Council who must judge this display of lack of judicial integrity.

In addition, it has also come to my attention that a close relative of Justice Lefsrud is a lawyer at Bryan & Company. This was never made known to me before Justice Lefsrud became case management judge and still has not been made known to me to date officially. I discovered the relationship informally on my own. There is a saying, that if you marry a mountain girl, then you also marry the mountain. This is aptly demonstrated by the fact that this relative is Ian Reynolds, Justice Lefsrud's son-in-law. If one takes into account the magnitude of this case with everything that is at stake one can understand Justice Lefsrud's reasoning behind his reluctance to decide any portion of this case in my favour when one also realizes he may have some allegiance to the law firm, Bryan & Company. In a conversation with Mr. Mechan, he informed me that the individual in question was acting against him as well as other associates, in another matter representing the lender of a property I used to own. Even Mr. Tkachuk referred to his Bryan & Company colleague's, Ian Reynolds, contempt application against Mr. Mechan I also understand that the contempt motion is being brought forward because of a scheduling problem between the parties. This is a clear example that this has not only become a bias issue, but it has become a personal issue with all the parties involved.

In closing, jurisprudence must rely on legitimate process to ensure judicial authority. On July 9th, Mr. Tkachuk was granted an order without proper application or motion, while on the other hand, on September 17th, I was denied the right to bring a properly filed motion forward. With all due respect sir, a letter from you stating that you have no further comment is unacceptable. The parties involved are using their vindictiveness masked under the cover of law to disguise and deflect their bias. Although difficult, the Court of Queen's Bench of Alberta is obligated to act as its own check and balance to ensure the rights of individuals. I submit to you that this has become such a quagmire that even the beleaguered General Jean Boyle would be able to recognize it. In spite of all this, I am prepared to meet with you to select a new Justice that can be mutually agreed upon. Thank you for your cooperation in advance.

MONIER M. RAHALL

cc: **The Honourable Catherine Fraser**
        Chief Justice of the Court of Appeal of Alberta
        Mr. Justice E. S. Lefsrud
        Court of Queen's Bench of Alberta
        Ms. Jeanne Thomas
        Canadian Judicial Council

This was an episode that only Rod Serling could appreciate. I kept clicking my heels together, hoping I would find myself in Kansas or perhaps I was in a scene from the movie, "Ground Hog Day" and I was reliving the same days over and over again. As you can see by the results, instead of becoming more sensitive to my rights, I had rolled an incredibly huge boulder up a hill only to have Justice Lefsrud roll that same boulder back down the hill, right over me. I next got out my atlas to confirm that I was living in Canada, not some third world banana republic.

I was right. This last letter definitely got the Associate Chief Justice's attention.

Dear Mr. Rahall:

Your letter of September 19, 1996, was brought to my attention upon my return to my office on September 24th after being absent for the past 10 days. This explains why you have not received an immediate reply to your letter. In this reply I do not intend to deal with every item that you have raised in your correspondence and I will deal with two issues, those being the matter of a Notice of Motion that you filed on September 12th returnable for September 17th to remove Justice Lefsrud as the case manager and your allegation as to his alleged allegiance to the firm of Bryan & Co.

As to the first matter I have reviewed the court records. My advice to you in my letter of August 30, 1996, was to file a Notice of Motion to have Justice Lefsrud removed as case management judge. It appears that you in fact did this, however, only two applications were to come before Justice Lefsrud at 8:30 a.m. on Tuesday, September 17th. Those were applications filed by Mr. Tkachuk. These applications were being heard at a time when Justice Lefsrud would not normally be sitting. Any applications that come before a judge outside of normal court sittings, i.e., at 10:00 a.m., will only be entertained if prior arrangements are made for the application to be heard by the judge. The record indicates that you never contacted Justice Lefsrud prior to September 17th to have your application heard. Nor did the Clerk's Office bring this matter to Justice Lefsrud's attention prior to this time. If you wish to make this application outside of normal court sittings you should contact the Trial Co-ordinators to ascertain when Justice Lefsrud is available to hear such an application. Such applications which would probably take more than an hour should not interfere with a judge's regular assignments. I can well understand why Justice Lefsrud would not hear your application at the time that you made it returnable as this would have obviously prolonged his morning and interfered with his regular assignments. More important, all parties who were involved in the case management proceedings are to be served with a Notice of Motion and affidavit in support. From the record it appears that this was not the case notwithstanding your representation that all concerned parties were already in the courtroom. This failure on your behalf necessitated an adjournment.

For you to allege that Justice Lefsrud has some special allegiance with Bryan & Co. because of the fact that he has a son-in-law associated with that law firm has nothing to do with the application that is before him. Many judges in our court have closer connections with member of law firms than Justice Lefsrud has with Bryan & Co. and this does not preclude us from hearing applications involving those firms. I personally find myself hearing all types of applications from firms wherein my son or daughter is associated and I, like other judges, have found both for and against those firms. In my view your complaint in this regard has no validity whatsoever.

If you intend to proceed with your motion to have Justice Lefsrud disqualified you are to arrange a suitable time for that matter to be heard by contacting the Trial Co-ordinator's office to set the time and ensure that all parties involved in the case management process are duly served.

Yours truly,

Allan H. Wachowich

Mr. Justice Wachowich was stealing from Groucho Marx--Do you want to believe me or do you want to believe your eyes? As you can see from the tone of the letter, it appeared that Associate Chief Justice Wachowich wanted to pull my jersey over my head and get in a few good punches. Since I had already elevated his blood pressure, what did I have to lose by writing him once again--so I did on October 8:

8 October 1996

Dear Sir:

Re: Your Letter of 25 September 1996

I find the first paragraph of your letter to be evasive. You say, "In this reply I do not intend to deal with every item that you have raised in your correspondence and I will deal with two issues". Why be so selective? <u>Are these other issues without merit, do you not have an answer for them, or is it, as Associate Chief Justice you feel that you do not need to deal with them</u>. All the issues that I raised have a bearing on the outcome of the proceedings. This is, I believe, what is known as an evidentiary foundation. Everything must be considered in order to formulate a proper answer.

One of the most crucial questions that you failed to answer, is how can Mr. Tkachuk be given an order on July 9th, 1996 for contempt when he filed no Notice of Motion or application. Then on September 17th, an even stronger order is granted, once again violating the Rules of Court. <u>If you refer to the transcript you will see that Rule 702 of the Rules of Court, dealing with civil contempt is clearly violated</u>. I refer you to page 797 of the Rules 702 note 1, wherein it states "Notice of the application must be given to the respondent; notice to counsel is not enough." And on page 802 according to Rule 702 note 6. "Respondent Must Be Given Opportunity to Explain." I quote further:

And subsequently for the Court of Appeal, Haddad J.A. said:

I am persuaded that having regard to the dire consequences a contempt citation is capable of yielding, the following principles have been recognized and are applicable in this case:

1. Caution should always be exercised to the extent that the person accused should be given the opportunity to retain and instruct counsel; and

2. He should be accorded the opportunity to offer an explanation or an apology before punishment is imposed...

The rule, well established, is that in applications to commit for contempt, the exercise of caution extends to ensuring, if possible, that a person accused of contempt is given notice of a motion to have him cited and committed. *250242 Alberta Ltd. v. Sohal* (1983), Alta. L.R. (2d) 382 (C.A.), at 388."

In the transcript, even Mr. Justice Lefsrud has a question on this point, but Mr. Tkachuk breezes over it. In the transcript this is plainly evident on page 3 at line 14: "COURT: Have you proper service on Mr. Mechan?" Mr. Tkachuk replies, "Sir, there is no need for service upon Mr. Mechan in the sense that your Court Order provided that if he does not provide the answers to the undertakings that he can be apprehended." Mr. Justice Lefsrud and Mr. Tkachuk were well aware that there was no Notice or application of this original Court Order. <u>Yet, in my case, with a motion, with adequate time, and with parties familiar with the evidence I relied on, my right to be heard is denied. I would ask that you please answer this question.</u> As well, concerning this order, I find it strange that you mention in your letter that you did not return until September 24th, and Mr. Justice Lefsrud did not sign his order until September 25th. Am I to assume that there is more than one Justice making the decision on these orders? [Note: It was over a week before the Justice signed the order.]

In your second paragraph, you address my concerns regarding the fact that my motion to have Mr. Justice Lefsrud removed was not heard. This seems to me to be somewhat convenient in that in the July 9th, 1996 proceedings, I followed the identical procedure and my applications made it before Mr. Justice Lefsrud with no problem whatsoever. It appears suspect that this particular motion for September 17th was not placed before the Justice as well.

In addition, my motion of 17 September 1996 was, in my opinion, the most sensitive motion of the case that Mr. Justice Lefsrud had to hear to date. Time was not a constraint as can be seen from the transcript. "COURT: Well, what I was saying to you before is that, you know, you're just fortunate today because I had a jury trial that didn't go or I'd be in real trouble at 10:00." If Justice Lefsrud did not feel prepared to hear my motion, then he should have adjourned all matters until he was willing to do so as the outcome of my motion would have had an effect on Mr. Tkachuk's motions.

If you check the transcript of the September 17th, 1996 proceedings you will notice a glaring inconsistency. In your letter you say that I never contacted Justice Lefsrud prior to the Court sitting to have the matter heard. Yet, Mr. Tkachuk continually advises me that it is improper for me to contact Mr. Justice Lefsrud directly. In the transcript, near the beginning of the proceedings, Mr. Justice Lefsrud says on page 6 at line 14, "Accordingly all proceedings will be dealt with formally. Although I can still be contacted personally to arrange applications at the earliest date possible." Later, same page, at line 22 he says regarding my application concerning his removal: "Accordingly, should you wish to make that application I invite you to contact the Trial Co-ordinators to determine my availability... and when that date is secured, you should file a Notice of Motion and Affidavit, serve copies of that material upon interested parties and at the appointed time, I'll hear the application." Further, page 8 at line 14: "I have invited you more than once and I have invited Mr. Tkachuk to contact me in order to arrange a time." On the next page: "So I suggest you go, once we're done this morning, you go to the Trial Co-ordinator to ask them." Near the end of the morning's proceedings, Mr. Justice Lefsrud continues to confuse the issue. Note page 51 at line 9. "You can talk to Mr. Tkachuk to find his available days and then one of you can give me a call and we'll set up a time at 8:30 in the morning to deal with that." Is there any wonder that I am not sure which way to make the application? It is readily apparent that neither you nor Mr. Justice Lefsrud can agree on the proper method either.

As I mentioned Mr. Tkachuk is continually talking to Justice Lefsrud but whenever I do so, he tells me it is improper to talk to a Justice. I received a prime example today of Mr. Tkachuk's hypocrisy and self-righteousness. Apparently it is perfectly acceptable for him to write a letter to Mr. Justice Lefsrud directly. He forwarded a copy of just such a letter dated 9 October 1996 and addressed to Mr. Justice Lefsrud. The different and discriminatory treatment of my application and correspondence when compared with Mr. Tkachuk is boldly and starkly highlighted in this instance.

It has also just recently come to my attention that it was you who made the assignment of Mr. Justice Belzil for the 11 September 1996 session and that it was outside the normal assignment. I was told that the reason for the choice was that there was an outstanding complaint concerning Mr. Justice Lefsrud that I had filed with the Canadian Judicial Council. Once again, I must question the consistency of decisions at the Law Courts Building. I find it passing strange that Mr. Justice Lefsrud was too controversial to handle the 11 September 1996 session and you found it necessary to have Mr. Justice Belzil preside. Yet, on September 17th, still after the complaint regarding Mr. Justice Lefsrud had been made to the Canadian Judicial Council, he was perfectly acceptable to you. Perhaps you could explain the difference in reasoning to me.

I must make another comparison of Mr. Justice Belzil with Mr. Justice Lefsrud. Mr. Sharek was given a Court time of 10:00 a.m., 11 September 1996. In this instance, it was the Associate Chief Justice who arranged for these two applications to be heard with a Court Reporter at 10:00 a.m. However, when it comes to my motion, it is handled with the greatest amount of obstacles possible in order to ensure that I am not allowed to be heard. How is it that a motion by Mr. Sharek against me comes to your attention immediately and it is given a time with a Court Reporter right away yet when I file a motion, I am led to believe that this does not come to your attention. Surely, it cannot be done both ways. That being said, let me make it perfectly clear that this is not meant to be seen as a criticism of Mr. Justice Belzil. He has treated me with the utmost respect.

It seems that lawyers have access to the Justice and are allowed to make private arrangements without my knowledge or consent. It is deemed to be unethical to talk to one of the Justices about the case without the knowledge of the other party. Nobody ever calls me to see if times are convenient or acceptable to me. I am merely expected to be there or be held in contempt. It appears that the level playing field does not exist for me at the Court of Queen's Bench of Alberta.

You deal with Mr. Justice Lefsrud's conflict of interest in that he has a son-in-law associated with the same law firm, Bryan & Company, as the Counsel for the Trustee. You missed my point entirely. Referring to your own son and daughter, would you hear a case in which your son or daughter was counsel for one of the parties? Or would you hear a case in which your son or daughter was acting against an associate of one of the parties in a related action? I suspect not. That was the point I intended to make and with all due respect my complaint is pertinent indeed. A Court of Queen's Bench Justice was a former tenant in one of my office buildings and that Justice would not even look at a file that concerned me, let alone hear it. In a normal rotation of assignments, I could see how such a situation could arise when the lawyers involved are not aware of which Justice will be presiding over a particular case, but in a case management scenario, this excuse is not valid. Everyone is fully aware of who the presiding Justice is going to be, and in such an instance, there is not reasonable excuse for not disclosing to all parties a potential conflict of interest.

Finally, let me say that my experience so far with the Court of Queen's Bench has led me to one conclusion. <u>When I was growing up I was always taught that a judge's duty was to ensure that the strong were just and the vulnerable were secure.</u> That conclusion is that the reverence I once held for the judicial system has been shattered and the cause of justice and the right to due process have been ill-served.

MONIER M. RAHALL

cc: **Ms. Jeanne Thomas**
      Canadian Judicial Council
      Mr. Justice Lefsrud
      Law Courts
      The Honourable Catherine Fraser
      Chief Justice of the Court of Appeal of Alberta

Once again, I would say that Associate Chief Justice Wachowich had had enough and declined to correspond with me personally again. Instead, he passed the gauntlet to Ms. Lori Ann Boychuk, legal assistant to the Chief Justice in Calgary. Just as I thought we were becoming pen pals, I was cruelly rejected by my pal. This, after he had given the false sense that he appreciated my legal writing.

It was obvious that the Associate Chief Justice was taking this personally. An individual in the Lebanese community informed me that I should see a gentleman named Terry Tarrabain, who was also of Lebanese descent. Apparently, he knew the Associate Chief Justice quite well, which he readily admitted. I went to his pawnshop on 96 Street and 111 Avenue in Edmonton to meet him. I gave him a brief synopsis of what had happened to me, and he asked who were the Justices involved. When I mentioned their names, he acknowledged he knew Justice Lefsrud and Justice Agrios. I simply asked if he could find out why I was being treated in such a manner. Mr. Tarrabain asked me to return, which I did on a couple of occasions, and it became apparent that he did not want to get involved. The only advice he gave me, after a two-week runaround, was that if you upset one of the Justices, you upset them all.

As a side note, there was another strange coincidence: I had put forth a motion in the Court of Appeal in the first week of September 1996. The actions of Justice Lefsrud led me to believe that I could receive a stay of all bankruptcy proceedings until the matter could be heard in the Court of Appeal. The Justice sitting in the Court of Appeal that day was Mr. Justice Belzil, Sr. Mr. Justice Belzil, Sr. flatly denied my stay of proceedings. In fact, the entire Notice of Motion took less than five minutes. A few days later, I appeared before a new case management judge, appointed by Justice Wachowich for the Law Society lawsuit. This Justice appointed by

Associate Chief Justice Wachowich was Justice Belzil, Jr. who was also appointed to handle the file of one of my associates. (Probably just a coincidence.)

Now, here is the missive that was sent to me by Ms. Boychuk on behalf of Associate Chief Justice Wachowich. It shows that if you can't be forthright, at least be vague.

By Fax: 426-3574

Dear Mr. Rahall:

The Honourable Allan H. Wachowich, Associate Chief Justice of the Court of Queen's Bench of Alberta, has asked me to acknowledge receipt of your most recent correspondence addressed to his office dated October 8, 1996, and to provide you with a response.

I note that you have expressed a number of concerns in your letter. You are not happy with the Order granted on September 17, 1996, by Mr. Justice Lefsrud and you allege that Associate Chief Justice Wachowich is being "evasive" in his reply to your earlier letter. A review of your past correspondence to Associate Chief Justice Wachowich indicates that your primary concerns have been the rulings made by Mr. Justice Lefsrud or the procedure he has followed when you have come before him. Please note, Mr. Rahall, that if you are unhappy with a decision made by justice of the Court of Queen's Bench, the appropriate recourse is to take steps to appeal the decision to the Alberta Court of Appeal. The Chief Justice Wachowich does not intend to be evasive. Neither he nor any other member of the

Court is in a position to interfere with, explain, or otherwise deal with a decision of another justice with respect to an ongoing proceeding which is before the Court. Once a decision has been rendered, this role is more properly performed by the Court of Appeal.

I emphasize that it is not Associate Chief Justice Wachowich's function to comment on Mr. Justice Lefsrud's decisions in this instance.

With respect to the matters which have been assigned to Mr. Justice Belzil, please be advised that the fact that you have filed a complaint with the Canadian Judicial Council concerning the conduct of Mr. Justice Lefsrud is of no consequence in this assignment. Rather, these matters simply are unrelated to those which are presently before Mr. Justice Lefsrud and, therefore, may be handled by another justice of the Court. [huh?]

As has been clearly indicated in previous correspondence, if is your wish to have Mr. Justice Lefsrud removed as case management judge on the files for which he has been assigned, you must bring a formal application in accordance with the Alberta Rules of Court. If a proper Notice of Motion, together with supporting affidavits, is filed and properly served, the matter will be heard by the Court. The reasons why you were not heard on September 17 have been explained to you both by Mr. Justice Lefsrud and by the Associate Chief Justice and there is nothing further that I can add. I can assure you, however, that there is no intention to "have more than one Justice [make decisions]" or otherwise act in a 'suspect' manner. <u>Perhaps our attempts to deal with your correspondence have created some confusion or seeming inconsistencies and this, I suggest,</u> would further support a view that your concerns should be directed, as appropriate, to the Court of Appeal and not to Associate Chief Justice Wachowich.

The Associate Chief Justice has asked me to reiterate that he is not in a position to continue to respond to your correspondence should your complaints be of the same nature.

Yours truly,

L. A. Boychuk

cc: *The Honourable Catherine A. Fraser*
Chief Justice of Alberta
The Honourable Allan H. Wachowich
Associate Chief Justice of the Court of Queen's Bench
Mr. Justice E. Lefsrud
Ms. Jeannie Thomas
Canadian Judicial Council

I remained defiant and continued to write the Associate Chief Justice directly.

28 October 1996

Dear Sir:

Re: Ms. Lori Boychuk's Letter of 16 October 1996

The tenor of the above-referenced letter is somewhat puzzling. <u>Ms. Boychuk says that you are not being evasive but yet you draft her to write your response to my letter.</u> I have yet to hear your reasoning behind the failure to answer all of my questions from the previous letters. It appears that you are now case managing the correspondence. Notwithstanding Ms. Boychuk's denial on your behalf, this is what I call being evasive.

Regarding the appointment of Mr. Justice Belzil, how can you say that the matters are of no consequence when it was you who informed Mr. Sharek that you had chosen Mr. Justice Belzil because there was a complaint against Mr. Justice Lefsrud that I filed with the Canadian Judicial Council? Justice Belzil has confirmed that he was appointed case management judge on September 6 and heard the matter within days (on September 11). Mr. Justice Belzil was appointed outside the normal rotation of assignments so that the contention that "these matters are simply unrelated" holds no water whatsoever. It is quite apparent by the appointment of Justice Belzil and the fact that Mr. Sharek's motions were given a time with less notice than my motion to remove Justice Lefsrud. It begs credulity for one not to believe that Mr. Sharek, the Law Society, and Graham McLennan were not favoured in this instance. The fact that you appointed a different justice in these new matters only confirms that we are in agreement that Justice Lefsrud should no longer hear any new issues.

Ms. Boychuk's letter becomes very revealing towards the end so let me return to the issue of evasiveness. Here is the telling quote: "Perhaps our attempts to deal with your correspondence have created some confusion or seeming inconsistencies and this, I suggest, would further support a view that your concerns should be directed, as appropriate, to the Court of Appeal and not to Associate Chief Justice Wachowich." The appointment of Justice Belzil to hear matters so quickly and not Justice Lefsrud who is the case management judge, can only be answered by you and not the Court of Appeal. This is an example of what I mean when I talk about evasiveness.

It is not my desire to correspond with you for the sake of correspondence. My preference is never again to appear in the Court of Queen's Bench of Alberta; it is the action of others that compels me to continue to appear. I am disappointed that in the Court of Queen's Bench I have become nothing more than an administrative process and that justice has become a result not a process in itself.

MONIER M. RAHALL

cc: **Ms. Jeanne Thomas**
Canadian Judicial Council
Mr. Justice Lefsrud
Law Courts
The Honourable Catherine Fraser
Chief Justice of the Court of Appeal of Alberta

As you can see, I never got any real, definitive answers to my questions. To make matters worse, I called the Trial Co-ordinator's Office and received the date of October 28, 1996, for my motion to remove Justice Lefsrud as case management judge. I prepared my documents for that date only to get a letter from Justice Lefsrud saying that the date was unacceptable even though I had it confirmed. After nearly four months, as of this writing, I have yet to get the matter heard. Compare this with the Alberta Treasury Branches Counsel who had been given every order that he had asked for and any time that he has sought. Justice for the few. The Counsel representing the Law Society, Mr. Sharek, had his motion to strike my lawsuit heard within five days of the appointment of Mr. Justice Belzil.

The words you have just read about the justice system may shock you and may even seem unbelievable to you. The wonderful thing about my case is that it is all on transcript for all to review. While I may be harsh in my judgment of the judiciary, I do understand some of the reasons behind the way things are done. The Justices are a very close-knit group. Justice Belzil, Jr. is a relatively young man and perhaps could stay in his position as a judge for another thirty years. If I have offended one of his brethren, he has to abide by an unwritten code to protect his colleagues, as well as himself. The likelihood of a fair hearing is drastically reduced. If he rules in favour of my position, he risks offending his brethren whom he must face each day for many years to come. If he rules against me, he throws the matter into the lap of the Court of Appeal and maintains his good relationship with the other Justices. It is quite logical when you think about it.

The Court of Appeal assumes that the Justices had no knowledge and wipes the slate clean, to start once again. As has already been seen, the Justices defend their position by telling the defendant that they have the right of appeal, thereby absolving them of any further obligation.

After reading this, the reader may believe that the Court of Queen's Bench of Alberta has no integrity. On the contrary, I know there are many impartial and decent Justices in the Court of Queen's Bench who find this chain of events equally as offensive. For instance, Madame Chief Justice Cathy Fraser, I believe, is fair and impartial, but she must come to grips with a dilemma. One of the major law firms that I describe in this book with several indiscretions is the firm of Cook, Duke, Cox. Madame Chief Justice Fraser's husband is a member of the same firm. I have copied Chief Justice Fraser on several of my letters, and I hope that she will begin an investigation. Although I had difficulty with a handful of these Justices, their behaviour should not colour the impression of all other Justices. Only those who would cast the system into dishonour--who dishearten those who grew up believing Justices stood for justice--should be exposed. While my faith in human reason was shaken, it was not destroyed.

PART TWO

WHERE THE BOYS ARE

CHAPTER 8
ALBERTA ADVANTAGE

"I always wanted to get into politics, but I was never light enough to get on the team."

- Art Buchwald

Everyone is probably aware of the career of one of the highest profile entrepreneurs in Edmonton, Mr. Peter Pocklington, alias Peter Puck, owner of the National Hockey League Edmonton Oilers, as well as a host of other enterprises. Mr. Pocklington also has had a turbulent relationship with the Alberta Treasury Branches and the Alberta Government which, by your leave, I intend to briefly document.

Mr. Pocklington is cat-like in his approach to business. Just when you think he has used all of his nine lives, he manages to pull a government official out of his hat to once again save him from the threat of extinction. Some hat trick! Premier Klein's Cabinet and Mr. Pocklington's hockey team have something in common: neither has many original members left.

During his days as a car dealer in Edmonton, Pocklington worked on perfecting his ability to use other people's money to finance his projects. His wholesale line of credit with Ford Credit, the Ford Motor Company of Canada's company finance arm, was frequently over extended because Mr. Pocklington was diverting the money for other projects. His vehicle orders would be placed on finance hold, but soon Mr. Pocklington would have invested the money in another project, made a profit and paid out his overdue line, and then gone on as before. It got to be a standard joke. As soon as the orders went on finance hold (i.e., vehicle orders held from production), the manufacturer's regional office staff would assume that Peter was financing some new endeavour. He was a master at extending the system to its limits for his own benefit and escaping by the skin of his teeth, or, more appropriately in the bearded Mr. Pocklington's case, by the hair of his chinny chin-chin.

In his dealings with the Alberta Treasury Branches and the Alberta Government, the story is twisted and convoluted to say the least. One of ATB's first forays into the Pocklington vortex came with the ill-fated Fidelity Trustco. In late 1982 and early 1983, the Federal regulators were already starting to sniff the odour that was coming from the propped up carcass of Fidelity Trust. The only thing that had Fidelity at the time was the stereo in Mr. Pocklington's car. It was the financial equivalent of "Weekend at Bernies". The ATB's indication was that Fidelity was in serious difficulty (a masterful degree of understatement). Notwithstanding this, the Alberta Treasury Branches in their infinite wisdom decided to lend 10 million dollars to Fidelity and Pocklington against approximately 90% of the shares by taking a hypothecation of those shares.

It was as if Mr. Pocklington was the captain of the Titanic and approached the Alberta Treasury Branches and said, "Iceberg, what iceberg? Full speed ahead!" The ATB, passengers on the sun deck, said here's the money as the water was splashing around their armpits.

While the Alberta Treasury Branches was funding Fidelity Trust, Mr. Pocklington was so strapped for cash that he borrowed over 700 thousand dollars from Arnold Portigal of Winnipeg at outrageous interest rates. Obviously, the ATB did not do any research before making the loan to Mr. Pocklington since the deal was consummated by the Superintendent of the Alberta Treasury Branches at the time, Mr. Fred Sparrow. It was Mr. Sparrow who signed the deal and arranged the designated credit. Once again the instruction to bail out Mr. Pocklington came from the top. File this following fact for future reference: the Honourable James Dinning, the Provincial Treasurer at the time the loan was made, was Director of the Southern Alberta Office of the Premier, Peter Lougheed.

The Canadian Deposit Insurance Corporation wanted the Alberta Treasury Branches to give up its hypothecation of the shares in Fidelity Trust, which it did without compensation from CDIC. Chip Collins, the Deputy Provincial Treasurer at the time, committed ATB to the release of shares. However, since Mr. Collins was in Mr. Lougheed's inner circle, it is inconceivable that Mr. Lougheed would not have known about it.

If you recall some federal history of the period, the aforementioned Peter Pocklington was campaigning for the leadership of the Federal Progressive Conservative Party. Given the ATB deal with Fidelity Trust, wouldn't it have made more sense to give the 10 million dollars directly to Mr. Pocklington's federal PC leadership bid? It certainly would have had more credibility than the hypothecation of the shares of Fidelity Trust which were worthless. As you know, both Fidelity and Mr. Pocklington's stab at federal politics failed miserably. Mr. Pocklington may, in fact, hold the world's record for the rapidity with which a loan went bad with no chance of recovery--no small accomplishment when considering the Alberta Treasury Branches' loan portfolio.

While Mr. Pocklington needed this infusion of approximately 10 million dollars in cash, the Alberta Treasury Branches soon found that they were left out in the cold. In order for Mr. Pocklington to go to the well again at the expense of the Alberta Treasury Branches, he had to make restitution of some sort. Mr. Pocklington had already leveraged the Edmonton Oilers with the Canadian Commercial Bank, the CCB, for approximately 25 million dollars. He went to the CCB and asked to place the Alberta Treasury Branches in the second position on the Oilers' loan. The CCB agreed to the ATB going to the second position, but this was all a ploy to set the ATB up for increased exposure. The CCB also placed a condition on the Alberta Treasury Branches that the loan remained non-performing and that no revenues would be diverted to the ATB. This was all a part of the plan and the ATB fell for it, lock, stock and barrel.

What happened next? The Alberta Treasury Branches knew that it was a very bad loan in that the placing of the second mortgage was a way of hiding the losses and protecting their balance sheet, as it was non-performing. Since the ATB were already halfway in, the

CCB was now prepared to test them, and you guessed it, CCB called the loan in the first position. Somehow, Mr. Pocklington was able to convince the Alberta Treasury Branches to pay out CCB's first position and become entangled with Mr. Pocklington and the Edmonton Oilers for years to come. In retrospect, the ATB should have taken its losses and walked away from Mr. Pocklington forever. There is a saying in the banking industry, your first loss is your best loss.

Over the years from the mid 1980s, this approximately 35 million dollar loan began to grow steadily to in excess of 40 million dollars. The ATB did not understand what they were getting themselves in to by paying out the first position on the Oilers. Mr. Pocklington's operating accounts were at Edmonton Main, one of the most corrupt in the system. The ATB had boxed themselves in. Mr. Pocklington kept writing cheques and the Alberta Treasury Branches kept honouring them. If they had not honoured those cheques, the National Hockey League would have stepped in, seized the franchise, and they would have been out over 40 million dollars. It would be highly unlikely then that the franchise would remain in the City of Edmonton. The ATB was damned if it did and damned if it didn't. Mr. Pocklington had masterfully manoeuvred them into a lose-lose situation which allowed him to push the ATB beyond rational limits.

The Alberta Treasury Branches formulated a plan that would dispose of Mr. Pocklington and leave the Oilers in Alberta. They found that trying to pin Mr. Pocklington down was like trying to nail jelly to a wall ... frustrating, diverting, and ultimately unproductive. In early 1993 for the first time ever, Mr. Pocklington put in writing that he would accept 85 million dollars for the team. While this was an expensive lesson for the Alberta Treasury Branches and Northlands (the City of Edmonton-owned operator of the Coliseum, the Oilers home arena) in hindsight, it was a relatively inexpensive way to rid themselves of Mr. Pocklington for good. But, once again the window of opportunity eluded them. Northlands got cute and offered Mr. Pocklington 65 million dollars. This was the beginning of the end for Edmonton Northlands and their control of the Coliseum. Mr. Pocklington led them through a long, dragged out lease negotiation that eventually gave him control of the Coliseum with federal government infrastructure money to remodel the building. This, in turn, would contribute to an increase in his revenue by adding private boxes and his acquiring the concession and parking monies. Instead of getting rid of Mr. Pocklington, he now had a stranglehold on the Coliseum, Northlands, and the ATB. Mr. Pocklington, Alberta's very own Rumpelstiltskin, continued to spin straw into gold.

Fast forward to 1996 and the Pocklington connection has ballooned to 128 million dollars since 1994 under the auspices of the now departed Acting Superintendent of the Alberta Treasury Branches, one Elmer Leahy. Why would Mr. Leahy, knowing very well that the public at large abhorred Mr. Pocklington's business acumen, increase the loan amounts that were fiscally irresponsible?

The answer to that question is relatively simple really and can be summed up in one word--graft. Mr. Leahy humbly availed himself of a number of skiing, golfing and fishing trips as a guest of Mr. Pocklington. It would be interesting to find out how the dutiful taxpayers of Alberta would have reacted had they known that the Acting Superintendent of the Alberta Treasury Branches had a history of casting, driving, and schussing compliments of Peter Pocklington's pocketbook (at least nominally--in reality at the public's expense). Mr. Leahy, that paragon of financial probity, not only stuck with Mr. Pocklington, but increased the exposure of the Alberta Treasury Branches to the detriment of the people of Alberta. As Mr. Leahy might have said after his appointment to his exalted position, "a few years ago I could not even spell corruption; now I have refined it." As you can see, Mr. Leahy was the recipient of these and other luxuries from Mr. Pocklington. Mr. Leahy's predecessors thought it necessary to have loan loss provisions in order to neutralize Mr. Pocklington's influence. Not only did he abandon this prudent policy, Mr. Leahy actually put the Alberta Treasury Branches in a worse position than they had ever been in with Mr. Pocklington. Mr. Leahy did not want to derail the gravy train, and his good living overshadowed his good judgment.

One of the major indiscretions ever perpetrated on the people of Alberta happened in conjunction with the Gainers loan guarantee by the Alberta Government. On one rainy day in 1987, Don Getty realized it was too wet to play golf so he decided to settle the bitter Gainers' strike. The result was that the Gainers plant was back in operation, and the taxpayers of Alberta were saddled with a 55 million dollar loan guarantee. First, Mr. Pocklington knew that the Government was sensitive to the issue and, as a result, he had them over a barrel. Second, Peter liked unions, as long as they were in Poland!

The story of the loan guarantee is interesting within itself. The Provincial Treasurer at the time, the Honourable Dick Johnston, stood up in the Legislature and said the Alberta Treasury Branches had nothing to do with the Gainers guaranteed loan. Mr. Johnston lied, or shall I say with proper parliamentary language, he misspoke himself. The Government guaranteed the loan and the Alberta Treasury Branches was a part of it from the beginning. The following letter from the newly departed Deputy Provincial Treasurer, A. J. McPherson, directed to Mr. Allan Bray, ATB's Superintendent, definitely destroys Mr. Johnston's version of the truth.

FROM: Deputy Provincial Treasurer
OUR FILE: EF 3584-G2
Finance and Revenue
443 Terrace Building   *YOUR FILE:*

TO: A. O. Bray   *DATE: October 1, 1987*

SUBJECT: Master Agreement made as of the 25th day of September, 1987 - $55,000,000 Guarantee for Gainers Properties, Inc.

We confirm that we have reviewed the above noted Master Agreement and related documents with our legal advisors. We are satisfied with the form and execution at this time, and that it is appropriate for you and your nominee company to sign the Master Agreement, Guarantee Agreement and other documents as presented to you or your counsel by the law firm of Lucas, Bishop & Fraser, and entrust the documents to that firm for release when they think fit.

The credit review appropriate to the terms and conditions attached to the Provincial Treasurer's memorandum to you of August 27, 1987, and to the Master Agreement and related documents has been undertaken by Treasury staff. In these circumstances we acknowledge you have not done a separate credit review and we are not relying on you to have done so.

We will also be monitoring all credits provided under the Master Agreement. At this time, the only thing we request is that you provide to us in a timely fashion the notices and other written information which are provided to you pursuant to the Master Agreement and related documents.

A. J. McPherson   cc: J.M. Drinkwater/L. Bellan   /jac

One may look at this and be shocked that the Provincial Treasurer, Dick Johnston, lied in the Legislature and to the people of Alberta about the loan guarantee, but the real problem was that Mr. Johnston and the Government now were beholden to Mr.

Pocklington. By lying in the Legislature, Mr. Johnston put a noose around not only his own neck, but also the rest of the Government, the Alberta Treasury Branches included. Mr. Pocklington was left free to jerk the rope as it suited him. This now allowed Mr. Pocklington the right of passage.

Right up front, let me give Mr. Allister McPherson, recently retired Deputy Provincial Treasurer, credit as the one who drafted the letter for the Pocklington guarantee. After all, it takes real talent to be able to put loan guarantees on a litany of financial sinkholes. Perhaps the names Novatel, Bovar, Gainers, CIC Canada, and Canadian Airlines sound familiar and bring a kind of queasy feeling to the pit of one's stomach. Mr. McPherson and his financial perspicacity was behind them all, and of course, he figures in my tale as well. A few words, then, are in order for the illustrious Mr. McPherson, who has hastily departed the vicinity of the Legislature, and floated his golden parachute into a senior vice-president and CEO position at Viridian, formerly Sherritt Gordon, which also has loan guarantees from the provincial government. (The current rumour mill has Mr. McPherson's former boss, Provincial Treasurer James Dinning, likely to resurface at the same corporation after his political career ends in the spring of 1997.) It appears that Mr. McPherson prepared his landing area quite well, indeed, although I like to think I was behind him all the way, pushing and shoving him out the door. I began writing letters to the Provincial Treasurer about Mr. McPherson in early August 1996. One of the questions I posed in those letters was why did the Provincial Treasurer need two Deputy Treasurers? Mr. McPherson retired within weeks of those letters.

During the Lougheed era, one of Mr. Lougheed's old associates from his Mannix Construction days was Chip Collins. Mr. Collins was appointed Deputy Provincial Treasurer in 1972 and remained so until his retirement in 1984 (who, until recently, worked with Provincial Treasurer, James Dinning, in an advisory capacity). It was Mr. Collins who in a highly unusual move, created two Deputy Provincial Treasurer positions, for what turned out to be overt and covert dealings. Throughout my investigation, my sources informed me that Mr. McPherson never used the front entrance to the Alberta Legislature. In fact, many consider him to be an Oliver North-type, the only difference is that he has a shorter attention span. His covert ability was more than evident when it came to my file; he exerted his influence over the Alberta Treasury Branches and the professionals that they employed so that their abuse of the process, which included me, could continue and be directed at the highest levels.

The reason Mr. McPherson received his wonderful aforementioned golden parachute and not the fate that he truly deserved was that he knew the intimate details of some of the most unconscionable deals put together by the Alberta Treasury Branches and the Alberta Government through loans and loan guarantees for nearly twenty years. This information could not be divulged, and therefore Mr. McPherson's golden parachute was necessary to ensure his silence. I believe that my letters, with their revelations about Mr. McPherson's meddling, prompted the Government's action in making a decision regarding Mr. McPherson, a decision that was long overdue. Those who attended Mr. McPherson's retirement party told me that it was quite evident that this career bureaucrat was forced from his position in an effort to create more optical purity, despite his desire to remain a bureaucrat. The government was willing to sever one of its limbs to ensure that the rest of the government body survived. This was once again an example of the damage control that continually occurred in response to my letters. When I turned on the light, the cockroaches scattered once more.

Before I started my letter writing campaign in 1995, the Acting Superintendent, Mr. Leahy, was ruthless and smug. When it started, Mr. Leahy became effectively neutralized, and his power as Acting Superintendent was usurped as I will explain later in Chapter 14. The Vice-Superintendent, Les Bellan, and Deputy Provincial Treasurer, A. J. McPherson, in their infinite collective wisdom thought that it would improve the public perception of the Alberta Treasury Branches dealings with Peter Pocklington if Mr. Pocklington would take his operating accounts out of ATB and move them to the Canadian Western Bank. Of course, the idea was ridiculous since all that happened was that the Alberta Treasury Branches were stuck with the loans while at the same time, it lost control of the cash flow. This control was vitally important because of Mr. Pocklington's history of not being able to control his spending. Mr. Bellan and Mr. McPherson acted on their idea to give the illusion that the ATB was no longer involved with Mr. Pocklington.

The Canadian Western Bank was laughing, dare I say it, all the way to the bank because now Mr. Pocklington placed his Oilers season ticket money in CWB in a current account. They now had millions on deposit with no risk. Obviously, Mr. Bellan's and Mr. McPherson's business acumen could be counted on to screw up a two-house paper route. The Alberta Treasury Branches and consequently, the people of Alberta, had the opportunity to mitigate somewhat their losses in dealings with Mr. Pocklington but thanks to the noted financial gurus, Mr. Bellan and Mr. MacPherson, that opportunity was lost. They proved that promotions in both the Government bureaucracy and the ATB were not based on performance nor intelligence.

As a concluding note, it goes without saying that Mr. Pocklington is a generous contributor to the PC Alberta Fund. Mr. Pocklington's lead counsel in his dispute with the Government of Alberta over the Gainers fiasco was none other that William J. Kenny of the law firm Cook Duke Cox. In a brilliant move by Mr. Pocklington, he not only manoeuvred hockey players, he managed to manoeuvre legal players into position for his own advantage once again. You see, Mr. Kenny was also the lead counsel for the Acting Superintendent of the Alberta Treasury Branches, a position coveted by many of the top legal minds in Alberta. I understand that Mr. Kenny and Mr. Leahy were, and perhaps are still, members of the same Catholic congregation.　With all due respect, I wonder if their priests have heard parts of this book in confession?

CHAPTER 9
THE END OF THE EARTH SALE

"Don't pay until the new Millennium"

"Greed has been severely underestimated and denigrated. There is nothing wrong with avarice as a motive as long as it doesn't lead to anti-social behaviour."

- Conrad Black

Maybe you've heard about Bill Comrie. If not, you've probably heard about his business, the Brick Warehouse furniture store chain. Bill is also well-known for his dedication to community service, but there is a side to Mr. Bill that you probably aren't aware of. That character is Mr. Bill Comrie, beneficiary of the great Alberta Treasury Branches loan system and Alberta government largesse. Mr. Comrie has suckled at the teat of the government for so long and so comfortably that they are unable to wean him.

Here's the story of an Edmonton apartment complex called Whitehall Square, one of those Alberta Treasury Branches' disaster relief funds that even the United Nations would envy. The deal to refinance the project was structured in a way to deceive Albertans covering up who was really involved in the loan. A numbered company of Mr. Comrie's (307657 Alberta Ltd.) was set up to facilitate the deal with mortgages through the Alberta Treasury Branches--specifically an 18 million dollar mortgage and another for approximately 4 million dollars. A prominent lawyer at the law firm of Bryan & Company and Tory fund contributor, Mr. Mike Crozier, is shown on the annual return as the numbered company's sole shareholder. (Bryan & Company is also the law firm of my Trustee--probably not important.) Why would a straightforward, honest arrangement need this simple deception of a numbered company?

The project was financed for approximately 125% of its true value at the time. Mr. Comrie was certainly headed for disaster. The only question that remained was when? Those ever-vigilant guardians of the public purse at the Alberta Treasury Branches elected to implement a soft receivership while allowing Mr. Comrie to continue to run the property as the receiver. This does not fall within proper or normal banking guidelines. The capturing of cash flow is the first order of business in a foreclosure or receivership.

A receiver has a legal obligation to act fairly and impartially. Mr. Comrie failed the test because he was in a conflict of interest, and his actions undermined the secured creditor for his own personal gain; thereby violating his responsibility as an official receiver. In this case, not only did Mr. Comrie receive an enormous fee to act as property manager, he knew very well that his actions had crossed the line when he then replaced all the appliances in the project bought and paid for from the Brick Warehouse. In all fairness to Mr. Comrie, the Brick Warehouse was the place with the highest prices.

How could anyone, let alone Mr. Comrie, be allowed to get away with something like this? Not only did he rape the project initially with the over-financing and the placing of the two mortgages, but he did it again on the way out, and the Alberta Treasury Branches never realized on any personal guarantees. Mr. Comrie's actions were absolutely amoral and he should have been held accountable; but he knew that the Premier at the time, Donald Getty, would not allow Mr. Comrie to suffer any repercussions for his illicit conduct.

Have you ever gone to a fast food restaurant and complained about the fries only to have them replaced by more bad fries? In order to rectify the damage that Mr. Comrie had done with Whitehall, the Alberta Treasury Branches sold the project to the Ghermezian family. There was no money down and extremely soft terms in the form of a preferential interest rate. Well, lo and behold, the Ghermezians got into a little trouble with their new acquisition, Whitehall Square, and so to remedy this, the ATB added another 5 million dollars in debt to the project, bringing the total to 27 million dollars. (Oh, by the way, the lawyer on this deal for ATB was Mark Gunderson, and the branch was First Edmonton Place--hardly a surprise.)

Four months after this additional 5 million dollars was funded to the project, the property was sold to Osgoode Properties, Inc. of Ottawa, who also got into trouble and who recently paid out to the Alberta Treasury Branches approximately 60% of their original debt. All in all, the lost interest and the original loan amounts, cumulatively would total losses of approximately 20 million dollars. Consistent with the modus operandi, Whitehall Square got passed through various incarnations. With each incarnation, the losses became greater and greater as each new owner pillaged the project for personal gain. This prolonged the agony. (Where is Dr. Kevorkian when you really need him?) How many orders of bad fries can one eat?

Prudent folks like you and me would assume that after all this, the Alberta Treasury Branches would want to end their relationship with Mr. Comrie. Alas, our assumption would be incorrect. The ATB was only too willing to continue doing business with Mr. Comrie; but now the story also includes the Bank of Nova Scotia as the victim and Mr. Comrie's enterprise, the Brick Warehouse, that I mentioned earlier.

Poor Bill got into trouble with the Brick Warehouse as well. At the time, he was approximately 115 million dollars in debt to the Alberta Treasury Branches. Mr. Comrie knew he had offended his friends at the Alberta Treasury Branches but not at the government. The ATB had come to an agreement that Mr. Comrie should move a portion of his Brick Warehouse debt from the Alberta Treasury Branches. To his credit, Mr. Comrie came up with a plan that ensured the viability of the Brick Warehouse as an ongoing entity for years to come. Many senior officials at the ATB have admitted that they doubted whether the Brick Warehouse had ever been profitable. Mr. Comrie was successful, however. The Alberta Treasury Branches and Mr. Comrie unloaded nearly 60%

of the substantial debt of the Brick Warehouse to the Bank of Nova Scotia for BNS shares. The ATB never actually got any money. The agreement between the two banks was such that neither lender could act on the loan without the other's approval. The Bank of Nova Scotia was duped by both Mr. Comrie and the Alberta Treasury Branches who knew that his operating accounts had been a mess for years. In fact, the ATB never actually knew what the Brick Warehouse had for inventory since Mr. Comrie would never allow them to do an inventory audit. However, they long suspected that Mr. Comrie was using old stock to shore up a shaky balance sheet.

Yet after all this, in 1994 when the Acting Superintendent, Elmer Leahy, took over the reins of the Alberta Treasury Branches, he saw fit to increase the loan exposure to the Brick Warehouse. Mr. Leahy did this knowing very well that the ATB had loan loss provisions of 100% of the loans to the Brick Warehouse, because they knew there was nothing to be recovered in a receivership. Before Mr. Leahy was the Acting Superintendent, the Bank of Nova Scotia wanted to place the Brick Warehouse in receivership, but needed the approval of the ATB to do so, as I discussed earlier. Mr. Leahy went out of his way to protect his friend, Bill Comrie, by ensuring that the Bank of Nova Scotia did not acquire the approval of ATB to place the Brick Warehouse in receivership.

Mr. Comrie can never be considered an intellectual, but he fancied himself as a developer. The sad truth, however, is that everything Mr. Comrie attempted to do in real estate turned into a huge mess for others but never himself; usually with the Government of Alberta and, therefore, the taxpayers of Alberta taking the proverbial haircut. One of the Brick Warehouse advertising gimmicks that was blasted over the air wares, ad nauseum, was the no down payment, no interest, don't pay until next year type of sale. Now you know the secret behind his marketing genius. He banked at the Alberta Treasury Branches.

Consider the City Centre (now Commerce Place) deal in downtown Edmonton. Mr. Comrie and Edmonton real estate developer and long time Tory bagman, Les Mabbott, got Premier Don Getty to approve a lease in the project known as the City Centre building (built by the Reichmans) for office space for the Government of Alberta, one of the main tenants--at inflated rates, of course. To add insult to injury, both Mr. Comrie and Mr. Mabbott, after the City Centre lease was signed, did a land assembly with a few of the Tory faithful. They then flipped the completed land deal to the Reichman family, Canada's best known bankrupts, for a profit. Mr. Comrie and Mr. Mabbott took a lease fee as well as a fee for arranging the land transaction.

In a depressed commercial rented market that was plagued by a glut of unleased office space, the Reichman's City Centre project should never have been built. Other landlords and developers were hurt in that City Centre was leasing AAA space at $5 per foot, a figure no one could compete with. Eventually, the Reichmans lost the project and the CIBC foreclosed on it. And you, long-suffering taxpayers, were paying for space that was never fully utilized by the government, and in some cases, the tenant improvements were never done.

There are those in the development community that believe the Premier benefited from his actions. There are many questions that are still swirling around a group of houses in San Diego, California, the site of Mr. Comrie's IHL hockey franchise. The relationship between Mr. Comrie and Mr. Getty was such that every time Mr. Comrie got into trouble, he would run to the Premier to help smooth things over. One former official at the Alberta Treasury Branches who declined to be named publicly thought that Bill Comrie was one of the worst individuals he ever dealt with. If Mr. Comrie couldn't get his way, he would enlist the aid of the Premier and the Provincial Treasurer.

Mr. Comrie is a 50% owner in the Edmonton residential development called Lewis Estates. The Churchill Group (more on them later) hold the other 50% (they also banked at the ATB and purchased Stuart Olson Construction with a huge loss to ATB). Mr. Getty has a lovely new home in this development, adjacent to the golf course where some people claim he did his best work as Premier. The choice of his residence was probably just a coincidence.

Mr. Comrie has a certain profile in the community for supporting various charities. I can't help wondering if his enthusiastic support of these fund drives (to which I understand he contributes very little monetarily himself) is a means to salve his conscience.

CHAPTER 10
THE ORPHAN THROWS THE HAIL MARY

First commandment of a Swiss banker: "Never lend money to someone who must borrow money to pay interest."

- as quoted by Lester Thurow

Whenever a sports franchise is involved in such a banking scandal as the Edmonton Oilers or the Calgary Stampeders, it becomes newsworthy. This chapter deals with the rise and fall of Mr. Larry Ryckman and the quandary he created for politicians and bankers. Mr. Ryckman's image was that of a winner and a rising star. His fall from grace to the position of one who is financially-challenged forced him to realize that he was indeed mortal. Mr. Ryckman is the living epitome of the adage that winners have many fathers, but losers are usually orphans. It is safe to say that now, Mr. Ryckman is up for adoption, and the guardian that put him up for adoption was the Government of Alberta.

As we all know, Mr. Ryckman had his $10,000 contribution to the PC Alberta Fund returned to his Trustee in bankruptcy, Coopers & Lybrand. If one looks at the list of ATB-designated credits and the list of contributors to the PC Alberta Fund, it is often confusing as to how to distinguish which list from which. Just think of the result: if all those who had loans at the Alberta Treasury Branches returned their donations, the PC Alberta Fund would be in a serious deficit position and would be the next target for some serious budget cutting by the Klein government.

Now allow me to narrow the general down to the specific. As you may be aware, a $10,000 donation to the PC Alberta Fund was not Mr. Ryckman's only foray into the rewarding world of Tory party support. On close examination of the PC Alberta Fund contributor lists, I find that Mr. Ryckman also exhibited a substantial degree of largesse ($5,000) in June of 1993 to support Tory campaign aspirations.

This was not the only occasion on which Mr. Ryckman contributed money to the PCs. During the 1993 election campaign, the Calgary Stampeders Football Club (at the time part of Mr. Ryckman's empire) supported both the campaign of Ken Kowalski, Deputy Premier, and the campaign of Premier Ralph Klein. His contributions became significant, indeed, especially in the case of Mr. Kowalski. In addition to his duties as Deputy Premier, Mr. Kowalski was also the Minister responsible for the Western Canada Lotteries, and, of course, lottery money flowed to the Stampeders (as well as other professional sports teams). Why didn't Mr. Klein order the return of these additional Kowalski campaign contributions, as well as the donation to his own campaign? These contributions certainly fall within the window for reversible transactions as specified in the Bankruptcy and Insolvency Act. As with the Multi Corp Affair, Mr. Klein is not concerned with dealing with the problem in its entirety. He is more concerned about adjusting the public perception from negative to positive.

Even more interesting is that Mr. Kowalski lent his support on behalf of the Alberta Government to back Mr. Ryckman's 8.5 million dollars in loans at the Alberta Treasury Branches. Mr. Kowalski, in florid prose, penned a letter of support for Mr. Ryckman to the Alberta Treasury Branches on behalf of the Government of Alberta. This letter supposedly gave Bill Tough, the Deputy Superintendent of the Alberta Treasury Branches, the authority to approve those loans, and which, eventually caused his demise (sorry, *retirement*, as the former Executive Director of Public Affairs for ATB liked to call it). The Alberta Treasury Branches were blamed for these bad loans to Mr. Ryckman. They were not guilty of approving bad loans, they knew they were bad. What they were guilty of was trying to justify those loans using Mr. Ryckman's suspect assets.

During May 1996, the Klein Government weathered a minor crisis when 2,000 copies of a government report on seniors was shredded as the government characterized it, "for recycling purposes only." As Premier Klein said, "I'm convinced there was nothing to hide and nothing to cover up" (The Edmonton Journal, May 15, 1996). At the time, when I was writing the Provincial Treasurer about Mr. Kowalski's shenanigans, I played on this penchant for the Tories to feed the paper shredders. Obviously, Mr. Kowalski's letter was serious stuff and because of that, most of the copies of Mr. Kowalski's letter ended up in the shredder ...

well, maybe not all of them. I'm sure that both Mr. Kowalski and Mr. Klein say this was "accidental." Right! The former Acting Superintendent of the Alberta Treasury Branches, Elmer Leahy, has admitted to shredding correspondence between him and government officials.

In my morning meeting with Mr. Kowalski on April 30, 1996, to discuss questions I had for this book, he tried to confuse the issue by saying that the loan guarantees were given by the Getty government to the Calgary Stampeders and the Edmonton Eskimos. I pointed out to him that was not the guarantee I was talking about, and instead of answering the question, he laughed nervously and did a creditable imitation of Marcel Marceau with lots of hand movement, uttering no sound.

The bankers, the politicians, and even the insolvency practitioners brought in to dissect the body are always consistent in their appearance. I pointed out in a letter to the Provincial Auditor General, Mr. Peter Valentine, that Mr. Bill Tough, Deputy Superintendent of the Alberta Treasury Branches and one of Mr. Ryckman's closest friends, approved loans and guarantees to Mr. Ryckman. This was done with Mr. Kowalski's backing, but none of these loans met proper and generally accepted banking guidelines. Mr. Ryckman, in addition to his political donations, also warmed up Mr. Tough by extending to him many and various luxuries. Significantly, when he defaulted, Mr. Ryckman was not pursued on any of his guarantees. Mr. Ryckman's personal residence is held by a corporation, 617578 Alberta Ltd., Mr.

Ryckman's lawyer. The ATB, in their infinite wisdom, put a 2 million dollar mortgage on this property in 1993. Mr. Ryckman continued to live in the house even after his problems with the ATB. Why wasn't this asset subject to personal guarantees? Now one of the recurring players took the stage once more. The Trustee for the Ryckman Financial Corporation was Coopers & Lybrand-- sound familiar? This was stage-managed by Mr. Tough, whose brother-in-law is a senior executive at Coopers & Lybrand in Calgary; thereby ensuring a known quantity would become the Trustee in this highly sensitive matter. That was why the Executive Director of the PC Alberta Fund, Peter Elzinga, only returned the most recent donation by Mr. Ryckman, as he was fairly certain there would be no more fallout. In order to try to cover up this fiasco and the additional unreturned PC contributions, Mr. Tough was forced to resign--er, retire. Mr. Tough realized that the price of his pension was silence. When the going got Tough, Tough had to get going.

CHAPTER 11
WEST EDMONTON MALL:
PHASE I

In Edmonton, Alberta, there exists what some have called the eighth wonder of the world--the West Edmonton Mall, the largest mall in the world. What thousands of tourists and Edmontonians don't know is that the term "wonder" more aptly describes the suspect financing that kept it afloat. This was the crown jewel in the Ghermezian empire, their calling card, the key to opening doors to new ventures including the Mall of America in Minneapolis, the largest mall in the United States. Hype over this great Mall became a way to seal many of their subsequent deals as they paraded dignitaries and financiers from around the world through its glittering and cavernous interior.

The Ghermezians were Iranian rug merchants who parlayed their buying and selling of oriental carpets into a massive real estate empire, all directed by the family, father and sons: Jacob, Bahman, Eskandar, Raphael, and Nader. They have become legendary in Edmonton, and Canada for that matter, for their skill at financial legerdemain.

The West Edmonton Mall has always had a tumultuous financial history, constantly being leveraged and releveraged. As one of the great American industrialists said, he who lives by leverage, dies by leverage. Caught in the middle of all this financing was none other than the Alberta Treasury Branches. While they were owed millions of dollars already in May of 1991, the ATB lent the Ghermezians another 20 million dollars for renovations to the Mall. The Ghermezians did superficial maintenance and whisked the lion's share of the 20 million dollars around the world, less the amount paid to the "friends of the Mall", the various brokers and bagmen who helped consummate the deal. This loan was, of course, processed at one of the designated credit branches, First Edmonton Place.

The power broker in all this was none other than Jake Superstein, prominent Alberta businessman. Mr. Superstein set the whole deal up and received a fee from the Ghermezian family for doing so. The branch manager at First Edmonton Place at the time was none other than Larry Leroux, the branch manager who did most of the designated credits at First Edmonton Place and Edmonton Main Branch. This is one of many deals that was done by Mr. Superstein and Mr. Leroux. They sound like a magic act (and in a way, they were). In return, Mr. Leroux received cash inducements, tailor-made suits by Pat Henning, as well as many other gifts. These benefits traveled all the way up the chain of command at the Alberta Treasury Branches. Mr. Superstein, the consummate broker, made sure of this. He has the Order of Canada and an Honourary law degree; but I wonder if there is a clause that allows these honours to be revoked for ethical indiscretions. He also was named outstanding Albertan in an Alberta Treasury Branches' sponsored program. It certainly does not require a superior degree of intelligence to realize why. To top ATB management, he **was** an outstanding Albertan indeed. The dynamic duo of Larry Leroux and Jake Superstein are responsible for some of the most magical deals ever to be realized at the Alberta Treasury Branches. Move over David Copperfield! For now, let us concentrate on the maneuverings surrounding the West Edmonton Mall.

It was evident that the Alberta Treasury Branches was never going to realize on the 20 million dollar loan and that they had been duped. This, in combination with the fact that senior officials had informed me that in all their years of banking experience, the Ghermezians were by far the most difficult customers to deal with (present company excluded!)

In late 1993 and on into 1994, the Alberta Treasury Branches began discussions with other creditors of the Mall, mainly Gentra Corporation, in order to get a consensus on how to deal with the financing of the Mall within normal banking guidelines. The individuals handling the negotiations were Mr. Doug Goebel, Executive General Manager, and his counsel, the lovely and talented Mark Gunderson of the law firm McLennan Ross. After many trips to Toronto, the ATB finally struck a deal with Gentra Corporation that fell within normal banking practices for non-performing loans.

The Ghermezians grew increasingly concerned with the inevitable fate about to befall them. The deal between the Alberta Treasury Branches and Gentra was in the final stages. The documentation was being prepared by the solicitors. The Ghermezians were desperate. They were about to lose their crown jewel and their calling card. Jake Superstein had once again bought them a little time, but even the influential Mr. Superstein could not prevent the inevitable.

In times of crisis, many of us become quite religious, hoping for some divine intervention to come to the rescue. The Ghermezians were no exception as you will see by the following letter addressed to Allan Bray, then Superintendent of the ATB:

February 14, 1994

PERSONAL AND CONFIDENTIAL

Dear Mr. Bray:

As you may know, the Ghermezian family is religiously orthodox. The Ghermezians have talked to a Kabalist in Jerusalem seeking his counsel and prayers with respect to the refinancing of West Edmonton Mall. This Kabalist has sent us the enclosed letter and insisted that we translate and send it to you. "Kabalist" is a religious man who dedicates his life to learning the secrets of our Torah (Jewish Bible) and everything in the world. The translation of the enclosed letter is as follows:

Dear Sir:

You are my respectable master. I, Yaghoob Negaran, a Kabalist, together with my other Kabalist colleagues of the holy Jerusalem, plea from the gates of Heaven, health, good ending and good deeds for you and your children.

Financial difficulties have surfaced for the Ghermezian brothers as a result of which they need your intellectual, humanitarian, good deeds help. It behooves you to participate humanly with them to resolve their difficulty. Your help and kindness will have life results for them to the end that their hard work of many years does not waste. This action of yours will cause our blessings and good prayers to continue with you and your children so that we would seek the gates of kind Heaven to grant long life, health and happiness to you and your children. I hope you do not hesitate helping them intellectually and financially towards their peace of mind. Through this good deed of yours, you will become well known and commendable in Israel and your name would remain eternal. Translate this into English.

Please accept my highest respect.

Signed by: Yaghoob Negaran

As you can see, the situation was so desperate that no accountants or lawyers could rescue the day. This letter was not a bad idea; but the likelihood of it having an effect were minimal, as it was a business decision and not a religious one. However the Ghermezians did not waste time and effort making a pilgrimage to Toronto or New York. Oh no, it was only the best for them; they went right to one of the holiest cities in the world. They appealed directly to Jerusalem, the City of Solomon. It would be interesting to discover their real rationale for sending this letter. Did they actually believe that holy intervention would resolve their problem or was it just a ploy to stall the inevitable signing of the agreement between the Alberta Treasury Branches and Gentra Corporation? But once again, the clock was ticking, and it appeared that even

Yahweh decided they should not own the Mall. What could they do?

CHAPTER 12
WEST EDMONTON MALL:
PHASE II

What the Ghermezians needed now was royal intervention--someone like Richard the Lion Heart, a King to lower a bucket into a well of their despair. That someone would be Ralph Klein, perhaps better known to Albertans as his Majesty King Ralph. What took place next was somewhat curious. Mr. Klein wrote a letter February 22, 1994, directed to Mr. Kowalski and Mr. Dinning requisitioning a government bucket. He wrote as follows:

To: Honourable Ken Kowalski   February 22, 1994
*   Honourable Jim Dinning*

Subject: West Edmonton Mall and Triple Five
*   [Owners of the Mall; the Ghermezians]*

Further to our conversation and our Priorities Meeting on February 14, it was clear that an Alberta solution would be preferable relative to West Edmonton Mall.

We need to protect the Alberta Treasury Branch (ATB) loans and, at the same time, ensure that the potential of West Edmonton Mall can be maximized for the economic benefit of Alberta.

It would be most helpful if Alberta Treasury Branch and Triple Five undertook very serious discussions to find a positive resolution to this matter. As we discussed, I would ask you to follow up with Alberta Treasury Branch to make sure there is "good faith" and good will in discussions with West Edmonton Mall and/or First Boston.

Our February 14th meeting agreed that no agreement between Alberta Treasury Branch and Gentra should be finalized.

It appeared that a quote from The Edmonton Sun on January 10, 1996, captured the very essence of Mr. Klein's metamorphosis into "more the downtown wheeler-dealer and less the working man's friend." Mr. Klein loves to promote his image as an average Albertan. Increasingly, the average Albertan bats last in Mr. Klein's line-up.

That the West Edmonton Mall deal had become a subject for discussion of one of the Cabinet's Priorities Meetings was puzzling. Not only was the arm's length relationship between the Alberta Government and the Alberta Treasury Branches violated, but the ethics associated with the highest elected office in the Province of Alberta were shamefully compromised. In fact, in the August 28, 1996, edition of The Edmonton Sun, when trying to avoid comment about another Alberta Treasury Branches public relations disaster, Mr. Dinning and Mr. Klein reiterated that the ATB operates like a bank and at arm's length from the government.[7] This was despite the great pains in the Legislature taken by the Government to make the arm's length relationship sacrosanct. Throughout history, any minister of the Crown would have to resign over such a breach of ethics. In Mr. Dinning's and Mr. Evans' (the Attorney General) case, they saw the writing on the wall and decided to jump before the electorate pushed them. Surely, Mr. Klein, if he has any honour, must be considering jumping as well.

How can Premier Klein reconcile his actions with the reputation and perception that he is a Premier who espouses less government and fiscal restraint. How does his laissez-faire attitude mesh with the propping up a massively non-viable commercial venture such as West Edmonton Mall? I guess he must view the West Edmonton Mall deal much the same as he views the new electoral boundaries. Both work just fine if you don't think about them. Secondly, Mr. Klein says that they need to protect ATB's loans. Guess what--that's what ATB management was trying to do. How did Mr. Klein know about those loans, and even more to the point, what qualified Mr. Klein to know the best method for protecting those loans? The Ghermezians were looking for a new arrangement that was surely to the detriment of the Alberta Treasury Branches' loans and not their protection. That was quite evident. Mr. Klein's feeble attempt to try to explain his position was to disguise the fact that the Ghermezians were lobbying successfully and calling in their political markers. They were one of the regular contributors to the PC Alberta Fund. These crafty politicians have made the Alberta Treasury Branches loan portfolio the Wile E. Coyote of banking.

---

[7] The Edmonton Sun. "Puck Defends Furniture Deal." Wednesday, August 28, 1996.

The Gentra Corporation had plans to close down the Mall's amusement park. As we can see from his letter, Mr. Klein intervened, as his conscience would not allow this to happen. Yet when Mr. Klein had closed down hospital beds, his conscience was conveniently absent. Now that Mr. Klein has admitted to ruining Alberta's health care system, I wonder when he is going to admit to ruining the Alberta Treasury Branches.

The Premier wanted Triple Five and the ATB to take on serious discussions. Prior to his letter, for nearly a year, there had been discussions and, as far as their getting serious, what does Mr. Klein imagine the ATB managers were doing--sitting around sipping herbal tea? There is another interesting and telling comment in the letter. Mr. Klein makes reference to First Boston. How did he know about their involvement?

Most of the lofty prose contained in the letter was the usual political window dressing. The last line, however, was the key: **"Our February 14 meeting agreed that no agreement between Alberta Treasury Branches and Gentra should be finalized."** Since when did the Premier and his Cabinet get involved in making loan decisions for the Alberta Treasury Branches? What qualified them to make such a decision? In his own words, the Premier has admitted his first-hand involvement with the West Edmonton Mall refinancing. It appears that I was a bit too hasty in my questioning the Ghermezian's request for God's influence: the Cabinet Priorities meeting and the request occurred on the same day. Jerusalem is ten hours ahead of Alberta. Well, it could be true, but it is a little difficult for me to believe that God's priorities and those of the Klein Cabinet are the same.

The curious part about his letter was that it was addressed to both Mr. Kowalski and Mr. Dinning. Mr. Dinning, I can understand. He is, of course, the Provincial Treasurer and the Alberta Treasury Branches does fall within his ministerial purview. But, why Kenny the K? Could it be because he was the Tourism Minister? But what would the Minister for Tourism have to do with the Alberta Treasury Branches? The Mall wasn't going anywhere, and it was not as if the Gentra Corporation could put wheels on it and push it to Toronto. Curious indeed. In my April 30, 1996, meeting with Mr. Kowalski, he pointblank lied by denying that he had any involvement in the Mall when I put that question to him. To reaffirm his denial, he then offered the coy comment that he had not been in an ATB branch in years. So what? How does the fact that he had not physically been in a branch preclude him from being involved? People do use telephones, faxes, and E-Mail, even Kenny the K!

The Premier's letter was so strong. Mr. Dinning sent it in its original form to the Superintendent of the ATB, Allan Bray. Mr. Bray, in turn, replied to the government with a detailed letter on why the ATB was entering into the Gentra agreement and that their actions were based on normal banking guidelines.

At this point, the Ghermezian family had thought that they had pulled out all the stops. Knowing that real men rule their own destiny, Nader Ghermezian decided to take matters into his own

168

hands by taking pen to paper and sending a letter to Mr. Klein; first dating February 22, 1994, then scratching out the date initialing it to show February 23. Normally, if someone writes a letter on one day and sends it the next, they don't bother to change the date. But in this case, not only did Mr. Germezian change the date, he initialed the change. Nader's missive follows:

February ~~22~~ 23, 1994

Dear Honourable Ralph Klein:

<u>*Re: West Edmonton Mall*</u>

Despite our opposition to the Gentra/ATB proposal, the representatives of ATB flew to Toronto yesterday and at this moment are negotiating to finalize an agreement with Gentra (an eastern lender presently under liquidation). We all know this would not be in the best interest of Alberta. Yesterday morning we met with Mr. Goebel of ATB to further stress the harm that the Gentra proposal will bring to us and the Alberta economy. During our meeting we provided ATB with the appraisal of 679 million which is twice the amount of the new financing that is needed and brought to ATB's attention that based on the Mall's audited statement, the present cash flow available for the debt service is 46 million, while we only require 26 million ($350 x 7.5% = $26 million) to service the debt.

Despite the above and even though ATB had been informed that First Boston, one of the world's major financing houses, is confident that financing on West Edmonton Mall in the $350 million range will receive an investment grade rating from the major bond rating companies. ATB is continuing their negotiations with Gentra.

*Now we see the end coming, all the doors have been locked
and you are holding the key.*

We anxiously await your response.

Sincerely,

Nader Ghermezian

*cc: Honourable Ken Kowalski
     Minister of Tourism and Economic Development*

For astounding revelations, Nader's letter to the Premier rivals
the Dead Sea Scrolls (it was even on better paper). First, let's deal
with the fact that the Premier's letter was dated February 22 and
makes mention of First Boston. If Mr. Ghermezian sent his letter
on the 23rd, how would Mr. Klein be aware of this? Obviously,
there were more conversations and meetings regarding this matter
than the public is aware of. Or, another possibility is that Mr.
Klein is the long lost brother of the Amazing Kreskin; but I need
more convincing on that last explanation. Why was Mr. Nader
Ghermezian writing the Premier? If the Alberta Treasury
Branches was being run at arm's length, what could the Premier of
Alberta do for him, as this was a banking decision, not a political
one--or so the Government would have you believe.

Next, Mr. Ghermezian states that the lender, Gentra, is "under
liquidation." That was incorrect. Gentra was set up to deal with
poorly performing or non-performing loans of the Royal Trust
Corporation by handling them as normal banking practice would
dictate. That can mean liquidating non-performing loans such as

the West Edmonton Mall. This is a concept that seems to elude Mr. Ghermezian from time to time. Mr. Ghermezian mentions that the Gentra proposal would not be in the best interest of Alberta. Who was he trying to fool? He must also have been a keen student of French history, recalling Louis XIV's famous epigram, "L'état cést moi!" It appears that Mr. Ghermezian thinks that the health of the Alberta economy is tied to him and the West Edmonton Mall. If this is the case, surely the end of the Province of Alberta's economy was near. Next, Mr. Ghermezian mentions an appraisal figure of 679 million dollars based on audited statements. Keep that figure handy since you will need it as we proceed to Phase III. Mr. Ghermezian then gives us a sample of his keen insight into the concept of debt servicing. For some reason, at this point as I read his letter, an indelible image of Jethro Bodine "cipherin'" lodges in my head. The end of Mr. Ghermezian's letter takes the form of a plea for the Premier to take action as "you are holding the key," similar to a prisoner's plea to a governor for an eleventh hour reprieve. Notice that Nader Ghermezian took care to copy his good friend and globetrotter, Ken Kowalski, on the letter. The construction of Phase II was now complete; but despite all the political interference, the Alberta Treasury Branches did consummate their deal with Gentra Corporation's Gary Whitelaw on March 10, 1994.

CHAPTER 13
WEST EDMONTON MALL:
PHASE III

What can I say about Phase III? The Gentra agreement was signed and the good guys, relatively speaking, finally won one--or did they? Two of the greatest questions of the twentieth century may be: 1) Did Lee Harvey Oswald act alone, and 2) How did the Ghermezians manage to break the agreement between Gentra Corporation and the Alberta Treasury Branches? Well, I can't help you on the assassination conspiracy question, as that will be debated for decades to come; but guess what, I can help you on the second question. What went wrong? This was a binding agreement reviewed by so many lawyers that it could probably be made required reading material at the Law Society.

Now, let's keep in mind that the senior management at the Alberta Treasury Branches did what was acceptable under normal banking guidelines, so quite obviously, it had become a political decision. If the order came from the Premier and it was defied, inevitably someone would have to pay the price for this defiance. What happened next was very strange. The Superintendent of nearly ten years, Mr. Allan Bray, retired suddenly *or* was the retirement forced?

Mr. Kowalski, the Minister of Cake and Circuses, was livid. The Alberta Treasury Branches had defied an order from the Premier and Cabinet. With little concern for his own reputation or what was left of it, Mr. Kowalski informed several individuals that he was going to have Mr. Bray removed as Superintendent of the ATB. Mr. Bray admitted to me that he saw the writing on the wall and would not allow Mr. Kowalski and the Premier the pleasure or satisfaction of removing him from his position. Therefore, he felt it was logical that he retire to avoid the inevitable confrontation.

Mr. Dinning, the Provincial Treasurer, knew that Mr. Bray was retiring to avoid the explosive situation on the West Edmonton Mall by defying Cabinet and signing the agreement with Gentra. Mr. Dinning told Mr. Bray that he was going to resign over the unconscionable West Edmonton Mall deal as well. He never followed through and became a party to the deal.

The retirement could not change the facts. There was a signed and sealed agreement which had to be honoured, or did it? The first order of business was putting someone in the Superintendent's office to do as he was told and not question directives. Mr. Leahy has a long record of indiscretions that have been documented internally at the Alberta Treasury Branches and which I have detailed in the following chapter. It was also quite evident that the Provincial Treasurer would have reviewed Mr. Leahy's file before selecting him to lead the ATB. Mr. Dinning knew exactly who and what he was getting. As an Acting Superintendent, lusting for the Superintendent's position, it made it difficult for Mr. Leahy to be independent, as the security of his job now hung even more in the balance. This only led to an increased level of political influence at the Alberta Treasury Branches by the Klein government in a period when they were giving the public impression that the ATB was to be more independent. In essence, he became Pinocchio to the Government's Gepetto. All the while they were pulling Mr. Leahy's strings, he wished to be a real boy, that is, the full title and power of the Superintendent. However, instead of his nose growing, his losses grew. I used to believe that the most powerful civil servant in Canada was the Secretary of the Privy Council. Now, I know it to be the Superintendent of the Alberta Treasury Branches. The Superintendent's position and monetary power were limitless.

So it came to be that Mr. Leahy was now the Acting Superintendent of the Alberta Treasury Branches. The first thing he did was to seize control of some of the most politically sensitive files that included West Edmonton Mall and Stewart Green Properties. To give one a better understanding of this, Mr. Leahy removed Mr. Goebel, the Executive General Manager, from the West Edmonton Mall file, as well as his counsel, the lovely and talented Mr. Mark Gunderson. Do the names look familiar? Mr. Leahy now took personal control of the file and his counsel was now William Kenny from Cook, Duke, Cox. (Many will remember Mr. Kenny from the Code Inquiry and more recently, he defended Peter Pocklington in the Gainers lawsuit.) What was so strange about this occurrence was not that a bank executive was removed from a high profile file, but that his counsel of record was also removed. This move would eliminate any continuity which was exactly what Mr. Leahy wanted, as Mr. Kenny was to turn a complete about face from his predecessor's path. As you will see, once again, a professional sold his integrity.

Now, the Government and the ATB found themselves in an untenable position. A loan which Mr. Leahy's predecessor felt was unacceptable and refused to do, was completed and put in place. To add insult to injury, through some legal leger demain to disguise the fact an additional 35 million dollars was tacked onto the debt to pay Gentra for breaking the March 10, 1994, agreement. This did not include millions in professional fees and payoffs, and as you will also see, millions leaked out along the way. Thus, a loan which was outside normal banking guidelines in its original form, now was made even more offside, and became part of the house of straw that ATB's loan portfolio increasingly resembled. On sober reflection, perhaps I am being too harsh. It could meet normal lending practices if there was such a thing as a 300-year amortization! Other than that, it was certainly not bankable.

As Mr. Klein's letter (which we saw in the last chapter) made evident, the Government was now directly involved. The down home prairie boys who orchestrated the reprieve for West Edmonton Mall were Ken Kowalski, the Ghermezians' attorney; Jack Agrios, an infamous Tory bagman; Bill Kenny; and Peter Elzinga, a former federal MP, provincial MLA and currently Executive Director of the PC Alberta Fund. He was also formerly the President of the Federal Progressive Conservatives. Also on board was a crew of Alberta's most influential and prominent

175

lawyers. Many of these individuals will be dealt with more fully near the end of this chapter. Patience!

To give you a feel for Mr. Elzinga's character, you should know that Mr. Elzinga's stint as Federal PC President corresponded with the elevation of the quality of his wardrobe. He was extremely fond of charging his suits, among other things, with the Party's credit card. Jack Agrios was well-connected with the provincial Tories since the days of Peter Lougheed and regularly had access to Premier Ralph Klein, as you can see from the accompanying photograph. Not only that, but Mr. Agrios was a member at Cook, Duke, Cox, the same law firm as Bill Kenny, now counsel for the ATB on the West Edmonton Mall refinancing package. This alone should have raised the alarm. However, if that was not enough, in the negotiations leading up to the West Edmonton Mall deal, Jack Agrios represented the Ghermezian family. The conflict of interest was so blatant, it became almost incestuous. The Alberta Treasury Branches not only did not recognize the conflict, they orchestrated it. It was less a straightforward business deal than a Gilbert and Sullivan operetta, sort of "H.M.S. Pinafore" meets "How to Succeed in Business Without Really Trying."

Premier Ralph Klein and Jack Agrios warmly greet each other.
From <u>The Edmonton Journal</u>, October 31, 1995.

The Alberta Treasury Branches had to address the foul odour emanating from the deal and its multi-layered conflicts of interest. To address this end, the deal was sent to Emmanuel Mirth, more familiarly known to his friends and colleagues as "Sonny", of the law firm Reynolds Mirth. This was such a large undertaking that Mr. Mirth enlisted the aid of one of his colleagues at the firm, Mr. Doug Stollery. Drafting a colleague for support was a regular tactic of Mr. Mirth's, as I observed first-hand on a number of occasions. Mr. Stollery and Mr. Mirth now became the ATB's de facto counsel taking instructions from Mr. Kenny. Mr. Kenny had done all the due diligence on the West Edmonton Mall deal along with Mr. Agrios, and the firm of Reynolds Mirth was nothing more than a glorified clerk, filing the documents. (Mr. Kenny used the firm Reynolds Mirth and the same individuals on the Stewart Green Property file.) Their job was to apply the purifying rubber stamp. In another scenario, their role was akin to the driver of the getaway car after an armed robbery--get the parties guilty of the dastardly deed out of sight and away from the scene of the crime as fast as possible.

Note here that Mr. Mirth was well aware of my antagonistic relationship with the Alberta Treasury Branches and the professionals they employed. In fact, Reynolds Mirth, was significantly present in the Courtroom on the day that I was petitioned into bankruptcy as a favour to their friends at the ATB. Sonny Mirth elected to proceed with foreclosure proceedings on behalf of Sun Life Trust and the Royal Bank against some of my property corporations only after I was petitioned, knowing it would be more difficult for me to fight back. Not surprisingly, this tactic mirrored the ATB strategy. Note that Mr. Mirth is a significant contributor to the PC Alberta Fund and one of the Tory faithful.

I began to review the links between the Ghermezian family and the Progressive Conservative Party. I noticed that the Triple Five Corporation Ltd. contributed $550 officially to the PC Alberta Fund. I wrote to Mr. Dinning and asked this question and I quote, "Could you please supply me with the figure representing the official and unofficial contributions?" Mr. Dinning never wrote me back on this specific issue. Perhaps, in retrospect, I should have softened my approach somewhat. That still does not negate the fact, however, that no where else that I am aware of could a $550 contribution be transformed into a 350 million dollar loan guarantee for the Ghermezians in addition to the ATB forfeiting their mortgage position creating an exposure of nearly half a billion dollars. Keep in mind that these guarantees were wide open and the ATB had no control over revenues. That is, should they so choose, the Ghermezians could strip the entire inside of the Mall and there would be nothing that the ATB nor the government could do about it. The Ghermezians had no personal guarantees that would have prevented them from doing so. They had carte blanche. It was completely legal and the ATB and the government would leave the people of Alberta holding the bag to reimburse any shortfall to the lender. I wonder if the people of Alberta will come up with a suitable method to repay the Conservatives for making such a great deal?

Exit one Superintendent, enter the new Acting Superintendent. With the final adjustments of the dramatis personae, the stage was set. Mr. Kowalski and Mr. Elzinga, hand in hand, the Bob and Ray of the Provincial PC Party, began a series of meetings with the Ghermezians and other parties that culminated in the most unconscionable deal in Alberta Treasury Branches' history and quite possibly in Alberta history.

We can analyze the deal itself, now that the cast of characters has been introduced. Firstly, the Ghermezian family had been trying to refinance the Mall for nearly a year. Now they were adding millions of dollars in debt plus adding approximately further millions in sundry fees to the players involved in bringing the deal to fruition. To have any confidence in the new deal for Gentra Corporation, Gentra needed the assurance that the Government and the Alberta Treasury Branches were supporting the Ghermezians. Because of the Ghermezians' track record, the covenant with the Government and the ATB were the only way the deal gained credibility with Gentra. The Government was well and truly buried in the deal, right up to its legislative eyeballs.

As can be learned from the Court Order of Justice E. S. Lefsrud (familiar name?) granted on October 26, 1994, the Order for Sale was granted to the purchaser 626110 Alberta Ltd. whose director and shareholder was Nader Ghermezian. What a surprise! The new owner of West Edmonton Mall was the former owner.

According to the same Court Order, the price that was payable was $419,630,000 to Mr. Ghermezian's new company, now known as WEM Holdings, Inc. I explained in Phase II how Mr. Ghermezian had written a letter to the Premier stating that the value of the Mall based on audited statements was 679 million dollars. How could this be? Mr. Ghermezian, a seasoned real estate entrepreneur missed the mark by nearly a quarter of a billion dollars. It is well known in business circles that over the years the Ghermezian family has kept several different sets of books, calling on which ever one served their purposes for the particular predicament of the moment. The manipulation could occur since no one was ever sure which one of the Mall's operating companies was involved at any particular time. The Ghermezian family was allowed to retain 100% of the Mall in a new corporation with new financing and no personal guarantees, and, in addition to financing the 419 million dollars 100%, another 20 million dollars was leaked to them. The final new financing was 440 million dollars. The transferring of the property from one Ghermezian corporation to the other was nothing more than a fraudulent transaction for the purpose of avoiding creditors, all guaranteed by the Alberta Treasury Branches and, by extension, the Alberta Government, with the whole process sanctioned by the Court. The application of the Court's rubber stamp was granted by Mr. Justice E. S. Lefsrud, my case management judge. Curious, is it not?

In my appearance before Mr. Justice Lefsrud, he admitted to me that he had been on the verge of insolvency himself as a result of bad real estate investments. One of Mr. Justice Lefsrud's problems was a piece of property he held in the west end of Edmonton. Several of the lawyers of my acquaintance in Edmonton have also told me that he was beholden to several lenders, and it was insinuated that one of these lenders was ATB. As the religiously orthodox Ghermezians would recognize from the Talmud, "A habitual borrower is unfit to be a judge," and soon you will see why.

To illustrate a point of how badly the Alberta Treasury Branches has been worked over by the Ghermezian family, the ATB had financed two buildings near the Legislature at 97th Avenue and 110 Street in Edmonton. One was an office building and one an apartment hotel where many of the members of the legislature (MLAs) stay when the Legislature is sitting. Also financed was a substantial parcel of land in west Edmonton called The Grange. These properties were financed for nearly twice their value--nothing new, right? They were finally taken back by the Alberta Treasury Branches. Well, they were not exactly taken back. They were moved into a corporation called Partow Park Holdings, Inc. whose shares were owned by the director of the company, Mr. William J. Kenny, of the law firm of Cook, Duke, Cox. Sound familiar? Senior ATB officials confirmed that these properties were transferred for 90 million dollars more than their real value. First of all, swearing a false affidavit of value can be a form of commercial fraud, so why was this risk taken? The main reason was to protect the balance sheet of the Alberta Treasury

Branches. Another reason is that as we head into an election, these kinds of losses could wipe out the ATB's profit for a number of years and reflect poorly on the government. I have heard the tired argument that doing this is to ensure the best value when selling the property. This is weak for two reasons: Any realtor worth his salt knows the story behind the property and its true owners. Next, in negotiations, the true owner can be revealed if the purchaser's lawyer does his due diligence.

The absolutely bizarre part of this story is that the Ghermezians still run the properties. They have shed their debt and responsibility while receiving a lucrative management contract. This was nothing new to the Ghermezians. The Gentra agreement with ATB allowed them to remain in a management capacity without control over revenues. Gentra discovered that they had tried to raise the management fee from 1.5 to 6.6 million dollars. That they are still running the project is a dead giveaway as to the real owner. The entire purpose of a foreclosure is to capture the cash flow for the secured lender and restore the integrity of the property. It appears you <u>can</u> have it both ways. The real reason that this was done was to protect the balance sheet, hoping that the values would change in the years to come, thereby protecting Mr. Kenny who has the dubious distinction of being the only employer of the Ghermezian family in Alberta. If the properties were sold immediately, the true value would become apparent. However, the same asset can be sold a year or two later for its true value which solves three problems. First, it protects the ATB's balance sheet until after the next election. Second, it creates enough gray area to justify Mr. Kenny's position on the Affidavit of Value. Third, having the Ghermezians run the property hides its true value based on cash flow.

Now comes the moment of truth and logic. Why would the Premier of the Province of Alberta, including the Cabinet, make this kind of decision given the following facts:

1. The former Superintendent and his staff felt that the loan could no longer be classified as a performing loan.

2. The Premier gave the directive that there should be no agreement with the Gentra Corporation.

3. The Acting Superintendent, Mr. Leahy, was given a mandate to help the Ghermezians.

4. The breaking of the agreement with Gentra added 35 million dollars to a loan that was already non-performing, in addition to millions in legal fees and various payoffs.

5. The people of Alberta were put on the hook for a wide-open loan guarantee for nearly half a billion dollars by the Alberta Treasury Branches and the Alberta Government with no benefit from interest revenues, yet all the risk.

6. A Premier advocates fiscal restraint, even though he ensures that the "Mind-Bender" roller coaster in the Mall's amusement park stay open while he closes hospital beds. After all, what was more important to the people of Alberta--the closure of hospital facilities or the closure of the "Mind-

Bender?" Considering the convoluted nature of the deal, perhaps the "Mind-Bender" was the appropriate choice.

7. The Ghermezian family signed no personal covenants and still control 100% of the Mall.

It was quite obvious that the Government would not receive political accolades for their role in this refinancing.

Let's take a look at the individuals involved for the Government. "It was if the motive for which they were originally sculptured was now revealed in scandalous actuality," to borrow the words of Carlos Fuentes. First, consider Mr. Peter Elzinga, one of the main cogs in the wheel, Executive Director of the PC Alberta Fund, and one of Mr. Klein's closest confidants. He has a new and extensively remodeled home in an exclusive area of Edmonton and several new vehicles, including a new recreational vehicle. He has even been considered a globetrotter of late. Perhaps Mr. Elzinga should replace the outgoing Mr. Dinning as Provincial Treasurer since his ability to manage funds is incredible. Surely the responsible Mr. Elzinga has duly reported all this to Revenue Canada. This must be why he was chosen as Executive Director of the PC Alberta Fund, a veritable Jesus of Nazareth, multiplying those loaves and fishes. One of the other main cogs, Ken Kowalski, has accepted many free trips from the Ghermezian family. A popular destination has been Las Vegas, Nevada--a place where no one goes empty-handed.

Lastly, there is the Premier of Alberta, the Honourable Ralph Klein. Why would he jeopardize his political career by getting involved in such a financial mess that had no benefit for the Province nor the ATB? Here is a leader who has advocated fiscal restraint, less government, and the privatization of Government agencies that are not profitable. How does a laissez-faire Premier mesh the propping up of a massive non-viable commercial entity such as West Edmonton Mall with his program of fiscal restraint? What truly motivated Mr. Klein? Mr. Allan Bray, the former Superintendent of ATB, admitted to me personally that Eskander Ghermezian invited Mr. Bray to his home and offered him half a million dollars to insure present and future loans. He declined, but one has to ask, who else did they attempt or actually pay off? Mr. Klein should remember that the horse that runs fast early, often fades in the stretch.

The stage was set and the first order of business was to annul the agreement between Gentra Corporation and the Alberta Treasury Branches with respect to the West Edmonton Mall. The Gentra Corporation was in an excellent position and hired Ernst Young to investigate the advantages of severing the agreement. The negotiations began and ended quickly. In addition to the payout of their first position, the Gentra Corporation was paid approximately 35 million dollars in excess to break the agreement that was signed March 10, 1994. In my conversations with several individuals at Gentra, they managed to interrupt their chortling long enough to tell me that the deal was quite satisfactory, and they only wished they had more West Edmonton Malls. All the legal maneuvering was intended to disguise what was really being done. Through sloppiness and just plain arrogance, the real intent was revealed. As Sholom Aleichem said, "Men make mistakes not because they think they know when they do not know, but because they think others do not know." Others know where the bodies are buried.

Are you puzzled that the Ghermezians were allowed to use an Order for Sale with the powers of a foreclosure to shed debt and retain ownership of the West Edmonton Mall? This bothered me the first time I heard the story. How was it possible, unless all the participants were part of the production? Could the parties all be on side and the Court rubber stamp the agreement to protect everyone from the inevitable fallout?

In fact, the Court proceedings were a total sham. All the actions of the parties involved (only select creditors, not all) show that there was no other objective than to shed the debt and have the Ghermezians retain control of the Mall. It was made quite obvious by the fact that creditors with judgments are trying to petition the old companies into bankruptcy today. For anonymity, the names of the defendants in the Order for Sale action were changed 24 hours prior to the October 26, 1994, proceedings to disguise what was happening from the creditors and general public. If these actions were straightforward, all creditors notified, and all arrangements legal, why the need to change the names to numbered companies? This ploy was so effective that it took The Edmonton Journal until June 1995 to report on it.

In a normal Court of Queen's Bench proceeding, the defendant has approximately two weeks to file a Statement of Defense to the Statement of Claim. In this case, the parties were in Court within two days. In contrast, consider the timing of these actions:

- 606881 Alberta Ltd. filed a Statement of Claim at 2:52 p.m. on October 25, 1994. (This corporation is controlled by Jack Agrios and purchased the second position.)
- Affidavit on Offer to Purchase, dated October 26, 1994, and Offer to Purchase dated October 25, 1994. (The Offer to Purchase came from 626110 Alberta Ltd., the new corporation owned by Nader Ghermezian.)
- Demand of Notice dated October 25, 1994. (The Demand Notice came from Jack Agrios who was representing the Ghermezians until this point.)
- Deposition of Keith Fraser who prepared Mall evaluation taken at 2:00 p.m. on October 24, 1994.
- Deposition of Martin Walrath taken at 3:18 p.m. on October 24, 1994. (Mr. Walrath is an employee of the Ghermezian family.)
- Court of Queen's Bench proceeding October 26, 1994. (Justice Lefsrud grants the Order Mr. Agrios is seeking.)

Talk about greasing the wheels of the legal machinery. The required documents were filed, select parties notified, examination conducted, proceedings held, and a decision rendered in the space of two days, a decision that involved nearly half a billion dollars! You don't suspect that there was collusion among the participants to get this handled before the other creditors, the press, and the public got wind of it, do you?

In the official record of the October 26, 1994, Court proceedings, Justice Lefsrud recognized the difficulty of getting through everything. The dialogue could easily come from any Abbott and Costello sketch. "I recognize just looking at the volume of paper, that it's a monumental task." Jack Agrios replies, "It's enormous." The most telling thing about these statements is that it was not humanly possible for Justice Lefsrud to review all the material. The examination of the appraisers, Mr. Keith Fraser and Mr. Martin Walrath, occurred less than 48 hours before the Court proceedings. The Court Reporter's preparation of the transcripts of the examination so quickly is important for two reasons: First, the usual time for transcript preparation is a week; second, it is highly unlikely that Justice Lefsrud had time to review them. How could Justice Lefsrud sign an order on a transaction of nearly half a billion dollars without reviewing the documentation fully.

Jack Agrios was shown on a registry document to be the sole director and shareholder of 606881 Alberta Ltd., the recent purchaser of the second mortgage on West Edmonton Mall.

(606881 was bringing the action of the Order for Sale as the plaintiff in order to sell it back to the defendants, the Ghermezians.) Yet, curiously, Mr. Agrios had recently represented the defendant Triple Five companies (now changed to Alberta numbered companies) in their tax dispute with the City of Edmonton. Before the Gentra agreement, Mr. Agrios was also trying to negotiate with the Alberta Treasury Branches on behalf of the Ghermezians. In fact, Mr. Bray, the Superintendent of the ATB at the time, offered 10 million dollars for Mr. Agrios' client, the Ghermezians, to walk away from the Mall without legal actions. The other solicitors who were there to represent all the parties, barely participated. They merely observed the Court's stamp of approval on a prior private agreement involving select creditors. In essence, they were legal pylons, not real obstacles, there to provide the illusion of legality. In one way or another, all the lawyers, with the exception of Doug Stollery representing ATB, were paid by the Ghermezians.

Consider the following section of the Court record that shows the various counsels at their pliant best:

THE COURT: Mr. Weir, have you any comments?

MR. WEIR: I have nothing to say, My Lord.

MR. WOLFF: Nor do I, My Lord.

THE COURT: And you're here --

MS. HOWELL: Nothing, My Lord.

THE COURT: Well, Mr. Agrios, I appreciate the manner in
               which you've handled this.

Mr. Jack Agrios was the producer, director, and main star of this entire proceeding. On October 24, 1994, two days before the Court proceedings, Mr. Agrios, the Counsel for his plaintiff corporation, conducted the examinations of Keith Fraser, the appraiser, and Martin Walrath, the employee of the Ghermezians. It appeared that Mr. Agrios had already arranged who was to say what and when.

The Court was also misled by the evidence and the lack of evidence that was presented in the examinations by Mr. Agrios of the appraiser, Keith Fraser. Prior to the 1993 appraisal Mr. Fraser had prepared for Gentra, he had done an appraisal on the Mall in 1992. He was not asked about the appraisal done a year earlier nor was it presented as value for comparison. In his testimony, Mr. Fraser had also mentioned that the property had been re-assessed for tax purposes, yet he was not asked about nor did he mention that value. If the proceedings had been conducted normally and properly and had all creditors been represented, surely those questions would have been asked. Mr. Agrios, a solicitor of vast experience in these matters, was avoiding sensitive issues.

Mr. Fraser's appraisal is somewhat suspect for several reasons. In appraising an asset of nearly half a billion dollars, the financial information contained in Mr. Fraser's report is scant at best. Mr. Agrios knew very well that the appraisal contained little financial information. To address this in the cross examination of Mr. Fraser, he asks Mr. Fraser on more than one occasion if he had access to all financial records pertaining to the Mall. Consider the following portion of the record:

MR. AGRIOS: And did you, during that period, have complete access to all records, be they financial, be they structured, be they plans, all material and all documents that were necessary to enable you to conduct a complete review and arrive at the necessary conclusion for you to formulate your opinion?

MR. FRASER: We had unlimited access to documentation ... Never were we denied any access with regard to our present assignment.

The most extraordinary question that Mr. Fraser was not asked was what would the value of the Mall be if soft terms were offered, for instance, a preferential interest rate or 100% financing without convenants? There was no cash and no liability. The West Edmonton Mall may have been sold to many real estate speculators for even more money than Mr. Ghermezian had paid. As stated earlier in the letter by Nader Ghermezian, based on audited statements of West Edmonton Mall, the value was 679 million dollars. Which financial statements and leases did Mr. Fraser review in order to make a mistake of a quarter of a billion dollars? The absolute avoidance of pertinent questions by Mr. Agrios can only lead one to conclude that Mr. Fraser was a part of the sham or monumentally unsuited to his work as an appriaser.

Mr. Agrios, wise beyond his years, knew the convoluted nature of the deal required a ringer to cover Keith Fraser's weak report. Enter Mr. Ed Shaske, another appraiser. Mr. Agrios brought Mr. Shaske to Court on October 26 rather than the appraiser, Keith Fraser. The following portion of the record of proceedings shows Mr. Shaske's contribution:

MR. AGRIOS: In reviewing Mr. Fraser's report, are there any--do you have any difficulties or any areas that you might disagree with?

MR. SHASKE: No. As I say, I would have likely come out with a far superior report, but the values would not have changed dramatically.

Mr. Shaske's statement is quite revealing. First, he agrees with my assessment that the report is of poor quality considering the magnitude of the property. Second, the fact that he reviewed Mr. Fraser's financial information and that he would arrive at the same value is logical. The math calculation does not change, but Mr. Shaske did not review the original financial material. Mr. Agrios attempted to make Mr. Shaske the second fall guy as can be seen, but Mr. Shaske outsmarted him.

In Mr. Agrios' cross examination of Martin Walrath, Mr. Walrath not once disagreed with Mr. Agrios' questions. Most of his answers consisted of, "I can confirm that." His counsel, Ms. Howell, appears on the transcript to such a limited degree that one would suspect she spent most of the examination helping Mr. Agrios.

Consider the lawyers individually in this proceeding. Mr. John Weir represented in Court the plaintiff corporation owned by Mr. Agrios. Yet only two days previous, Mr. Agrios represented his own corporation in the cross examination of Mr. Fraser and Mr. Walrath. During the Court proceedings of October 26, 1994, Mr. Weir uttered ten words from an eight thousand word court application. Very strange considering it was his action. The purpose of an examination is to flush out the facts for the Court so it can make a decision. Mr. Weir did not cross examine Mr. Fraser or Mr. Walrath. It was highly unlikely that he was prepared to make an argument in Court. Maybe next time Mr. Agrios will allow his lawyer to conduct the examination rather than the client. Mr. Weir is known in legal circles as one of the best, if not the best, in Alberta at conducting cross examinations. One has to wonder why Mr. Agrios did not avail himself of such litigating expertise, especially when Mr. Agrios was known as a corporate lawyer, not a litigator. He was out of his element. Perhaps I am being too hard on Jack. He may have just been trying to save on legal bills for the Ghermezians.

Mr. Horst Wolff was representing the new buyer 626110 Alberta Ltd. whose director and shareholder was Nader Ghermezian; go figure! Mr. Wolff was the perfect legal pylon example. Allow me to repeat his words once more as to where he stood in the Court proceeding, "I have nothing to say, my Lord." Certainly Mr. Wolff was not being paid by the word.

The Ghermezians' counsel, Ms. Howell, disarmingly spoke approximately ninety words in the Court proceeding of October 26. Surely in a proceeding deciding the fate of approximately half a billion dollars, her defense would have entailed reference to Mr. Ghermezian's appraisal for 679 million dollars and audited financial statements--crucial to her arguments to fend off the steam rolling Jack Agrios. If she had introduced these exhibits, Mr. Agrios' argument would have been moot.

Doug Stollery from Reynolds Mirth was representing the Alberta Treasury Branches on behalf of Bill Kenny, one of the original architects of the deal, and was nothing more than a stand-in for Sonny Mirth, taking the blows while Mr. Mirth collected the big fee. Remember that Mr. Stollery and Mr. Mirth were merely filing documents on Mr. Bill Kenny's behalf. This was not the only time Mr. Kenny called upon Mr. Mirth and Mr. Stollery. They were also involved with Stewart Green Properties as counsel for Coopers & Lybrand. There may have been a perception of conflict of interest because both Mr. Kenny and Mr. Agrios were from Cook, Duke, Cox. How fair of them!

Consider also the mysterious disposition of funds in the transaction that was ordered. 606881 Alberta Ltd. (Mr. Agrios) had purchased the second position mortgage from American interests for 15.25 million dollars, barely three months after these American interests had purchased the 50 million dollars mortgage from the ATB and its seven co-lenders. However, in the refinancing, 606881 Alberta Ltd. sold the position for 56 million dollars for a fast profit of over 40 million dollars. This money apparently went to Gentra Corporation who held a 362 million dollar first position (including interest) to induce them to step aside. Gentra was paid out the nominal sale price, which I mentioned earlier was 419 million dollars. But the TD Trust mortgages totaled 440 million dollars. Where and to whom did the other 20 million dollars go?

The actual transaction that resulted from the Order for Sale was also curious. There was no cash that went from the buyer to the seller. The buyer, 626110 Alberta Ltd. (Nader Ghermezian's company), had no assets prior to the deal to pay the 419 million dollar purchase price. Additional assets were transferred without valuation which included a substantial amount of cash, even though 626110 Alberta Ltd. put up no cash.

The defendant corporations had lawsuits claiming damages of 15.4 million dollars that was transferred to the purchaser, also without valuation. However, any lawsuits seeking damages against the Ghermezians were left behind to proceed against defendant corporations which had no assets. The transferred cash and lawsuits were not valuated nor were they shown on the record. The inevitable conclusion can only be that they were either gifts or an absolute fraud on the creditors. There was not even an attempt to create an environment with regard to legal propriety.

The transaction was merely the execution of a private deal that the Court was asked to rubber stamp its approval. This was a protective cloak to deter other creditors not properly notified from pursuing the matter. The owners and supposed group of select creditors needed the Court to help deflect other creditors in order to have exclusive rights to the assets. Mr. Agrios himself admitted in Court that the transaction had been agreed to by all parties, with counsel for the parties present. This was an absolute fraud on the Court, as many of the creditors who were not notified have since received judgments and are currently trying to petition the old West Edmonton Mall corporation into bankruptcy.

Once again, the Court of Mr. Justice Erik Lefsrud was suspect. Notice was not given to all creditors, nor did they have an opportunity to be heard. Any Justice in the Court of Queen's Bench of Alberta knows that the West Edmonton Mall was always embroiled in litigation in one form or another. The list of lawsuits, creditors, and judgments was and is lengthy. The Disney Corporation had a well-publicized lawsuit against the Ghermezians over the name "Fantasyland" (the Mall's amusement park) which Disney eventually won. Surely Justice Lefsrud had heard of that. Only a few months previous to this application, Justice Lefsrud had granted an application by MacDonalds Restaurants of Canada against West Edmonton Mall. I would have to say that the good Justice was playing possum. When Justice Lefsrud signed the order for sale, he was being professionally dishonest because all the creditors had not been notified. Mr. Agrios' change of the corporations back to numbered companies 24 hours before the proceedings helped ensure the avoidance of creditors. How was it possible that Justice Lefsrud could be so thorough on my file and so slipshod on the West Edmonton Mall matter?

With my Court appearances before Justice Lefsrud for his removal as case management judge, Justice Lefsrud said he could not proceed with the application unless everyone was notified. It was strange for two reasons: He had already given the counsel acting against me what they wanted. And, the counsel for the Trustee agreed that all the parties necessary for the proceeding were present. Apparently, there were two sets of rules to be observed, the Alberta Rules of Court and the Justice Lefsrud abridged version. Given the rules that applied to my case, the Order for Sale is fraudulent, should be overturned and Mr. Justice Lefsrud should do the honourable thing. The way Justice Lefsrud handled my file, one can reach no other conclusion but he is beholden to certain interests. The Court of Queen's Bench cannot afford nor tolerate such conduct on the Bench. Mr. Justice Lefsrud's role in the fraud should be examined and he, along with Mr. Agrios and all the lawyers involved, should be examined and investigated for their role in this financial sham.

It became quite evident to me why Justice Lefsrud was my case management judge, as he had already set an unconscionable precedent. If he was prepared to sign an order such as he did on the West Edmonton Mall deal, neutralizing me was a piece of cake. Justice Lefsrud's merciless pounding of me in Court, his disregard for fairness, seems to be a character trait. But more importantly, Justice Lefsrud had an interest in providing the authority for the witch hunt. Justice Lefsrud was appointed to the West Edmonton Mall file and my file by Associate Chief Justice Allan Wachowich. Justice Wachowich was also the one who was to sign my first attempt at the CCAA, as you will recall.

Earlier in the book, I described the resignation of Justice Agrios, brother of the aforementioned Jack Agrios. Justice Wachowich himself confirmed that I did not ask Justice Agrios to resign and that I had mentioned him only obliquely in a letter to the ATB which he was not privy to or so I thought. After Justice Agrios resigned, I appeared before Justice Lefsrud on a number of occasions. The first few times Justice Lefsrud would scold me about my criticism of Justice Agrios. On one of these occasions, I was puzzled as to which criticism Justice Lefsrud was referring. He replied, "You know what you said." What I want to know is if Justice Agrios was not supposed to know, how did Justice Lefsrud know?

If he knew about the letter in which I mentioned Justice Agrios, then logic would dictate that he was aware of my letter writing campaign to the Alberta Treasury Branches and the Alberta Government. The most sensitive of those letters was pertaining to the West Edmonton Mall refinancing. The whole picture only fell into place when Justice Lefsrud's signature appeared on the Order for Sale dated October 26, 1994. Only then did I fully understand the reason for my treatment in Justice

Lefsrud's Courtroom and why the first thing he did was strike my lawsuits against the ATB. Mr. Justice Lefsrud was appointed to the Bench November 29, 1991, after some strong lobbying by the provincial Progressive Conservatives. He regularly socializes with many of the same individuals involved in the West Edmonton Mall refinancing. To make matters even worse, the Ghermezians were given a gag order that stopped <u>The Edmonton Journal</u> and <u>The Edmonton Sun</u> from reporting on their affairs. It was now easy to understand Justice Lefsrud's attitude toward me as I outlined in Chapter 7, The Honourable Erik the Red. He was not only protecting the Alberta Treasury Branches and all his friends, but more importantly, himself.

PART THREE

WHO'S SORRY NOW?

CHAPTER 14
THE ETHICALLY-CHALLENGED CLUB

"Some men rob you with a gun, other men rob you with a pen."

- Woody Guthrie

Mr. Leahy is the classic "Prairie Boy" and in this case, a classic Alberta Treasury Branches employee, rising through the ranks over more than thirty years, finally becoming the Acting Superintendent officially in June 1994. Mr. Leahy also was the catalyst for my story, as well as the story of the Alberta Treasury Branches. Not only was he weaned on the culture of willful blindness, he perpetuated it. It was his forte and he was in his element: the Charles Keating of his time.

Mr. Leahy has a chequered past of questionable deals. In fact, he became well-known for doing the offside deal. "Let us return to those thrilling days of yesteryear," to review Mr. Leahy's influence in the debacle known as the North West Trust Company, NWTC for short. It seemed that Mr. Leahy liked to specialize in politically-sensitive deals. Mr. Leahy approved an approximately 20 million dollar loan package to Mr. Kipnes and Mr. Rollingher to assist them in their acquisition of North West Trust from Carma Developments. The ATB Superintendent at that time, Mr. Holgate, did not approve of the deal nor the way in which Mr. Leahy was able to make the approval well above his lending limits. Why was this extraordinary assistance given to Mr. Kipnes and Mr. Rollingher? Alas, Mr. Kipnes' and Mr. Rollingher's adventure into the wonderful world of Canadian banking was ill-timed. You will recall that in the mid 1980s, NWTC had run into a spot of trouble, and the company was burdened by a portfolio of overvalued real estate. For all intents and purposes, NWTC was insolvent.

Mr. Leahy is from the Vermilion, Alberta, area and while he was doing his lending magic at the Alberta Treasury Branches, back at the ranch so to speak, Mr. Leahy and his brother, James Leahy, were becoming hoteliers with the purchase of the Vermilion Inn. This is a classic case of the hometown boys doin' good. In a telephone conversation with James Leahy in October 1995, he acknowledged that he was a shareholder in Spayside Investments Ltd., the holding company that owned the Vermilion Inn. He also said that he was not involved in the mortgage negotiation with North West Trust in 1985, although this would seem to be a curious lack of diligence given that there were so few shareholders involved in the multi-million refinancing package. Further investigation revealed why James Leahy had such a fuzzy recollection of the details surrounding the Vermilion Inn deal. A director of North West Trust at the time confirmed that the loan was done for Elmer Leahy, not James Leahy, Elmer Leahy negotiated all the terms of the financing. Elmer Leahy, to use gambling parlance, called in his marker with Mr. Kipnes and Mr. Rollingher. James Leahy was merely the conduit or, more accurately, a sort of financial pylon.

Please, pay attention now because events happen rather fast and furiously at this point in our little summary. In November 1984, a mortgage of 1.035 million dollars was placed on the hotel through North West Trust. One year later, another mortgage, again with North West Trust, was placed on the hotel for 2.97 million dollars, nearly a 300% increase in financing. Now, in 1986, the hotel was sold to Mr. Philip Milroy for 1.345 million dollars and mortgaged for 1.285 million dollars with--can you guess--yes, North West Trust! This would be the same North West Trust that would be bailed out by the Alberta Treasury Branches to the tune of 95 million dollars and whose principals, Mr. Kipnes and Mr. Rollingher, were friends of Elmer Leahy. In the words of that sage, Mr. Rogers, can you say "conflict of interest?" Mr. Milroy's engraved invitation to the party was the refinancing of his own Bonnyville, Alberta hotel. That is, in order to finance the Bonnyville Hotel, he had to take over the Vermilion Inn. Kipnes and Rollingher, knowing Mr. Milroy's desperation in obtaining financing for the Bonnyville Hotel, pressured him to take over the Vermilion property to allow the Leahy gang to get out of town without getting hurt financially. Surely, this must be considered the epitome of the rugged individualism the Prairies were known for.

Mr. Milroy subsequently sold the hotel in 1990 for 600,000 dollars. Certain implications arose out of that figure. Considered on a conventional mortgage basis, 450,000 dollars was the maximum that could be mortgaged. Cast your mind back to the original deal. The 2.97 million dollar mortgage suggested that the hotel was worth 4 million dollars for financing purposes. The market for small town hotels was not exactly bullish at that time, not even Conrad Hilton would believe the Vermilion Inn was worth 4 million dollars. There was an obvious question to be asked. How was it that the deep thinkers at North West Trust accepted the financing? And, there was an even more obvious question to be asked--where did all the money go?

Mr. Leahy's character can be questioned in many ways, and he has demonstrated it in many forms. He was known not only as Acting Superintendent of the Alberta Treasury Branches, but also as a jet-setter and bon viveur. He was an avid sportsman, well, actually an outdoorsman to be precise. His reputation as an angler and skier of renown was forged as a guest of Mr. Peter Pocklington on a number of free pleasure trips. This, of course, was the same Peter Pocklington of Gainers meat packers fame who had some highly public financial arrangement with the Alberta Government. The mode of travel was either Canadian Airlines International paid for by Gainers and other Pocklington companies or on Mr. Pocklington's private jet. Elmer was indeed a jet-setter, worthy travel companion and confidant of the rich and powerful. In fact, I suspect that most of Mr. Leahy's friends fart through silk.

Free trips and graft were not the only thing Mr. Leahy was interested in. Mr. Leahy wanted a permanent resort he could call his own. Who better to help address Mr. Leahy's desire than Mr. Klein's constituency president, Hal Walker. Mr. Walker and Mr.

Leahy became quite close after one of the famous designated credits helped fund one of Mr. Walker's Canmore developments. For personally attending to Mr. Walker's needs, Mr. Leahy acquired two pieces of property in the Canmore area from Mr. Walker. There will be more about Mr. Walker later. Mr. Leahy, being a very private person, decided that his personal lawyer, Norman Simons, should hold the property in trust through an Alberta corporation in which Mr. Simons appears as the director and shareholder. Mr. Leahy has tried to explain his position on this issue, but the bottom line was if the deal was not ethically questionable, why the need to hide it?

Senior officials at the Alberta Treasury Branches were well aware of Mr. Leahy's questionable ethics. It was well-documented within his personnel file, especially after his dealings with Mr. Kipnes and Mr. Rollingher of North West Trust Company. Mr. Leahy was moved to an administrative post for several years because of this and other sundry dealings. The purpose of this move was to try to neutralize Mr. Leahy's ability to influence loans. It was not a totally successful gambit.

Then, there was a most curious chain of events. Mr. Allan Bray, the Superintendent, retired suddenly after the consummation of the Gentra deal that concerned the West Edmonton Mall. Mr. Dinning then appointed Mr. Leahy as Acting Superintendent. Surely, Mr. Dinning reviewed Mr. Leahy's personnel file before appointing him to such a powerful position that had no checks and balances. If Mr. Dinning was interested in the perception of his choice, the cracks and crevices in Mr. Leahy's character were recorded within his personnel file. Or, could the flawed character of Elmer Leahy be a prerequisite and that Mr. Leahy was perfect for Mr. Dinning's requirements? Mr. Leahy in his two years as Acting Superintendent increased the loans to West Edmonton Mall, the Brick Warehouse, the Pocklington connection, to mention just a few. He also dealt with many politically-sensitive files such as Stewart Green Properties, Ryckman Financial Corporation, among others. It appeared in this case that the Provincial Treasurer, Mr. Dinning, had a strange method of disciplining corrupt employees at the Alberta Treasury Branches. He promoted them.

To prove how amoral Mr. Leahy really was, I offer the following example. As you will recall earlier in this chapter, I described the relationship between Mr. Leahy and Mr. Rollingher. Here's the rest of the story. Mr. Leahy as Acting Superintendent, began almost immediately to lend millions of dollars once again to Mr. Rollingher. This was like a bad movie. The actors were older, but the storyline was still the same. Their past dealings had cost the people of the Province of Alberta millions of dollars in the debacle that was North West Trust. A former director of NWTC told me that Kipnes and Rollingher stole equal amounts of money from the trust company, and both should have been criminally investigated, but at least Mr. Rollinger did it in a nice way. Mr. Rollingher was also a very close friend of the Premier, Don Getty, a fact which kept a criminal investigation from reaching Mr.

Rollingher. How could it be possible that Mr. Leahy was still able to make these loans and yet not be reprimanded or dismissed for his actions? Mr. Dinning must have been extremely naive or Mr. Leahy had some extremely sensitive information concerning certain members of the Government of Alberta that afforded him administrative carte blanche.

To make matters worse, these loans were given to projects that had little or no cash flow. A prime example was Mr. Rollingher's acquisition of the former Belmont Correctional Facility in the northeast part of Edmonton. Mr. Rollingher borrowed several million dollars from the Alberta Treasury Branches to purchase the property, which had no viable cash flow and whose developmental viability was many years away. Mr. Leahy had provided a loan that was known as land banking that had not been seen for many years, and at a time when Edmonton land development was at an all time low. This was only one of many deals that Mr. Leahy had arranged with Mr. Rollingher during the short time that he was the head of ATB. But make no mistake about it, Mr. Leahy did not arrange the loans out of the kindness of his heart, but rather, as was the rationale ten years earlier, it was for financial gain. The greatest motivator in the world is still money. Before Mr. Leahy became Acting Superintendent, it was ATB policy not to lend Mr. Rollingher any more money.

It is important to jump ahead just now to understand the players involved. A couple of the key players that interacted with Mr. Leahy on the refinancing of West Edmonton Mall were the ubiquitous Peter Elzinga and the garrulous Ken Kowalski, whom humility never touched. Mr. Leahy's relationship with both was necessary for him to cement his position as Acting Superintendent of the ATB.

Mr. Elzinga, the Forrest Gump of Alberta politics, is at every major political event but no one really understands why. After he and Mr. Kowalski, the bridge linking the various components in the West Edmonton Mall refinancing, showed their wares, Mr. Klein put Mr. Elzinga in charge of the Redwater by-election, which the PC's eventually lost. To give you some insight into Mr. Elzinga's brilliance, he elicited the help of "Pavement" Peter Trynchy as his right hand man for Ralph's team in the Redwater by-election. If one is to question Mr. Elzinga's character and intelligence, it can be done on this issue alone. Anyone who thinks that "Pavement Pete" lends credibility to the electoral process should be questioned, but I digress.

I am quite Orwellian in that I believe that everything has a political undertone or significance. I also believe that Mr. Leahy is Orwellian, whether he knows it or not. My letters had put into question Mr. Leahy's promised position of Superintendent in return for the refinancing of West Edmonton Mall. Mr. Leahy also knew that Mr. Elzinga was Premier Klein's right-hand man and Executive Director of the PC Alberta Fund. He began to lobby Mr. Elzinga in his quest for permanent status as Superintendent. The following is a thank you note from Mr. Elzinga to Mr. Leahy:

12/94

Dear Elmer,

Special thanks for the lovely lunch and the scotch and leather case. It was a delight to get to know you better.

Wishing you a blessed Christmas Season.

Warm regards,

Peter E

When I saw this letter originally, a wave of nausea flooded over me. Mr. Elzinga is a "schmoozer" of wide repute, knowing the value and persuasive power of a political contribution. Mr. Elzinga is such a dull speaker that after his visits to a constituency office, hardware stores in the vicinity have learned to ban the sale of rope or any sharp implements to protect the public. Mr. Elzinga's letter is the culmination of the relationship that began to blossom at the genesis of the West Edmonton Mall refinancing. Mr. Leahy knew that Mr. Elzinga was one of Mr. Klein's closest confidants. Therefore, cementing a relationship with Mr. Elzinga would help ensure his permanent status.

Mr. Kowalski's actions are documented in more detail elsewhere, but suffice it to say for now that it was Mr. Kowalski who was one of the catalysts in reversing the West Edmonton Mall deal with Gentra Corporation, and he was not above personal gain for services rendered. In this case, the Government dropped him from the Cabinet on the Western Lotteries issue before he fulfilled his promise to Mr. Leahy of permanent status as Superintendent. The conduct of both Mr. Elzinga and his cohort, Mr. Kowalski, showed that they are strong advocates of situation ethics. You know, feel good now, rationalize later.

My letter campaign against the Alberta Treasury Branches began in October 1995. Mr. Leahy admitted to me that my letters caused a slide toward what he considered a mental breakdown. On August 1, 1996, he informed me and I quote, "I had been meeting with myself at the kitchen table at three and four in the morning." He also informed me that he was promised the job of Superintendent before the receipt of my letters. In addition, he was forced to give all the senior ATB executives golden parachutes as a part of the damage control implemented by the Provincial Treasurer and the Auditor General because of my letters. The Auditor General and the Provincial Treasurer had known about the activities for two years and only exposed them when they were forced to. Rather than institute a criminal investigation into the activities of the senior executives, they were allowed to resign or retire with their benefit package intact. The bare minimum was done to soften public perception. As ridiculous as it sounds, it was a cover up of a cover up.

Mr. Leahy had gotten rid of the senior management who supposedly retired on March 31, 1996. The Auditor General, Peter

Valentine, was the impetus behind these forced retirements. Mr. Valentine was covering his own ass. He had been informed about the improprieties and irregularities surrounding these individuals in early 1994 by Mr. Brian Sutherland and Mr. Geoff Perkins, both former ATB employees. There should have been a criminal investigation, but the Auditor General chose to protect his political friends. Mr. Leahy was called to Mr. Dinning's office in early April 1996 and offered a package to step down that he could not refuse, or perhaps more accurately, was not allowed to refuse. He informed me that he would have been prepared to stay another five years but was not given the option. Because of my letters, the Provincial Treasurer believed that Mr. Leahy had become a political liability. Mr. Leahy candidly admitted to me that the letters had ended his career. Mr. Leahy told me, and again I quote, "Your letters have changed the ATB for a generation." In short, Mr. Leahy removed all the senior officials and then the Government removed Mr. Leahy.

You may have wondered why Mr. Leahy was being so forthright. Frankly, I did too at the time. His main objective was to apologize for the abuses that I had been suffering and he informed me that the Auditor General was in charge of the file. His real intent was clear, however. It was his mea culpa and being aware that I was working on this book, an attempt to soften his portrayal. Allowing me to be treated the way I was, he said, was the biggest mistake he ever made in his life. Too little, too late! His actions allowed the thin layer of respectability to be peeled back, exposing the rottenness at the core of the Alberta Treasury Branches.

CHAPTER 15
STOP ME BEFORE I LEND AGAIN

It has been well over a year since I started my letter-writing campaign. In those letters I asked the questions concerning many Alberta Treasury Branches' accounts, so many questions they could be a book in themselves and may be yet. A litany of scandal follows, since I do not have enough space to discuss them all in detail. While these made the book, all the others I discussed in my letters deserve to be in the Hall of Shame. Warning: May not be suitable reading for taxpayers with high blood pressure. Consult your member of the Legislative Assembly before reading.

Up first is Strathmore Investment Services Ltd. and the settlement agreement with the Alberta Treasury Branches. Strathmore had a total outstanding indebtedness of 4.4 million dollars in early 1994. During the course of that year, a settlement agreement was reached with the Alberta Treasury Branches to settle this indebtedness with a single payment of 1.65 million dollars, saving Strathmore 62% of the total loan. Even beyond that, Strathmore then was allowed to split the required lump sum payment by paying just over a million dollars in 1994 and the remaining 630,000 dollars subsequent to the 1994 year end interest free. Such a deal! This was notwithstanding guarantees, security on amounts receivable, and postponement of claims by shareholders. Strathmore's principal, Mr. Rasmussen, a chartered accountant, had a net worth that would have allowed the repayment of the loan in full, yet it was written off by the Alberta

Treasury Branches. Another stellar member of the Alberta Treasury Branches' rogues gallery, Mr. Larry Leroux (now hastily departed manager of Edmonton Main Branch), set up the loan originally. Mr. Leroux was prominent on a list of ATB employees implicated in unethical behaviour I included in a letter to Jack Briscoe, the Executive Director of Public Affairs for the Alberta Treasury Branches. Mr. Briscoe has been shown the door as well. (It must be noted here that Mr. Leroux had hired Brian Beresh, the well-known criminal lawyer, to represent him.)

Now back to our story about Strathmore Investment. Mr. Leroux advised Mr. Rasmussen to hire the lovely and talented Mark Gunderson from McLennan Ross as his solicitor in the negotiations. Sound familiar? The entire matter was stage-managed since this was the same Mark Gunderson who also acted for the Alberta Treasury Branches on a regular basis. In return for facilitating the deal, both Mr. Gunderson and Mr. Leroux benefited from kickbacks. Mr. Gunderson also had similar arrangements with other ATB employees, and Mr. Leroux was well known as one of "Elmer's boys"; and if you were a friend of Elmer Leahy and Larry Leroux, the loan repayment terms were sweet indeed. You have probably guessed it already, but Mr. Rasmusssen and Strathmore Investments were consistent contributors to the PC Alberta Fund.

Next, on the "hit" parade, General Composites of Nisku, Alberta, obtained financing from the Alberta Treasury Branches' Strathcona branch for a new manufacturing venture. Included in that financing was 1.75 million dollars of Government of Alberta guarantees on the loans. The whole enterprise was upside down before the first products were ever made. The Alberta Treasury Branches did not want to do the deal in the first place but because the principal, Donald Wolfe's family, was strong PC Alberta Fund contributors, the political pressure was on to do the deal. To give you an idea of how far outside normal loan guidelines the deal was, consider these highlights. The Government of Alberta guaranteed 1.75 million dollars while Mr. Wolfe was so confident in the viability of his project, he could only manage to guarantee 36 thousand dollars, a scant 2% of the value of the Government guarantee. Apparently, Mr. Wolfe was such a financial genius, he could bend loan guidelines at will. From what I was able to gather from this failed venture, the best thing that General Composites manufactured was this loan agreement.

Now, let us look at Norm Green of Stewart Green Properties Ltd. and one-time owner of the Dallas Stars National Hockey League franchise. Mr. Green's relationship with the Alberta Treasury Branches dates from the Lougheed era. Mr. Green was a part of Mr. Lougheed's inner circle and was able to rally that influence in the form of loans from the Alberta Treasury Branches. Mr. Green was not the only luminary from Mr. Lougheed's inner circle that benefited. You will remember Mr. Ron Southern of ATCO fame who was an undercapitalized trailer manufacturer in the early 1970s and now, through Canadian Utilities Ltd., ATCO, has become one of the largest utility companies in Canada. Mr.

Lougheed now sits on the Board of Directors of ATCO. ATCO dealt at the Calgary Northhills branch of the Alberta Treasury Branches, the Calgary home of the designated credit. Note that Mr. Lougheed is now a member of the law firm Bennett Jones Vechere. The great majority of legal work for ATCO is done by Bennett Jones, and members of the law firm have also become directors of ATCO. Finally, Mr. Green used the same law firm to implement his dealings with the Alberta Treasury Branches.

There are more interrelations here than an Arkansas wedding, but I digress. Mr. Green on the other hand, dealt at Calgary Main, another burial ground for the designated credits. It must be remembered that Mr. Green dealt with Wayne Peterson, Wally Peters, and Bill Tough. This is the key problem that has plagued the ATB. By knowing that the politicians were tied to these types of deals, Mr. Tough, Mr. Peterson, and Mr. Peters, among others, ensured they were insulated from disciplinary action when it came to their own personally beneficial deals. This was how corruption survived, and, in fact, honour among thieves made sure the sordid details remained covered up. Mr. Peterson, Mr. Peters, and Mr. Tough remained immune from prosecution, and the Auditor General allowed them to retire with full pensions because of the political fallout. All knew where the bodies were buried and used that knowledge to their full advantage.

The first asset of major significance of Norm Green's to be disposed of was the Dallas Stars NHL hockey franchise. The purchase price was 89 million dollars. The Alberta Treasury

Branches was owed 54.4 million dollars by the Dallas Stars. This amount represented a discount from the full loan of nearly 3 million dollars. The ATB was going to lose millions upon millions of dollars on Mr. Green's property portfolio when they could have realized 100% of their loan to the Dallas Stars. Why would ATB do this? This loan payout had become high profile, the details of which had received considerable play in the press in the fall of 1995. It was inconceivable that the Superintendent of the Alberta Treasury Branches would give such a reduction without the blessing of Cabinet. Mr. Green and his corporations have been major contributors to the PC Alberta Fund over the years, making specific contributions directly to Mr. Dinning's and Mr. Klein's election campaigns. During the Lougheed years, Mr. Dinning was the Director of the Southern Alberta Office of the Premier and was very familiar with Mr. Lougheed's inner circle.

This arrangement was unique. Instead of trying to retrieve assets, the Alberta Treasury Branches were releasing money. Mr. Green also had a home in San Diego, California that ATB did not act on nor were they even remotely interested in the fact that part of the deal for the sale of the Stars allowed Mr. Green to be on the Board of Directors for ten years with a 5 million dollar consulting fee. The Alberta Treasury Branches also allowed him to keep 3 million dollars from the proceeds of the sale of the Stars. Even with the huge black hole sucking up millions of dollars through his property holdings, Mr. Green's political friends were not going to allow him to go away empty-handed or even spend one night in a men's hostel.

I asked some puzzling questions about Stewart Green Properties Ltd. First, why were the assets that the ATB was a secured lender on transferred to Stewart Green Holdings, Inc.? This is a federally incorporated company of which Mr. William Kenny of the law firm Cook, Duke, Cox is the shareholder and director according to registry documents. Notice that Stewart Green Holdings, Inc. was federally incorporated while its predecessor, Stewart Green Properties Ltd. was provincially incorporated. Why the difference, considering that the Alberta Treasury Branches are part of the Alberta Government and their mandate is to do business only in Alberta? This was done deliberately to deceive the people of Alberta. The names, while different for legal reasons, are strikingly similar. It was legal legerdemain. Second, a federal incorporation makes it much more difficult to discover the identities of the shareholders and directors, since the information must be requested through Ottawa. This was a page out of the North West Trust saga in which government-owned assets were moved into a private corporation at inflated values to protect the financial institutions balance sheet. A private corporation is also not obligated to report financial information publicly. It was the same old story except Mr. Kenny, the ATB's lead counsel, had refined the devious process.

This was done to protect the financial statement of the Alberta Treasury Branches in a precautionary move before the next provincial election. The same method was used with Partow Park Holdings, Inc. that I discussed earlier in Chapter 13. The move gave the ATB the chance to avoid massive capital write-downs on the Stewart Green portfolio. If the Stewart Green assets were properly written down, it was highly unlikely that the Alberta Treasury Branches would have shown any profit at all for 1995. It has been confirmed that Mr. Kenny received a higher than normal legal fee for becoming director of the new company. In a letter to Mr. Kenny, I asked him this very question: How does one put a price on impropriety? It proved that Mr. Kenny was not above trading money for embarrassment.

As proof, the historic Hudson's Bay Department Store in downtown Edmonton had a first mortgage from the Royal Bank, as well as corporate guarantees from Stewart Green Properties. When Mr. Kenny moved the Stewart Green assets into the new corporation, a part of his rationale for doing so was the avoidance of creditors in a manner he had so recently refined, the aforementioned Partow Park Holdings, Inc. One is left wondering how many other creditors were left holding the bag. To ensure this transition, the Alberta Treasury Branches and Mr. Kenny enlisted the help of Coopers & Lybrand Ltd. Coopers & Lybrand hired their counsel, D. R. Stollery and Sonny Mirth, from the firm of Reynolds Mirth. The Alberta Treasury Branches seem to resort to the same old cast when mounting any new production.

We know that Mr. Green was paid 3 million dollars to walk away from his hockey team. Did Stewart Green Holdings, Mr.

Kenny's company, pay Mr. Green a fee to walk away? Does Mr. Green have first right of refusal to purchase the properties back? And finally, one of the shopping centres was sold from the Stewart Green portfolio by Mr. Kenny to a company called Centrefund, and one of the major shareholders in that group of corporations is a gentleman by the name of Robert Green. (It's probably just a coincidence.) This property was controlled in Alberta by John Little, a lawyer at Witten Binder. Why didn't Mr. Green use his own name on the documents? Oh well.

The next financial boondoggle on the list was the new Links Clinic in Edmonton. The Links Clinic operated under three different companies: Westmount Med City Properties Ltd., Roc Terrace Holdings Ltd., and the Links Clinic. The loans policy of the Alberta Treasury Branches stipulated that no loans of over ten million dollars were to be made to one connection or one party. The Vice-Superintendent of ATB, Les Bellan, circumvented this policy by lending to three separate corporations in a hope that the deception would go undetected. The breakdown for each company was as follows: Westmount Med City Properties Ltd. was lent the lion's share, $8.4 million; the Links Clinic received $1.3 million; and finally, Roc Terrace got $1 million for a total of $10.7 million in financing, $700,000 over the ten million dollar loan limit.

Several of the guarantors on the loan and the clinic itself as per standard operating procedures were contributors to the PC Alberta Fund. This loan originated at one of the several designated credit branches, in this case, Edmonton Strathcona. No one at the branch level all the way up to Mr. Bellan's position wanted to grant the loan, as it was not economically viable. Yet, Mr. Bellan insisted that the loan be funded. What was curious about this loan was that knowledgeable bankers in the Edmonton area knew that the project was a white elephant and no one was prepared to fund it. In order to make the clinic profitable, estimates of $30 to $35 per foot in gross rent would be required. This at the time the best office space in Edmonton was being rented for $7 to $10 gross per foot. Edmonton had the most inexpensive office lease rates in the world for a major centre and vacancies were at an all time high. Not only was the loan bad, but the terms of the loan were bad. The interest rate was fixed, and the compounding interval was semi-annual. I understand that this loan has been restructured at least once and possibly more.

The loan, not surprisingly, failed miserably. Why would the Alberta Treasury Branches (Les Bellan) insist that the loan be made despite that the entire financial community thought it was a bad loan, unless he was pressured to do so by a government official? (Mr. Bellan was no stranger to government pressure. He had been copied on the Gainers' guarantee letter from Deputy Provincial Treasurer, A. J. McPherson.) I posed this question in one of my letters, and the damage control began to be deployed. The clinic was foreclosed on and moved into one of the famous CK Holdings companies, kind of a burial ground for bad deals and a place to protect the balance sheet. The estimated losses were well over five million dollars. The ATB worked in reverse. Upper management approved loans that middle managers disagreed with. A very dangerous way to run a bank.

The next exhibit in the Hall of Shame is Alberta Bakeries Ltd. This corporation had been in business since 1928. The principals had been trying to sell their business for quite some time, but nobody would pay the asking price. The enterprise was in a run-down condition and some of the equipment was so old, it was churning out buns when Bill Aberhart was Premier. What could they do to get rid of it? In walked "Uncle Jake" Superstein. If you can't sell it, refinance your buns at the Alberta Treasury Branches, proferred Uncle Jake. It was unconscionable what happened next. Mr. Superstein agreed to arrange for a new loan at Mr. Leroux's First Edmonton Branch, which was his previous assignment before Edmonton Main Branch. It was the *yeast* he could do.

Jake Superstein was able to refinance Alberta Bakeries for approximately 2.5 million dollars, and for doing so he received a large fee which was included in the financing package. Then, he paid Mr. Leroux a paltry 5 thousand dollars for a deal that cost taxpayers millions. But, please don't worry about Mr. Leroux. He had his house re-sided by the Sunset Eavestroughing Company, one of his customers, so he did not need a lot of money.

Lo and behold, Alberta Bakeries failed. Coopers & Lybrand was appointed the receiver of the corporation. To give you a sense of how bad the deal smelled, it even offended Coopers, no small feat. The liquidators and auctioneers were so appalled by the quality of the assets, they could not even get bids on some of the equipment. In fact, most of the equipment, including the delivery trucks, was not functional. The results could be categorized as dismal at best. When all the assets have been sold, including the building, it is unlikely that the Alberta Treasury Branches, after paying all the legal and accounting fees, will realize anything approaching four hundred thousand dollars. A few crumbs compared to 2.5 million. The value of the equipment was most accurately determined by its weight according to the prevailing market value of scrap metal. John MacNutt, Senior Vice President of Coopers & Lybrand, as you will recall from a previous chapter, not exactly a candidate for beatification himself, thought that Mr. Superstein should be investigated for his *roll* in the refinancing of Alberta Bakeries. The best *bread* that came out of the Alberta Bakeries was that which changed hands when the loan was funded. More disturbing is that the Alberta Bakeries' heist was one of many of Jake Superstein's forays into arranging loans for friends at the Alberta Treasury Branches. Realize that Mr. Superstein is from the Willie Sutton era. When asked why he robbed banks, Willie replied, "Cause that's where the money is!" These loans were perhaps a cry for help, "Stop me before I lend again" which leads me to wonder if there is a twelve step program for ATB branch managers? I hope that Mr. Haggis implements such a program. The least the Klein Government could do would be to cover the program under Alberta Health Care.

CHAPTER 16
WON'T YOU BE MY VALENTINE?

"He looks like the guy in the science fiction movie who is the first to see The Creature"

- David Frye

How to describe Mr. Peter Valentine, Alberta's watchdog of the public purse? Well, here is how his duties are set out in the Auditor General Act. In part, he is responsible for overseeing a:

> Council or a Minister of the Crown or by any combination thereof, that is responsible for the administration of public money or assets owned by the Crown .... (e) 'public money' means public money as defined in the Financial Administration Act and includes money forming part of the Treasury Branches Deposits Fund.

First, let me address Mr. Valentine's duties with reference to the Auditor General Act. As you will see, given Mr. Valentine's actions it is highly likely that he has never seen or read the Act. He is supposed to be the financial watchdog for the taxpayers of Alberta; instead of barking when sensing a scoundrel, the only thing this watchdog is interested in is burying things. What Mr. Valentine managed to prove is that even idealism has its own vices.

Many years ago, I read an article about the great South American general and statesman, Simon Bolivar. The article described one of the general's theories of government. Bolivar believed government was made up of not three but four branches: the legislative, the judiciary, the executive, and the bureaucracy. He felt all were accountable to a system of checks and balances with the exception of the bureaucracy. It was subject to no checks whatsoever and therefore, the greatest threat to the state. I never thought much more about his theory until my dealings with Mr. Valentine; then I realized that Mr. Bolivar was ahead of his time.

Mr. Valentine, it must be remembered, is no paragon of virtue in his own right. In early 1996, the Auditor General caused a flap with taxpayers, the Opposition, and even Premier Ralph Klein got into the act. Not only was the Auditor General's budget larger by a third than Ontario's, but he was asking for a 1996 increase of $300,000. On top of that, he asked for nearly $800,000 to purchase new office furniture for his staff, notwithstanding 5,000 surplus government desks and chairs that were sitting idle in Edmonton. Mr. Valentine is a truly amazing man. When it comes to a company such as Career Designs that overcharged the Government a few thousand dollars, he is able to uncover the facts immediately. When it comes to politically sensitive files concerning millions of dollars such as Trimac and Bovar, his investigation wallows in indecision. It's fairly simple! Mr. Valentine should just follow the money.

Mr. Klein said in The Edmonton Sun on January 11, 1996, "I would have to say honestly that [a pay increase] would set a very, very bad precedent." Apparently, Mr. Valentine's personal credo is do as I say, don't do as I do. With all fairness to Mr. Valentine, while Ontario's population dwarfs Alberta's, their books are easy to maintain as they are straightforward and follow generally accepted accounting principles. The fact that Alberta's Auditor

General budget is larger than Ontario's means that the Premier should cut Mr. Valentine some slack; it costs a great deal of money to keep two sets of books and to come up with creative new ways of formulating a massive cover up.

The following letter was sent to Mr. Valentine on October 11, 1996:

11 October 1996

Dear Mr. Valentine:

The recent release of your Annual Report, specifically that part of the Report dealing with the Alberta Treasury Branches raises some disturbing questions. I would like you to validate my research surrounding those questions for my book, **Banksters and Prairie Boys**.

Firstly, I would like to deal with a personal issue. It has come to my attention that <u>you have personally attacked me with racist epithets such as "Unabomber", "Third Would Terrorist", "Arab Terrorist", "Camel Jockey", "Sand Nigger", and that my tactics are of the Third World vein</u>. A person who usually resorts to these tactics is unable to deal with the real issues at hand. I understand however, that things have changed for you and that you are no longer a practising racist, because apparently, you no longer need the practice.

It has come to my attention that <u>the entire chain of command from the Alberta Treasury Branches and the Alberta Government knew about the loan irregularities and improprieties</u>. There is a record of meetings that you were involved in that clearly show you were aware of irregularities and improprieties in the ATB loan portfolio, long before you addressed them in your report. In fact, you were hand-picked by Mr. Dinning to overlook the problem as you were one of the Tory faithful that could be relied on. When signing off on the 1995 ATB Financial Report surely you must have abandoned normal CA guidelines as well as your responsibility for accurate financial reporting. I have to call you a liar; otherwise I would have to assume that you're so incompetent that you actually believe that the ATB's financial statements and the Annual Auditor General's Report are correct. However, I should thank you for giving me anonymous kudos on page 200 of your most recent Annual Report for making you "aware of, allegations of inappropriate business practices at the Alberta Treasury Branches" - as if you didn't know! It's the best written statement I have ever seen for someone trying to cover his severely exposed backside. Surely, the CICA would be interested in your abilities to formulate and cover up some of the most fraudulent financial statements and annual reports of the Auditor General. How can the Auditor General, the watchdog guarding the tax dollars of the people of Alberta, in good conscience affix his signature to these reports, especially when you were aware of the improprieties that had taken place? Why haven't you called for a criminal investigation to purge these fraudulent transactions?

In my case, you have allowed the Alberta Treasury Branches and their agents to spend millions in fees by ruining me and trying to keep the truth suppressed about my file as well as others. The Auditor General continues to condone the funding of this abuse. Would you please comment on why you continue with these actions? There is much more to consider but that is for next week.

MONIER M. RAHALL
cc: **Mr. Jack Briscoe   The Honourable James Dinning**
Alberta Treasury Branches   Provincial Treasurer
The Honourable Ralph Klein
Premier of Alberta
The letter campaign that I started in the fall of 1995 confirming

information for this book has been a constant source of irritation for Mr. Valentine, even to the point of him using racial slurs referred to in the letter. You might think that I was a touch sensitive about these racial slurs and references made by Mr. Valentine. Not at all. In fact, I was probably the last one to take them seriously until I had met with someone who had heard them first-hand. Others, however, lawyers, professionals, and ATB employees for the most part were telling me what Mr. Valentine had said, seeking my reaction. One lawyer from the law firm of Duncan & Craig, Darcy Readman, said that senior ATB managers were using these same racial slurs. Even Elmer Leahy told me himself that this was happening and confirmed Mr. Valentine's attitude. I am not the most politically correct guy around, but my reaction was, of course, that it was not appropriate for any kind of government officials, let alone the Auditor General, to use or condone that kind of derogatory language. What did bother me about the remarks, however, was that they were filtering through various levels of the government, and ATB employees and officials without qualms were using them regularly in reference to me.

Interestingly, if anyone cares to examine the list of employees in senior ATB management, you will find virtually no minorities-- most are prairie boys, tried and true. I am a Canadian and Albertan born and raised; so I thought that Mr. Valentine overstepped the bounds of propriety and good taste and was totally unbecoming to someone of his position. This episode does provide a small insight into the man's character, character which was more fully exposed by his handling of the improprieties as I have pointed out to him elsewhere in my letters. Besides, I wanted him to know that I was aware of his racial slurs.

The more corruption that was exposed, the more the level of racism spiraled upward in the Auditor General's office. In a letter to Premier Klein, I pointed out being called an Arab terrorist was just pure bottom-line racism. For those of you whose surname suggests an ethnic background, watch out. They will, regardless of your Canadian values, also characterize you as wearing a headdress, baggy pants, and pointy slippers that curl up at the toes. I do not drive a carpet. The only camel I ever saw was in a zoo. I have never spent any time in the desert, nor do I encourage terrorism. Rather than deal with the real issues and with the corruption within the ATB and the Alberta Government, certain individuals resorted to name-calling to divert attention away from their own corruption.

This was not the first time the issue of racism was brought up in these matters, as when employee of the Alberta Treasury Branches, Brian Sutherland was dismissed by the ATB. He had informed senior ATB officials of the sundry dealings of Mr. Superstein and Mr. Rollingher. These gentlemen replied by hiring a lawyer named Sol Rolingher to take legal action against Mr. Sutherland for his anti-Semitism if he became a problem. The difficulty I had with this was that their action does not deal with the issues. If Mr. Rollingher and Mr. Superstein were not guilty of any impropriety, this would reflect on Mr. Sutherland's character.

In essence, they were practicing reverse racism to deflect attention from their own impropriety.

The irony in all this, of course, is that the Alberta Treasury Branches has just authored a new Code of Conduct dated December 20, 1996. The issue of racism is specifically addressed in section 6(iii), the Rights of Others:

> Discrimination, whether against an individual or a group, is to be neither practiced nor tolerated. Standard of conduct established by law, whether included in the Bill of Rights or the Individual's Right Protection Act, are to be adhered to.

This is the same Code of Ethics which has been greatly expanded. I wonder why! This is also the same Code of Ethics that the Auditor General recommended in his Report, but defended by saying it was not triggered by impropriety.

It is important that racism *does not* play a role in any of this and that it does not cloud the issues at hand. My revelations are based on fact and fact only. There are no ulterior motives at work here. I *am* sensitive to anti-Semitism, as I *am* a Semite. There are many people in the Jewish community who are worried that this scandal will reflect on them adversely, schande fun die goyim or embarrassment in front of gentiles. In the end what really matters is that the facts are investigated and in this instance, if there is an issue of racism, it should be addressed and dealt with when all the facts are known and not before.

It was quite obvious that Mr. Valentine could not defend his position in covering up the corruption at the Alberta Treasury Branches so he launched a personal attack against me hoping it would discredit my criticism of his illicit actions. Apparently, the mere mention of my name sent Mr. Valentine into an apoplectic rage, and the only way in which he could deal with my letters and questions was for him to be heavily sedated. (Okay, okay, perhaps I don't know that he needed to be heavily sedated, but he certainly should have been and I do like the picture!) This heavy sedation could explain how the Auditor General has been hiding the true facts of the practices of the Alberta Government, as well as the Alberta Treasury Branches from the people of Alberta. To use an analogy here, what made Watergate so corrupt was not a third-rate burglary, but rather the cover up of the burglary. The Auditor General, with whom we entrust our tax dollars, has been covering up fraudulent transactions that have a political fallout. So, in short, Mr. Valentine has been protecting his political friends and allies rather than the people of Alberta which is his mandate.

My letters forced the hand of the Auditor General compelling him to address the matters in his Annual Report as part of the damage control that was taking place. The Auditor General cannot change history, only how it is recorded. It always fascinates me how scandal and impropriety are just like deadbeat relatives and just won't go away. He was derelict in his duties by not reporting this earlier, which indicates a cover up.

The reason the Auditor General became so testy on the receipt of one of my letters was that he had to investigate all the matters that I raised. The investigation required that reports had to be written. I can understand why he would be so upset, since he was probably running out of ways to cover up the improprieties and irregularities. The worst thing that one can do to a bureaucracy is send it a letter, because the letter takes on a life of its own and each of these creatures is quite different in its effects and fallout. Don't hate me because I am inquisitive.

Upon the instructions of the Provincial Treasurer and the Acting Superintendent of the Alberta Treasury Branches, my inquiries were to be directed to Jack Briscoe, the Executive Manager, Public Affairs for ATB. After the receipt of several of my letters in September and October of 1995, Mr. Briscoe wrote me with the following letter:

October 18, 1995

Dear Mr. Rahall:

I acknowledge receipt of your letters of October 13 and 16, 1995.

The information contained in the above referenced correspondence appears to be from a sick and demented source. It is also inaccurate and libelous.

As we are in litigation with you and your companies, the entire matter has been turned over to our solicitors to handle now and in the future.

Yours truly,

J. L. Briscoe
Executive Manager
Public Affairs

What followed was a series of retirements, resignations, and terminations of senior ATB officials, finally including Jack Briscoe himself. Note that the Alberta Treasury Branches and the Alberta Government have never started a legal action against me nor the facts contained within my letters. Of course, to bring such a libel suit, the Government and the Alberta Treasury Branches would have to produce documents to show what I said was not true; something that is anathema to them.

A senior official at the Alberta Treasury Branches confirmed for me that when I sent letters to Jack Briscoe, these letters were whisked away to the Office of the Chief Inspector, Andrew Wingate, the former Acting Auditor General. Mr. Wingate then duly reported them to Peter Valentine, the Auditor General. Mr. Briscoe volunteered that he was out of the loop for over a year, and was not allowed to see or read any of the letters. If what was contained in the letters was not true, why the need to take Mr. Briscoe out of the loop? Could it be that Mr. Valentine was worried about his own reputation and did not want any ATB officials privy to any of the information with political implications? After all, Mr. Dinning had advised me to correspond with Mr. Briscoe. Was Mr. Valentine defying Mr. Dinning, or had Mr. Dinning changed the rules after viewing the contents? Or, was Mr. Valentine freelancing and trying to protect his own funny valentine?

I had many more questions about the Auditor General's letter. I sent another letter to Mr. Valentine and co-addressed it to Mr. Dinning, the Provincial Treasurer on October 11, 1996.

11 October 1996

Dear Gentlemen:

To further validate the information that will form part of my book, **Banksters and Prairie Boys**, I must question your handling of certain situations with respect to the Alberta Treasury Branches in your recently released "Annual Report of the Auditor General of Alberta".

In your report, on page 200, you make the following statement: "As a result of this work, I made a number of recommendations designed to address the problems identified. These recommendations called for: a more business-like approach to administering large commercial loans; better quality due diligence when approving credit; improved control over temporary credit facilities; better financial reporting by customers; a more effective chief inspector function; an expanded code of conduct and ethics; and a better process for dealing with allegations of improper behaviour received from staff and others. These recommendations have since been discussed with, and have the support of, the new Board of Directors." I find this comment somewhat puzzling and ironic when viewed in the light of your conduct and ethics. The degree of both were aptly illustrated in recent newspaper articles in which you state that none of the rash of retirements and resignations over the last few months have anything to do with the irregularities or improprieties. I know for a fact, sir, that most of those individuals did not wish to leave but were forced to based on the circumstances that you deny. This was an astoundingly hypocritical comment if not disingenuous in the extreme. If these gentlemen were not forced to resign or retire for improprieties, then why would you need a new code of conduct and ethics; why would you need a more effective Chief Inspector function; why would you need a better process for dealing with allegations of improper behaviour? In conjunction with my file, it has been admitted under oath that ATB employees were forced to retire and resign. Surely, between you and Mr. Wingate, who was once the Acting Auditor General that you would have been able to recognize the improprieties and irregularities. When you made Mr. Wingate the new Chief Inspector after having been the Acting Auditor General did some metamorphosis occur when his title changed to see these improprieties and irregularities that he could not see before? Just like the Bible, a miracle must have happened and the scales fell from his eyes. The fact is, Mr. Valentine, that if you tell the truth, you never get yourself caught in these little bothersome inconsistencies.

I know for a fact, Mr. Valentine, that you were well aware of the improprieties. I refer you to a gentleman, one Geoff Perkins by name, who was once an Alberta Treasury Branches employee but who now works for the Bank of Nova Scotia. Mr. Perkins informed you of some of these improprieties and irregularities in the banking practices of the Alberta Treasury Branches. To try and cover your severely exposed backside and to whitewash the situation, you called for the firm of Peat Marwick to produce a report on the matter. So, for you to deny that you had any knowledge of these events is just a bald-faced lie....

However, what concerns me most about your conduct is that your signature appears on the Alberta Treasury Branches financial statements. If you are saying that you did not know about these improprieties and irregularities, then you must be incompetent in your role as Auditor General of the Province of Alberta. On the other hand, if you did know about these matters, and I have it on reliable authority that you did, and covered it up, <u>I suggest you seek legal advice. I suggest you seek legal advice. (Sorry, that's not a typo, it was just fun to write</u>!). This is a fine example of the classic Catch-22 situation, Mr. Valentine. In either instance, you should do the honourable thing as Mr. Dinning the individual who hand-picked you for your current post has done and resign as the Auditor General of the Province of Alberta.

However, as you are still the Auditor General as of this writing, I will be forwarding to you a time line of the chain of events on my file to date and since you claim to be able to recognize irregularities and improprieties, the events listed should keep you busy indeed. In the time line, you <u>will recognize classic conflicts of interest such as Coopers & Lybrand Limited being allowed to work for both the debtor and creditor on the same file</u>. Or, as another example, the instance in which unsecured creditors were allowed to rank ahead of secured creditors. These are samples of the litany of misdeeds only. There are a host of others for you to exercise your perspicacious powers on.

You should also be aware that I have gone to a public inquiry under the auspices of Robert Clark, the Privacy Commissioner, in an effort to verify what professional fees the Alberta Treasury Branches have spent on my files. This information was denied. As the Auditor General, could you please explain to me and the people of Alberta how you could justify the continued expenditure of the fees on my file and, in fact, why you allow this abuse to continue? It would be interesting to me to know what the fees are for your other investigations compared to my file and their justification. Note here also, that the CICA is currently investigating the role of certain of its members with regard to my file. Perhaps it would be worthwhile contacting them and reacquainting yourself with the Rules of Professional Conduct, as you seem to have lost your perspective.

Now, I should like to draw your attention to an additional remark made in your report that I also find ironic. "I have no evidence that any of Alberta Treasury Branches' customers were financially disadvantaged by the inappropriate business practices." Well, let me say that this comes as a complete shock to someone who has had both his life and his businesses ruined by these "inappropriate business practices." I would have to guess that you do not characterize such a file as being severely disadvantaged even though the Alberta Treasury Branches have already admitted that two of their managers were forced to resign for unethical behaviour that dealt with my file. On the other hand, as I have pointed out to Mr. Dinning and others on numerous occasions over the past year, several Albertans (those who are a select cadre closely associated with the PC inner circle) that has been supremely advantaged as a result of ATB's efforts. In fact I believe that it was the ATB's dealings with these individuals that gave rise to the slogan, "the Alberta Advantage." Fortunately, for the Government, the vast majority of Albertans do not realize that this is a double entendre, - yet. If you do not understand the concept of the Alberta Advantage, I suggest that you have Mr. Dinning or Mr. Klein explain it to you as they have come to rely on it in several instances.

Now, I direct some comments specifically at you, Mr. Dinning. You and Mr. Evans were able to resign or retire (however you characterize it) before the Auditor General's Report was released. I must say your timing was impeccable. <u>The concrete beneath your pedestal that has been erected for your service to the people of Alberta just nicely dried before the Report was released</u>. Apparently, you did indeed learn a thing or two from the master, Mr. Lougheed. In the famous words of Al Jolson, always leave when they still want you. You knew very well, Mr. Dinning, that soon they would not want you. Your timing was deliberate in that it accomplished two things: first, it allowed you to duck questions concerning the Auditor General's Report and, second, it made all the issues moot since you were on your way out. Well done, sir!

Would you gentlemen verify the contents of my letter and send me a response by the end of October, 1996, or otherwise, I must assume from your silence that you concur that the information contained herein is factual as described?

MONIER M. RAHALL

cc: **Mr. Marshal Williams**
Chairman of the Board, Alberta Treasury Branches
The Honourable Ralph Klein
Premier of Alberta
Mr. Paul Haggis
Superintendent, Alberta Treasury Branches

After considering the letter to Mr. Valentine, it was evident that the Auditor General had caught himself in his own web of deceit by making recommendations for problems he says don't exist. In reference to my personal file, it was Mr. Leahy, the Acting Superintendent, who told me that Mr. Valentine had control of my file since November 1995 and was well aware of the improprieties and irregularities of the professionals who worked for the Alberta Treasury Branches. If the Auditor General was investigating this matter properly and understanding what was happening, why did he not stop the funding of the abuse? He continued the funding and, in fact, escalated it. The only possible explanation is that now that the ATB employees were slowly being removed, was he protecting the politicians as well as himself? He needed to discredit me to ensure that his own reputation remained unsullied.

The resignations of the Provincial Treasurer, Mr. Dinning, and the Attorney General, Mr. Evans were stage-managed in relationship to the timing of the release of the Auditor General's Annual Report. I received no response from Mr. Dinning nor Mr. Valentine--their silence was deafening.

I wrote to both Mr. Valentine and Mr. Dinning concerning further issues again on October 21, 1996:

21 October 1996

Dear Gentlemen:

In order to round out the litany of corruption associated with the dealings of the Alberta Treasury Branches for my book, **Banksters and Prairie Boys**, I have additional information that I need you to validate. I notice that in your 1994 and 1995 Report of the Auditor General, there is no mention of irregularities or improprieties, even though they predate those reports. However, in 1996, you had a moment of enlightenment for the current Report and miraculously ferreted them out. (By the way, I acknowledge your thinly disguised tip of the hat for raising these issues.)

The first thing that I should like to deal with is the loan loss provisions of the Alberta Treasury Branches. As Auditor General of the Province of Alberta, you would definitely have to review and approve these loan loss provisions for the financial statements of ATB. Specifically, I should like to draw your attention and your powers of recollection to three accounts in particular: The Brick Warehouse, West Edmonton Mall, and the Pocklington connection. My information is that loan loss provisions were put in place that covered 100% of the loan for both the Brick Warehouse and for the West Edmonton Mall loan; as well, a loan loss provision equal to 25% of the loan was set up for the Pocklington loan with respect to the Edmonton Oilers Hockey Club for the fiscal 1994 financial statement. Now, for the clincher, I also have reliably-sourced information that these loan loss provisions were put into profits in order to cover up irregularities and improprieties. I have a very serious question to ask at this point. Why would the Auditor General of this province allow these loan loss provisions to be moved into profits? It makes no sense at all. Senior ATB management considered that these loans were of the highest risk in nature and that is why these loan loss provisions were created in the first place, which is within normal banking guidelines.

What makes these loans even more suspect is the fact that all of these loans have increased through additional funding or guarantees, some nearly five-fold. Now please forgive me for not being a financial mind of the first order like yourself but let me humbly submit it to you that putting the loan loss provisions back into profits on suspect loans and increasing those loans and guarantees does not fall within the guidelines of normally accepted banking practice. How can the Auditor General of Alberta spout on that these improprieties and irregularities have been properly investigated when it is the conduct and professional ethics of the Auditor General himself that have led to these improprieties and irregularities and that begs investigation. Your actions in this matter would lead one to conclude that you are not one of the pre-eminent financial thinkers in Canada; nor in Alberta for that matter.

Allow me to analyze your stiletto-like critical thinking a little further. For the sake of discussion, assume that even if the Brick Warehouse loan and the Edmonton Oilers loan for Mr. Pocklington were servicing their debt with interest payments (which is highly unlikely) that still leaves a huge unanswered question. How can you, in good conscience, sign off on the West Edmonton Mall loan, and massive loan guarantee that has absolutely no financial benefit but all of the risk to the Alberta Treasury Branches and the people of Alberta? Yet, in the 1995 Alberta Treasury Branches financial statement your signature appears on the Auditor's Report page sanctioning these actions officially. Logic has dictated that it was not a sound, conventional commercial financing and that it was not based on economics but rather politics by which you have allowed yourself to be influenced. You are derelict in your duties, sir, and on that basis alone you must resign as the watchdog and the guardian of sound financial practices for the people of Alberta. Your stewardship role is irrevocably compromised.

The fact that you sanctioned the West Edmonton Mall deal, which is not commercially viable, is a clear indication that there was political influence being exerted. Since you still report to the Provincial Treasurer and are a part of the Public Service Act, there is no other explanation for a loan with no revenues from interest but nearly a half-billion dollars of exposure to the Alberta Treasury Branches and the people of Alberta. It is once again a case where future Albertans are on the hook for loans arranged by politicians for the current benefit of their political cronies.

The Alberta Treasury Branches has lost over ten thousand borrowing accounts over the last couple of years. I refer to your recently released "Annual Report of the Auditor General of Alberta" and on page 200, the following statement appears: "I have no evidence that any of the Alberta Treasury Branches' customers were financially disadvantaged by the inappropriate business practices." What would be sufficient evidence - the exodus of twenty or thirty thousand borrowing accounts? Customers are obviously frustrated that the ATB has serious problems and is not meeting their financial needs.

Sources close to me have confirmed that in meetings, you have a tendency to become highly agitated upon the receipt of one of my letters or even the mention of my name. These would compel you to investigate my concerns and write a report. I have to ask why you become so upset and begin to use racist slurs, which I have documented previously and are too odious to repeat. Was it because you actually had to do your job or was it because you were running out of ways to cover-up the improprieties and irregularities at the Alberta Treasury Branches and in the Auditor General's office? I would ask that you comment on why you investigate only whatever is necessary but continue to cover-up the rest. You seem to operate on the theory that if you cut a cat's tail one inch at a time, it will hurt less. These same sources also tell me that you are one of the main agents in continuing to fund my abuse through the instrument of the Bankruptcy and Insolvency Act. I am sure that you thought that the use of the Act properly funded would serve to suppress me. As you have seen, especially over the last few days, it has accomplished the opposite which is, I am sure, another reason why you are upset. Since I am told, time and time again, that the Auditor General is involved in my file, I am curious as to what you have reported on it. I am told by several senior officials who have reported to you that there have been improprieties directed at me and my corporations causing financial ruin. You have refused to recognize this and to continue to authorize the funding of the abuse to discredit me and disguise the improprieties of ATB. I must point out to you that no matter how you fund the abuse, be it in the millions, it still doesn't change the truth nor absolve the guilty.

I would require your response by the end of October 1996. If I do not hear from you by this time, I will assume from your silence that you concur with what I have said and have no reason to disagree with any of my points.

MONIER M. RAHALL

cc: **Mr. Marshal Williams**
Chairman of the Board, Alberta Treasury Branches
The Honourable Ralph Klein
Premier of Alberta
Mr. Paul Haggis
Superintendent, Alberta Treasury Branches

It was evident from the findings I addressed in this letter that all the actions and investigations by the Auditor General's office were reviewed for their political ramifications before a proper investigation was initiated. Time and time again, the major theme in most of my letters has been that self-investigation is **improper**. The credibility of the investigation must be based on the integrity of the process, otherwise the results of the investigation will remain suspect.

What remains consistent about my findings is that the names of the same professionals surface time and time again. This is to be expected, as they have become part of the culture that condones wilful blindness.

On October 31, 1996, Halloween and fittingly, the phantasmal figure of the Auditor General, responded to my letters. Well, sort of....

Dear Mr. Rahall:

This letter is written in response to your letters addressed or copied to me from August 20 through October 28, 1996. I will respond only to comments in your letters that directly involve matters related to the statutory mandate of the Auditor General and the Office of the Auditor General. This letter will not comment on various remarks directed at me personally, except to categorically reject them as being false, and, in some cases, defamatory.

Your letters contain a number of allegations, opinions, facts and purported facts relating to Alberta Treasury Branches and its business practices. I have taken very seriously your allegations regarding inappropriate business practices, as I do any other allegations respecting the operations of Alberta Treasury Branches and its officers. My staff has carefully examined all factual assertions contained in your letters, to determine whether they can be verified or otherwise. Facts that can be verified have been taken into account in our audit investigations, which are still in progress. If you have anything in the way of new, verifiable evidence that would assist in these ongoing investigations, you may be assured that it will be examined and evaluated carefully.

I await your further factual information.

Yours truly,

Peter Valentine, FCA
Auditor General   *PV/GA/BL/sd*

Did my eyes deceive me? Was this a response from the Auditor General or the longest suicide note I ever read? Whatever the case, I could not restrain myself. I found the need to take him at face value and point out numerous other examples of irregularities in the business practices of the Alberta Treasury Branches and wrote him again, almost immediately. This letter follows:

31 October 1996

Dear Sir:

Re: Your Letter of 31 October 1996

I am in receipt of your letter and find it only fitting that you would send it on Halloween as it has become a tale of horror. However, I think you must have your special days mixed up as the contents of your letter would make me think you believe it's April Fool's Day.

"I will respond only to comments in your letters that directly involve matters related to the statutory mandate of the Auditor General and the Office of the Auditor General." This is an astounding comment made in the first paragraph of your letter. You have violated many of the rules that govern generally accepted accounting principles. I will list these in detail later on in the letter. Failing to report properly is one of these principles that you tend to ignore on a regular basis.

I quote again from your letter. "This letter will not comment on various remarks directed at me personally, except to categorically reject them as being false, and, in some cases, defamatory." Firstly, it is my belief that this letter was written either entirely by a lawyer, or at least in close consultation with a lawyer. The verbiage would dictate that. It is quite obvious that you are treating the comments made in my letters seriously and cautiously. I invite you to pursue legal action if what I have said is not true. [Author's Note: As of publication, no legal action has ensued.]

Let us deal directly with the racial remarks you made against me. In a meeting on 1 August 1996 at 2:00 p.m. in my

246

lawyer's office, I met with the former Acting Superintendent of the Alberta Treasury Branches, Mr. Elmer Leahy. It was Mr. Leahy who informed me about the racial slurs that the Auditor General and Les Bellan had been making against me personally. To lend credibility to what I have said let me tell you that this is not the only source of this information but just one of many that have confirmed your attitude and remarks concerning me, so your letter becomes a feeble and ultimately futile attempt at denial.

Mr. Leahy also informed me that it was now the Auditor General's Office that was in control of my file, and as the Acting Superintendent of Treasury Branches, he was unable to correct the abuses as you have refused to listen to reason. You are well aware of the improprieties of the professionals working on my file for ATB. Lastly, the fact that I was petitioned into bankruptcy in a hope of quelling my actions against the Alberta Treasury Branches (which was confirmed by Graham McLennan, the ATB solicitor) was absolutely abusive.

Also, in that very meeting, Mr. Leahy physically broke down and apologized to me for the abuses that myself, my family, and my associates have been subjected to. He also admitted to me that the ATB were in complete control of the Trustee and its Counsel. This is an absolute violation of the Rules of Court. Surely, a CA of your experience can recognize how serious tampering with a Court-appointed officer can be. Mr. Leahy informed me that the inappropriate manner with which he and others had dealt with my file was the biggest mistake that he had ever made in his life. I was informed by him as well, that he had gone to you directly and asked that you reconsider your position on funding these abusive actions and you refused to settle the matter. On the contrary, you became quite upset and informed Mr. Leahy that you would continue to fund the abuse and give directions and receive advice through Mr. Bellan.

<u>The last thing in my meeting with Mr. Leahy was that he candidly admitted to me that it was my letters that ended his career and that he was forced to retire by the Provincial Treasurer when he would rather have remained for an additional five years.</u> Here is another example of your professional dishonesty. On one hand, you tell the media that none of the resignations or retirements of ATB employees were related to wrong-doing but the former Acting Superintendent of the Alberta Treasury Branches admitted that this was indeed the case.

"I have taken very seriously your allegations regarding inappropriate business practices, as I do any other allegations respecting the operations of Alberta Treasury Branches and its officers." I must assure you Mr. Valentine that I was born at night but not last night. Let us first deal with the Ryckman Financial situation. The person who approved those loans was William Tough. All of these loans did not meet proper banking guidelines. It is a fact that Mr. Ryckman showered Mr. Tough with several gifts among other gratuities and it is also a fact that Mr. Kowalski supported these loans through written correspondence. <u>It is a fact as well that ATB employees have been given orders to shred documents</u>. In this case, Mr. Ryckman was not pursued on any guarantees whatsoever and, in fact, the <u>Trustee for the Ryckman Financial Corporation was once again Coopers & Lybrand. This was completely stage-managed by Mr. Tough as his brother-in-law is a senior partner at Coopers & Lybrand</u>, therefore ensuring a friend became the Trustee in this highly sensitive matter. Mr. Tough should have been dismissed without approval of his pension by the Auditor General's Office. The Auditor General, however, looked the other way as this file had political implications. I believe the term is "wilful blindness".

Let us now deal with the next corporation, Philadon Construction. <u>Surely, you</u> remember this file Mr. Valentine.

The Alberta Treasury Branches wrote off 9.5 million dollars. Mr. Wally Peters and Mr. Wayne Peterson had several indiscretions on this file: the use of vehicles, private jet trips to Atlanta to play golf at the world famous Augusta National, private jets to Phoenix to play golf, and a long list of other gratuities. In the infamous words of K-tel, the T.V. hucksters "There's more, much more!".

The loan for Philadon had been classified as a non-performing loan and the bizarre part here is that the Alberta Treasury Branches issued a $100,000.00 guarantee to a branch of the CIBC in Toronto when this loan was non-performing. How in the world can this be classified as proper banking practice? This guarantee was unique. It was used to fund a venture for Wally Peters' daughter in Toronto. Since you have difficulty with the terminology Mr. Valentine, the term is "fraud". Senior accounts managers refused to sign the credit, so Mr. Wayne Peterson valiantly volunteered to give his approval of this fraudulent transaction.

Even after writing off 9.5 million for Philadon, not only did the ATB not realize on Mr. Remington's guarantees, but it released its security on a large parcel of land near Raymond, Alberta, close to the U.S. border. Mr. Peters and Mr. Peterson had compromised themselves as well as the Alberta Treasury Branches in order to keep Mr. Remington quiet. This sad tale, however, does not end here. This same piece of property that the ATB walked away from its security on, was then used again as security on a new ATB loan. This is absolutely fraudulent activity. You, Mr. Valentine had first hand knowledge of all these facts which has been confirmed to me. You allowed Mr. Peterson and Mr. Peters to retire with pensions when they should have been fired and criminal charges laid. This is another prime example of the Auditor General covering up to ensure there would be no political fallout. The reason these gentlemen were given their pensions is that they had handled many politically-sensitive files over the years, for example, Stewart Green Properties and the powers wished to ensure their silence and complicity.

The next corporation is Garden Developments with its principle, Mr. Eric Proppe. It is <u>a well-known fact that both Mr. Peters and Mr. Peterson received monetary gratuities for generous approval to Mr. Proppe and his multitude of corporations for total loans of approximately 25 million and an anticipated loss and write-off of nearly 15 million dollars</u>. (Author's Note: Gifts were from all three corporations: Philadon, Garden Developments, and Paradise Canyon.) To prove how ridiculous these loans were, Mr. Proppe borrowed money from the Alberta Treasury Branches to buy raw land in Phoenix, Arizona for development. I believe this violates the rules governing loans that the ATB can make. Mr. Peters and Mr. Peterson continued to loan money to Mr. Proppe having Mr. Proppe create new entities, and then failing to report the loan connections properly. <u>This is another prime example of why these gentlemen should have been fired, investigated criminally, and not allowed to receive their pensions.</u>

This is not the end of this flagrant corruption. In addition, Mr. Peters approved the Paradise Canyon development in Lethbridge, Alberta. <u>This is such a cozy arrangement that the Alberta Treasury Branches shares a box at the Calgary Saddledome with the principal of this corporation. This loan of approximately 40 million has a real value of only 20 million</u>. I will let you do the math on this one.

Now, Mr. Valentine, this is how you become involved. Let's look at what happened. When Mr. Peters and Mr. Peterson retired, Vic Neufeld became head of the Main Branch in Calgary. <u>The cover-up begins with the significant fact that Mr. Neufeld used to be the Chief Inspector of the Alberta Treasury Branches. It was quite obvious that Mr. Neufeld was aware of the improprieties and irregularities in the loans</u>

and would keep things quiet, which has been verified by his earlier conduct. He should have been aware of those things you see, for Mr. Neufeld was the former long-term manager of the North Hill Branch. The designated credits or special credits of the ATB primarily vested in five branches: Edmonton Main, First Edmonton, Edmonton Strathcona, Calgary Main, and Calgary North Hill. The fact that Mr. Neufeld was moved in signifies a cover-up and not an investigation. Why else would Mr. Neufeld move back to branch manager from the position of Chief Inspector? The cynical among us would say it was to shepherd the politically sensitive files and prevent the truth from coming out. The North Hill Branch was famous for ATCO and, of course, the Hal Walker deals. The Auditor General merely applied a band-aid to what was in reality a gaping political wound.

Speaking of bleeding, I understand that the write-offs at Edmonton Main Branch are in the neighbourhood of 150 million and that this is just one branch! One shudders to think what the total may be. Of course, this leaves a burning question unanswered: how can the Auditor General sign off on financial statements knowing that the massive write-offs are being held in reserve? Allow me to provide the answer to that question. The reason is that we are about to head into an election campaign and there can be no scandal surrounding hundreds of millions of dollars of losses, especially to political cronies.

It has also come to my attention that several would-be board members refused to accept the appointments because the ATB, the Government and the Auditor General's Office refused to have an outside firm audit the statements. All that I have revealed to you is confirmed by this affirmation that no outside parties should be privy to the Alberta Treasury Branches books. We don't have corruption in Alberta, we have the Government for that. The financial statements have been stretched thinner than your conscience. Your letter to me gave me the same creepy feeling that I get when I think about the West Edmonton Mall refinancing.

The Auditor General was also derelict in his duties as these problems began to arise in late 1993 and continued through to 1994. What is shocking is that you were directly involved Mr. Valentine; I know this to be a fact. If you were not trying to cover this matter up, why was it not mentioned in the Annual Report, of the Auditor General for 1994/1995? Once again, Mr. Valentine, I must point out that you are the watchdog supposedly guarding against fiscal mismanagement and impropriety for the people of Alberta. Because of your professional dishonesty, I strongly suggest that you do the honourable thing and immediately resign as the Auditor General of this Province. By the way, is this enough further factional information for you? Since you replied so late, I shall allow you
some time to reply to this letter. Should I not hear from you by close of business, Tuesday, November 5, I shall assume that you concur with the facts as presented.

MONIER M. RAHALL

cc: **Mr. Marshal Williams**
   Chairman of the Board, Alberta Treasury Branches
   The Honourable Ralph Klein
   Premier of Alberta
   The Honourable James Dinning
   Provincial Treasurer
   Mr. Paul Haggis
   Superintendent, Alberta Treasury Branches

While hopeful I would get into a dialogue with the Auditor General, November 5 came and went without a response from Mr. Valentine. Perhaps I had offended him. In my need and haste to return the correspondence, I left out a few items that I would like to share with you now. First, in reference to Mr. Wayne Peterson and the Philadon Corporation, Mr. Peterson put an extension on his house as well. He also was in charge of doing Mr. Jake Superstein's Calgary loan portfolio. In the case of Wally Peters, and the Paradise Canyon file, Mr. Pat Shimbashi was lent $50,000 by the Alberta Treasury Branches to purchase his half of the Calgary Flames Hockey Club box seats; the other half was held by the ATB itself. What makes this totally inappropriate is that, at the time, one of Mr. Shimbashi's loans of nearly 10 million was in a non-performing category. Even more ridiculous is that that loan had been rewritten at 3% annually (interest-only) and Mr. Shimbashi was still unable to service the debt. All of these gentlemen were given golden parachutes that I have mentioned in letters. The Auditor General was absolutely derelict in his responsibilities by not calling for a criminal investigation, thereby making him a party to the cover-up. The Auditor General was misguided. His position was to protect the finances of the people of Alberta, not his political friends. He may be the equivalent to a financial Judas Iscariot in his betrayal of the trust of the people of Alberta. I wonder how many pieces of silver Mr. Valentine received for **his** betrayal?

CHAPTER 17
KNIGHTS IN DULL ARMOR

The first Knight in Dull Armor is the soon to be ex-Provincial Treasurer, the Honourable James Francis Dinning. I have been unable to confirm this, but as a young child Mr. Dinning was asked, "What do you want to be when you grow up?" He would always reply, "a Progressive Conservative!" First of all, it was ingrained in him genetically, as his grandfather was the first head of the Alberta Liquor Control Board. Then he married Mr. Fred Peacock's daughter. (Mr. Peacock was a Cabinet Minister in Peter Lougheed's Government.) He has a Master's Degree in Public Administration and held a variety of positions associated with government in his career. Secretary to Cabinet Committees, Government of Alberta, Executive Assistant to the Provincial Treasurer, Director of the Southern Alberta Office of the Premier, and Deputy Minister of Federal and Intergovernmental Affairs are highlights of his resumé before his current position. Mr. Dinning is probably the model you would use if you were trying to build a career politician and bureaucrat. As you will see, it may have been better for Mr. Dinning to stay a bureaucrat. They say that the boys run for politics to be someone, but men run for politics to do something. Some guys never grow up.

The reason I call Mr. Dinning a Knight in Dull Armor is that his career path would lead you to believe that he was being groomed to be a Premier someday and the equivalent of a Knight in shining armor for the people of Alberta. Mr. Dinning never found that formula to make his armor shiny. He has had a great life as a follower. Along with some character flaws, it appears that like the line Auntie Mame used, Mr. Dinning believed that "Life is a banquet and most poor suckers are starving to death." You may recall that Mr. Dinning had trouble explaining a private slush fund in the past, approximately 18 thousand dollars. During the government ownership of North West Trust Company, Mr. Dinning's friend, Mr. Gary Campbell, who was appointed head of NWTC to clean up the financial mess by the Tory Cabinet (of which Mr. Dinning was a member), was making political donations on behalf of NWTC to the PC Alberta Fund and to the coffers of James Dinning's campaign fund. The directors of NWTC, Mr. Rob Peters and Mr. Roy Wilson, also made personal contributions to the James Dinning campaign. The NWTC donation was from a company that could not afford to have its financial statements prepared so that it had to have two years done together.

Were campaign contributions a prerequisite to be appointed to the NWTC Board of Directors? The fact that Mr. Campbell was the Executive Director of the PC Alberta Fund and Mr. Dinning was the career politician and bureaucrat, surely they must have understood the ramifications and perception of such campaign funding. Their arrogance in thinking they could use public monies to fund the Tory campaigns was immorality of the highest degree. It is clear to see how the Tories remain in power; they use public money to fund their campaigns. In a letter to Mr. Dinning, I asked him why he accepted such a donation to his campaign. I received no response.

In discussing one of Mr. Campbell's other ventures at NWTC, let's also keep in mind that North West Trust Company was literally given away to the Canadian Western Bank, as will soon become evident.

The directors and employees of NWTC used to refer to the Santa Fe Plaza as Santa Claus Plaza. It was the project that just kept giving. Even the late Billy the Kid would have envied this heist of the Santa Fe. The borrower was a numbered company whose majority shareholder was Denny Andrews. You will recognize Mr. Andrews as the owner of Denny Andrews Ford or from one of his original enterprises, the Denny Andrews Good Times Centre, a Kawasaki dealership.

This deal on Santa Fe Plaza was Mr. Andrews' version of the "good time" loan. The original loan from NWTC was for 7.5 million dollars for constructing seven free-standing buildings on a large site in West Edmonton, just north of Denny Andrews Ford. The loan was given to the lending staff to be written up by the President, Don Farnell. This loan was approved by the investment committee of the Board and the initial disbursement for land acquisition was made. As no one on the lending staff wanted to take credit for this doomed loan, the loan officer on the application was Donald Farnell. Note here that the legal documentation for the loan was not written, let alone registered when the first loan advance had been made. The legal firm that acted for North West Trust Company was Cook, Duke, Cox which also acted for Mr. Andrews. How could these stewards of the law not recognize a conflict of interest, or did they have something to hide? Finally, it should be noted that the aforementioned Mr. Campbell was a member of Cook, Duke, Cox before his term at NWTC, as well as after. This is the same law firm that handled the West Edmonton Mall refinancing.

The equity in the project was derived in a large part from leasing revenue of the project, which was quite strange since it had yet to be leased or even built, for that matter. It was blatantly obvious to the lending staff presented with the task of administering the mortgage that it could not be completed without a substantial injection of equity from Mr. Andrews. The lending staff informed Mr. Farnell that the ability of the proposed buildings to provide the necessary cash flow to service the debt was impossible. Many commented that the probability of seeing God was more likely than this loan servicing its debt.

Each time a loan advance was requisitioned by the project manager, Ernie Stevens (the brother-in-law of NWTC Chairman, Gary Campbell, and also President of the Churchill Group), the lending department asked for additional equity since the project budget was dreadfully undercapitalized from the beginning. Each time this happened, Mr. Stevens or Mr. Andrews would call the executive of NWTC and the request for additional equity was overruled. To try to appease the lending staff, they used the excuse that the project was a joint venture with North West Trust Company, although no documented evidence of that is known to exist. Even so, the project was undercapitalized and the debt burden too severe. The borrowers (Mr. Andrews and Mr. Stevens) confessed and understood that the project was undercapitalized. It was never hidden. Yet, they continued to rely on the supposed relationship between NWTC and themselves to override that fact.

A thumbnail business biography of Mr. Stevens is now in order. The Churchill Group (with Mr. Stevens as President) banked at the Edmonton Main Branch of the ATB. Stuart Olson Construction became a part of the Churchill Group after it had run into some financial difficulty. The ATB lost several millions of dollars on Stuart Olson. The Stevens family had a parcel of land on 97 Street and 127 Avenue in Edmonton that was such a useless piece of property that not even used car operators would consider leasing it. Guess which piece of land the ATB leased? Right! The fact that Ernie Stevens and ace Tory bagman, Gary Campbell, are brothers-in-law probably lends interesting insight into the ATB site selection criteria.

A number of Alberta Treasury Branches should be examined as to their placement and the individuals connected with that placement. Consider the Terrace Plaza branch located in a building once owned by Mr. Zeiter who had taken the ATB for millions in bad real estate deals; or, consider also our old chums, the Ghermezian family who ATB had leased the many locations.

We all know their relationship with ATB. In fact, all the placement of the branches deserve to be investigated. Once again, staunch PC supporters and relatives of prominent Tories had the keys to the bank, literally.

In the end, the Santa Fe loan was fully advanced, all 7.5 million dollars and then some, with only four out of the originally planned seven buildings actually constructed. The appraised value of the project, including the excess land (based on income) was only 4.25 million dollars. Mr. Stevens and Mr. Andrews continued to receive substantial management fees out of the advances. Those fees were 10 thousand dollars monthly and paid nearly to the end.

The project never met its obligation with regard to the debt service requirements of the mortgage. The initial interest accruals were covered out of the reserve built into the project budget but was totally inadequate. The NWTC started legal action, but a deal was worked out between the NWTC executives and the borrowers that saw NWTC take over the project. Lo and behold, Mr. Andrews was absolved of his responsibility for a 500,000 dollar personal guarantee that was a condition precedent to the original loan. It took the mortgage department nearly a year to get the mortgage and the commitment letter signed.

What made the project even more suspect was the leases. The north perimeter of the site was supposedly leased to Public Works Canada at a high rental rate for a minimum five-year term. The tenant turned out to be Statistics Canada for the use of their census staff on a one year gross rental basis. Next, the first building constructed was leased to a private warranty company whose director was Dennis Horne, a lawyer from Duncan & Craig. Mr. Horne was a long-time personal legal advisor and friend of Mr. Andrews.

The lending department was preparing to put in a property manager once NWTC had control of the project. Mr. Farnell, the President of NWTC, overruled this plan, saying that the project was so large it needed an asset manager. He engaged Western Asset Management to take control of the property. Mr. Guy Scott, long time friend of Mr. Farnell's, was the person in charge. The fee agreed upon by the executive of NWTC was 15,000 dollars per month plus expenses. There was little, if ever any direction given by Western Asset Management on the project, and their reporting was pathetic. In the end, the lending department confirmed that there was never any need for an asset manager. An appraisal was done by John Weisgerber AACI and was based on the entire project being leased at $10.50 per square foot for office space and $6.50 per square foot for warehouse. The Edmonton market has never, ever come close to achieving these types of rates. On that basis, the valuation was approximately 6.45 million dollars. Then, NWTC sold the entire project to the "Softco" at the appraised value with Softco selling several properties back to NWTC. Keep in mind that these assets were moved into the Softco to avoid public scrutiny. This unconscionable chain of events was orchestrated to avoid showing substantial losses on the Santa Fe property.

A valid offer to purchase the Santa Fe project was presented by LTD Realty, Inc. for approximately 4 million dollars, from a purchaser named Jack Peat. This offer was rejected by Softco upon its acquisition of the property for a simple reason. Had the offer been accepted, they would have confirmed the commercial fraud that had just been perpetrated. Here was the truly strange part. The project was sold nearly two years later to the same purchaser, Jack Peat, for only 3.8 million dollars. Enough time had passed to muddy the waters so that the fraudulent transaction would be difficult to confirm. But now, Mr. Robert Taylor, head of N. A. Properties and Softco who was famous for his slight of hand with respect to the value of Government assets, was paid a commission. Mr. Taylor's actions at N.A. Properties also deserve investigation.

This entire amoral activity was condoned under the chairmanship of Gary Campbell. The saga of North West Trust Company was another horror story in its own right. So for our purposes here, it is enough to know that Mr. Campbell was placed at NWTC, not as a financial messiah, but rather as the gatekeeper of the Governments's reputation. How can the people of Alberta ever thank Mr. Dinning and his Cabinet colleagues at the time for appointing Mr. Campbell to his position?

There were times that Mr. Dinning influenced loan agreements at the Alberta Treasury Branches. The first company I will deal with is Airlite Neon Sign Manufacturing Company Ltd. It banked at First Edmonton Place Branch and became a recipient of the ubiquitous designated credit. One of the principals, Ms. Denise Layton, admitted that she was a relative of James Dinning. The designated credit came directly from the Superintendent's office. The Laytons had dealt directly with Mr. Leahy who was responding to a request from Mr. Dinning "to talk with the Laytons" about this loan agreement, the code for designated credit. To make a long story short or a loan story tort, Airlite Neon's loans were approximately a million dollars. The company ran into financial trouble. A receiver, Coopers & Lybrand, was appointed (probably just a coincidence), but the company was never shut down. Coopers came in, monitored the situation, and then sold the assets back to the principals for less than ten cents on the dollar. I *repeat,* the company was <u>not</u> shut down by the supposed receiver. This was a small favour from an Acting Superintendent who wanted to be a Superintendent. There was no realization on the personal guarantees, and the loan was not administered under normal receivership practices.

Another one of Mr. Dinning's friends was Ric Forest of Forest Construction. There was an interesting twist to Mr. Forest's story that involved me. I talked to Mr. Forest a couple of times on the phone concerning Nancy Betkowski's (the eventual runner up to Ralph Klein) bid for the leadership of the Progressive Conservative Party of Alberta. Mr. Forest contacted me about a vacant space in the Liberty Building on Jasper Avenue that he and the supporters of Ms. Betkowski (which included Mr. Dinning) asked that I donate for her leadership campaign. I agreed to this, but then the campaign declined as the space was too small for their needs.

Mr. Forest's accounts with the Alberta Treasury Branches are at Edmonton Main, a branch known as one of the most corrupt in the system. It seems that Mr. Forest's companies had run in to a spot of trouble with a shortfall of 5 million dollars, but when one of your closest friends is the Provincial Treasurer, you can continue to carry on business. Mr. Forest has certainly taken the phrase "friends in high places" to heart. He has even gone one better, taking it right to the bank. Mr. Dinning, the Provincial Treasurer, revered for his fiscal restraint, seems to have a Sybil-like financial personality depending upon the circumstances in which he finds himself.

Mr. Dinning has been around politics a long time, and he learned at the knee of the Master, Mr. Lougheed, as can be seen by some of his political choices. Firstly, let's deal with Mr. Peter Valentine, the Provincial Auditor General. When picking a provincial Auditor, the Provincial Treasurer has a responsibility to pick somebody independent minded. Choosing the best qualified person Auditor General ensures the integrity of the Government for the people of Alberta. Mr. Dinning shrank from his responsibilities by appointing Mr. Valentine. Mr. Valentine, well-known as a Tory faithful with political aspirations, was hand-picked by Mr. Dinning to ensure the least amount of criticism to the Provincial Treasurer for obvious reasons. For one who was groomed through the Lougheed and Getty administration, Mr.

Dinning understood the underlying rationale, the necessity of choosing the *right* individual.

The new Chairman of the Board of the Alberta Treasury Branches was Marshall Williams, the retired chairman of Transalta Utilities and an old acquaintance of Mr. Dinning from the Lougheed era.

I understand that Mr. Dinning was so upset by the West Edmonton Mall deal that he informed Allan Bray, the Superintendent of ATB, that he was also going to quit if the deal was approved. I believe that Mr. Dinning understood that the political fallout would be devastating while there was no benefit to the people of Alberta, but at last he changed his mind. Then, he became an accomplice. By finally agreeing to the deal, Mr. Dinning became Alberta's version of Galileo, but recanting his belief to save his life before the Inquisition. Living the political equivalent of Galileo, Dinning quit politics. As I wrote to him, politics is the art of compromise and his actions were living testimony that he was no dogmatic ideologue. By compromising on his convictions, Mr. Dinning had assigned himself to the backwaters of political history by abandoning ship before his career was wrecked on the shoals of the West Edmonton Mall refinancing.

Mr. Dinning was well aware of the questions I had been asking of him directly, as well as being copied on letters I had sent to others. After several months, Mr. Dinning finally sent the following weak response:

July 4, 1996

Dear Mr. Rahall:

I wish to acknowledge receipt of your several letters over the past few weeks.

These matters are being investigated and appropriate action will be taken in light of the findings and conclusions.

Yours sincerely,

Jim Dinning
Provincial Treasurer

AJM/skg

It was quite evident that Mr. Dinning's letter was written by a lawyer. He obviously did not understand me, mistaking insolvency for naiveté, and there may have been more dignity in Mr. Dinning remaining silent. The following is my reply to Mr. Dinning:

12 July 1996

Dear Mr. Dinning:

Re: Your Letter of 4 July 1996

I thank you for your reply. However, you have not taken issue with any of my research findings for my book, <u>Banksters and Prairie Boys</u>, and I have a question regarding the delay in response. You will recall that when I wrote to you last fall, you replied within a few days. In contrast, your

July 4, 1996, response comes over two months after I began the latest series of letters. What accounts for the inordinately lengthy delay this time?

As you will also recall, in my earlier letters, you replied to specific questions with appropriately specific details as to how those questions could be handled. Your current letter is form letter generic. It really says nothing.

I refer to your assertion, "These matters are being investigated and appropriate action will be taken in light of the findings and conclusions." My immediate reaction is investigated by whom and what actions are deemed appropriate? If you will remember, my bone of contention was that the Government of Alberta could not properly investigate itself. You do not address the problems surrounding the Superintendent, senior management, and employees of the Alberta Treasury Branches, the Provincial Treasurer, and the Auditor General. Am I to assume that you have requested the Attorney General of this province to do the investigations? Would you please confirm who is doing the investigations and what it is that they are investigating? There is another burning question here. Mr. Dinning, above all, how do you investigate yourself? In the spirit of cooperation and in a sincere attempt to resolve these issues, I would be prepared to turn over the documents in my possession to the Attorney General of another province to assist in the investigation of the Alberta Treasury Branches and the Government of Alberta.

"Appropriate action", as you term it, has never been taken. Individuals have been forced to resign or retire from the Alberta Treasury Branches in order to save the Government and the ATB embarrassment. Do you deem such actions appropriate?

Am I to assume that you are also investigating my file at the Alberta Treasury Branches and the fact that I was petitioned into bankruptcy in order to take away my right to due process, all because I dared to tell the truth about the rampant corruption throughout ATB? Am I to also assume that you are investigating the premeditated conflict of interest in conjunction with my file? Are you also going to investigate senior ATB officials who are continually, even to this day, harassing me, my family, and my associates, even in light of the fact that they have admitted under oath that certain senior ATB officials were forced to resign for unethical behaviour in connection with my file? Which is it? Some, all, or none of the above?

It appears that your letter was written by a solicitor and that you are reluctant to answer clearly and concisely. If you would like to discuss the matter in person, you may phone my office to arrange a mutually convenient time and place for a meeting. However, I should make you aware of one small caveat. I have previously met with Mr. Kowalski and if you choose to meet, I would hope that our conversation would be frank and earthy, unlike my encounter with Mr. Kowalski.

MONIER M. RAHALL

P.S.   Just a note, my middle initial is "M", not "J".

P.P.S. I apologize that I have fallen somewhat behind in our correspondence, but I have had six lawyers in the service of the Alberta Treasury Branches monopolizing my time lately. I do hope that you have not given up on me as your pen pal.

cc: **The Honourable Ralph Klein**
     Premier of Alberta
     Mr. Jack Briscoe
     Alberta Treasury Branches

It is my belief that rather than a thorough investigation, a form of damage control took place after this and every letter.

Mr. Dinning has played a role in all the Tory governments to date. As history has shown, after the Liberals had been in power in Ontario a few years back, after 43 years of Conservative rule, they found the Province's books to be in impeccable condition. I do not believe that Mr. Dinning could leave this kind of legacy. He has been a witness to the abuse of the Alberta Treasury Branches for nearly a quarter of a century. Mr. Dinning had no intention of changing the culture of wilful blindness that was cultivated over so many years by the Progressive Conservatives. Their maxim was, "Lead us not into temptation--just tell us where it is; we'll find it!"

CHAPTER 18

THE SINGULAR CASE OF MR. BRIAN EVANS

"How often have I said to you that when you have eliminated the impossible, whatever remains, however improbable, must be the truth?"[8]

Allow me to pose for you, faithful reader, a question regarding the logic of the actions of Mr. Brian Evans, Minister of Justice and Attorney General. The question is this: Why would the Attorney General of the Province of Alberta, an ascending star in Ralph Klein's firmament, resign his position only a few months before an impending election? In the announcement of his resignation from the Cabinet, Mr. Brian Evans cited family reasons as the rationale for not seeking re-election. While I believe that he did want to spend more time with his family, I also believe the overriding reason was that he was pressured by moral and ethical concerns about his role in the Cabinet of Premier Ralph Klein. All the senior officials, both in government and in the Alberta Treasury Branches, have told me that they regard the government of Premier Ralph Klein as the most corrupt of the Conservative administrations they have ever been involved with.

Mr. Evans' workload was tough, as well, especially inventing new ways to avoid investigation of the corruption within the Alberta Treasury Branches and the Alberta Government. He also said that he was not keen on a long political career. If the voters

---

[8] The Sign of Four. Sir Arthur Conan Doyle.

had known at the time of the last election what is known now, they would not be keen for a long political career for Mr. Evans either. Once again, the timing of Mr. Evans' announcement (as was that of Mr. Dinning) can be seen as crucial and deliberate, certainly not accidental. Mr. Evans hinted to the press before the release of the Auditor General's Report that he probably would announce his resignation October 1, 1996, thereby fielding the questions immediately. On October 1, we saw an announcement with very little press and few questions because most of these questions had already been answered.

The Alberta Treasury Branches debacle bore the unmistakable imprint of Ralph Klein. No matter how much it was denied, no matter how many ministers resigned or retired, it was obvious that the direction came from the top. There was a joke that circulated during the Watergate affair about President Richard Nixon. His press secretary, Ron Ziegler, came to him at the lowest point of the crisis and said that all avenues of explanation were exhausted and that there was only one person left who could take the blame for the Watergate cover up. Mr. Nixon shook his head. "No, no, there must be someone else." Mr. Ziegler replied, "There is no one else, Mr. President, only you." Nixon, downcast, went reluctantly to the scheduled press conference and slowly began his remarks. "It can now be revealed that my wife, Pat, led and instigated the Watergate break-in. I am shocked and deeply saddened." Mr. Klein cannot even use Colleen as an excuse after Multi Corp.

I had written Mr. Evans on several occasions requesting an investigation into the operating practices of the Alberta Treasury Branches. He never responded directly but always passed that duty on to an underling. Here are the replies I received from the Office of the Attorney General.

May 30, 1996

Dear Sir:

Your letter to the Attorney General dated May 13, 1996 has been sent to my attention for a response. In it you indicate that the Attorney General's Department is conducting an investigation into
the operations of the Alberta Treasury Branches. I am unfamiliar with such an investigation being carried out and I am therefore unable to respond to the concerns raised in the second paragraph of your letter.

With respect to your letters dated February 29, 1996 and March 26, 1996 they are, as you know, directed to the Law Society and the Chartered Accountants of Alberta and relate almost entirely to the behaviour of professionals governed by those bodies. Although reference is made to misbehaviour on the part of Alberta Treasury Branch officials a more detailed account of such misbehaviour together with an evidentiary foundation more reliable than a simple narrative would be required before any decision could be made as to whether a police investigation should be requested.

Yours truly,

TERRENCE J. MATCHETT
Director, Special Prosecutions   *TJM:wef*

Mr. Matchett's letters are prime examples of the bureaucratic "no comment" reply. I took issue with this limp reaction to my letters. I wrote Mr. Evans as follows:

26 June 1996

Dear Sir:

Re: Letters of Terrence J. Matchett Dated 14 May 1996 and 30 May 1996

I should like to respectfully disagree, with Mr. Matchett that an evidentiary foundation is lacking in this instance to initiate a criminal investigation. On the contrary, such evidence does exist. The law firm of McLennan Ross has confirmed in writing information from cross-examinations and undertakings that certain Alberta Treasury Branches employees were forced to resign for unethical behaviour. This is not just narrative, it is a fact. Examples of such conduct include graft, gifts accepted for favourable loan terms, self-funding of loans for corporations that ATB employees were either principals or parties of. In addition to the employees admission, Detective Terry Pitcher of the Calgary Police Service Commercial Crime Division is currently investigating such an instance involving a now terminated senior Alberta Treasury Branch official in the Calgary general head office. An investigation of this magnitude should not be fractured into small segments. It should be investigated not as an isolated incident - but rather as symptomatic of a more widespread problem.

As I have frequently pointed out to the Provincial Treasurer, Mr. Dinning, the Attorney General of a province other than Alberta should do this investigation since it is essential that the government not be seen to be investigating itself as the Alberta Treasury Branches is a part of the Government of

Alberta. However, notwithstanding that I would ask that you reconsider your position and look more closely at the facts. The recent rash of senior level "retirements" at the Alberta Treasury Branches is not mere coincidence, despite what Mr. Briscoe, the Executive Director Public Affairs at the Alberta Treasury Branches, would have you believe. It falls in line with the other forced resignations but are characterized as retirements for the sake of public perception.

MONIER M. RAHALL

cc: Honourable James Dinning
     Provincial Treasurer
     The Honourable Ralph Klein
     Premier of Alberta

I had met with Detective Terry Pitcher of the Calgary Police Service Commercial Crimes Division at his request. Mr. Pitcher told me that it was indeed my letter that triggered the investigation of Terry Semeniuk, the terminated manager of ATB's Calgary general office. In our conversation, Detective Pitcher confirmed that Mr. Semeniuk had received two money orders from Corporate Realty for a total of 40 thousand dollars. This was 10 percent of the commission that was paid to Corporate Realty for the sale of a Calgary hotel, the Marlborough Inn. Mr. Semeniuk's relationship with Corporate Realty and kickbacks went back a number of years, as he had grown up with Corporate's owner. On a final note, Corporate Realty does not have an office in Calgary.

For Mr. Matchett to deny that the Attorney General's Office did not know or monitor criminal investigations being done begs credulity. As I pointed out in my letter, the Calgary Police Service

Commercial Crimes Division was and is conducting an investigation of ATB employees. Mr. Matchett's denial showed that he failed to check on whether or not there was a criminal investigation ongoing. He was either derelict in his job function or was told to disavow any knowledge of such investigation.

Throughout my writings, I have continually pointed out that self-investigation is not a proper form of investigation as the Alberta Treasury Branches are wholly-owned subsidiaries of the Alberta Government and such obfuscation as that of Mr. Matchett's becomes the Government line. In the investigation of the Devine Government in the Province of Saskatchewan, the Government realized that self-investigation was improper and sought the assistance of another province to ensure the integrity of that investigation. A reporter in Saskatchewan believed it was the Alberta Attorney General's Office that lent this assistance, but repeated requests to confirm this with Mr. Evans' office were rebuffed. After my June 26 letter above, Mr. Matchett did not respond, but the torch was passed to Gregory Lepp (ostensibly, Mr. Matchett was on vacation). My response addressed once again to Mr. Evans appears below:

15 August 1996

Dear Mr. Evans:
    Re: Mr. Gregory Lepp's Letter of 16 July 1996

Concerning Detective Pitcher's investigation, by assigning such an investigation to the Calgary Police Service, the scope of the investigation is too narrow. As I attempted to point out to you, this is a province-wide problem within the Alberta Treasury Branches and <u>I am left wondering if fracturing the investigation of these matters among the various police forces, demonstrates a lack of desire to fully investigate the situation</u>. A province-wide cohesive investigation by the RCMP, the federal police force would be much more effective. The biggest fish are still in the sea.

In Mr. Lepp's letter, and I quote "There is no need for this case to be transferred out of the province for investigation." Mr. Lepp's statement defies credulity. The fact that the Alberta Treasury Branches are owned by the Government of Alberta puts additional pressure on the Attorney General to act impartially. The perception of the government investigating itself and whitewashing the investigation cannot be dispelled in any other way. I believe there is a legal maxim that says that justice must not only be done, it must be seen to be done.

<u>Therefore Mr. Lepp's narrative that an Attorney-General from another province is not necessary to investigate these matters would lead one to believe that impartiality is already a casualty since your department views self-investigation as proper</u>.

The law firm representing the Alberta Treasury Branches, McLennan Ross has admitted that several ATB employees were forced to resign for unethical behaviour. In Mr. Lepp's letter, and allow me to quote him again ... "an evidentiary foundation is required before we can decide whether further police investigations are required<u>". Surely, a confession of guilt and unethical behaviour is one of the most solid evidentiary foundations one can have</u>.

Overlooking these facts only reinforces my belief that the Attorney-General from another province must be requested to direct the investigation in order to lend credibility to the process.

MONIER M. RAHALL

cc: **The Honourable James Dinning**

I have asked several lawyers many questions as to what constitutes the strongest form of evidence. The answer was invariably that a confession is one of the strongest forms of evidence, if not the strongest, and I had a mountain of evidence brought to Mr. Evans' attention that even a Sumo wrestler could parachute from. As Winston Churchill said, "He occasionally stumbled over the truth, but hastily picked himself up and hurried on as if nothing had happened." Such was the approach of the Attorney General. He and his Office never responded further to this last letter. What followed shortly thereafter was the resignation of the Attorney General. (It's probably just a coincidence). Given the choice between investigating Mr. Evans' friends and remaining as Attorney General, his choice was to end his career.

Consider Mr. Klein's constituency president, Mr. Hal Walker for a moment and his selfless devotion to the Premier. It goes without saying that Mr. Walker and his corporations were major contributors to the PC Alberta Fund. Mr. Walker's Stone Creek Properties, Inc. was the fortunate recipient of a 7.4 million dollar loan for his Canmore developments. The curious thing about the loan was that it was not done by the closest branch of the ATB in

Banff, but rather by the Calgary North Hill branch known as one of the breeding grounds for the designated credit for political friends.

I have often wondered if Premier Ralph Klein ever cast any logic on his arguments. He vehemently denied having any influence over Mr. Walker's 7.4 million dollar loan at the Alberta Treasury Branches for Walker's Canmore development. You may recall the picutre in the <u>Calgary Herald</u> of Premier Ralph Klein turning the sod for the project. This alone should call into question the Premier's integrity. Think about it. Mr. Walker was Mr. Klein's constituency president. Surely he would understand the perception of the funding of a loan by the Alberta Treasury Branches, a bank wholly owned by the Government of Alberta. Why didn't he acquire the loan before the election? A constituency president with even the merest hint of political savvy must have understood the detrimental perception and political fallout of such financing. The Alberta Treasury Branches are known as a lender of last resort. If the deal was bankable, why didn't Mr. Walker go to other financial institutions? Since ATB generally charges a higher rate of interest than other banks, again, why did Mr. Walker get his financing at ATB? In short, if Mr. Walker was really concerned about Mr. Klein's public perception and his project was financially viable, why did he not go to an independent financial institution to avoid the embarrassment to the Premier?

After Mr. Klein's coronation on June 15, 1993, everyone knew that Mr. Walker's project was undercapitalized. Nearly three months to the day after the election, Mr. Walker's loan at the Alberta Treasury Branches was finally funded. Surely, someone like Mr. Walker deserved immediate attention to his post-electoral needs. Once again, my August 13, 1996, letter to Premier Ralph Klein tells "the rest of the story." As recently as January 1997, Mr. Walker accompanied Premier Klein on his Asian economic tour and signed a deal in which Asian investors agreed to invest in Mr. Walker's Canmore development with the enthusiastic support of the Premier and the government. (The reference to MLA Julius Yankowsky in the August 13 letter was about his book-banning tirade. He banned a book he had not even read, instead relying on a bad book review in a newspaper column. For his ill-considered outburst, he was being mercilessly pilloried in the press.) The letter to Premier Klein appears below.

13 August 1996

Dear Mr. Klein:

Today's letter is to validate some additional information contained in my book **Banksters and Prairie Boys**. However, this letter will deviate from the usual in that rather than dealing with just one prairie boy, the questions will concern an entire posse. (Hint: Don't let Julius Yankowsky see the word "deviate"; he may try to ban this letter!).

In fact, this posse puts me in mind of those visionaries who tamed the mountain vistas for the Canadian Pacific Railway.

Their names ring in the imagination - Cornelius Van Horne, Sir John A. MacDonald, Hal Walker. Perhaps Pierre Berton will take up the story but if not, I shall try to do it justice worthy of the "Last Spike".

Mr. Walker was the head of the posse that also was comprised of a host of PC fund faithful, luminaries like Bill Dickie, J. R. McCaig, Ken Lambert, Gordon Stollery, and Hal Walker. In fact I believe these gentlemen could be considered some of the "Fathers of the Alberta Advantage". I am positive you are aware of this background information since as environment minister in the Cabinet of Donald Getty, you were charged with protecting Alberta's pristine mountain areas or so thought the people of Alberta.

However, even though you are thoroughly familiar with the story, just humour me for the moment, if you will. Mr. Walker had his grand vision for a resort development in Canmore but in order to ensure the viability of his Alberta Treasury Branches loan, he needed to create equity. It is well known that Mr. Walker was seriously under capitalized with this project before 15 June 1993, a day that will live in infamy. (Sorry, I guess someone else had used that already). It was an auspicious date, anyway, lets leave it at that. Mr. Walker needed to re-apportion his land in Canmore to increase the utilization and thus the profitability. The Minister of the Environment at the time could not help him until he received his new mandate from the people of Alberta as Premier of this province. But, after 15 June 1993, lo and behold the gods of politics (and land development - they were covering both portfolios with the cut backs and what-not) embraced Mr. Walker benevolently and all was well in Canmore. The election of the Klein government was able to fuel not only his inspiration but also his project.

    The environmentalists and conservationists never understood before 15 June 1993 what they were able to recognize easily only a few short months after the election.

It is amazing how they learned to appreciate Mr. Walker's position in this brief period with the help of your new government. Mr. Walker was able to re-apportion his development to increase his utilization which thus increased his equity. He was able to convince environmentalists that his new condominiums were going to be more scenic than a bunch of boring old pine trees. After all, they had been cluttering the landscape for hundreds of years. Amazingly, the environmentalists and conservationists agreed with Mr. Walker. This in itself is somewhat amazing (not to mention ironic) in that the Klein government has had some difficulty with the concept of re-apportionment i.e. electoral boundaries, for instance.

Here, please allow me to digress for a moment. Mr. Walker was so dismayed before the election that he was unable to continue with his project; he felt the need to re-define himself as a developer who believed in democracy. Why not make the ultimate sacrifice? Why not commit and dedicate himself to the preservation of democratic principles? He thus devoted himself to becoming your constituency president, the very best damn constituency president he could be. This spirit of democracy invigorated Mr. Walker so completely, it elevated him to another **plateau**. Mr. Walker's new enthusiasm brought him a new lease on life (well, the property anyway).

What you could not deliver as Environment Minister, Mr. Walker knew you could deliver as Premier. That explains his determination. To paraphrase a certain bank's commercial slogan, Mr. Walker recognized that when you succeed, he succeeds.

Would you please comment on Mr. Walker's life affirming decision to help you become the Premier of Alberta? Would you please comment of Mr. Walker's vision for eastern slope development? Would you please comment on Mr. Walker's altruism? Would you also please compare your reasoning regarding land re-zoning versus electoral boundary re-alignment in addition to your motivations? Would you also please comment on your role in increasing the utilization of Mr. Walker's property? Would you please comment on whether you would be using Mr. Walker as an example for your election theme that this is another case of the "Alberta Advantage".

I hope that you agree that the cultivation of your relationship with Hal Walker could be summed up by the words of no less a personage than the world famous historian Arnold Toynbee. He describes "what he calls the phenomenon of withdrawal and return as a disengagement and temporary withdrawal of the creative personality from his social milieu and his subsequent return to the same milieu transfigured in a newer capacity with new powers."

MONIER M. RAHALL

cc: **Honourable James Dinning**
    Provincial Treasurer

At the time of this unconscionable deal for Mr. Hal Walker, it must be remembered that the Honourable Mr. Evans was Environment Minister. These are the facts surrounding the Canmore development. First, while now the Minister of Justice and Attorney General, Mr. Evans is also the MLA for Banff-Cochrane. Second, Mr. Evans was the first lawyer to start a full-time law practice in Canmore in 1976. Third, he belonged to several clubs which included the Canmore Golf Association, and the Calgary and Bow Valley Chamber of Commerce. It would be quite evident that Mr. Evans was a known entity to the politically-active Mr. Walker.

A short time after Mr. Walker received his favourable re-zoning and financing, Mr. Evans was promoted to the high profile portfolio of Attorney General (October 1994). Perhaps it was just coincidence or could it be that Mr. Evans was supremely talented?

It's not as if Mr. Walker's exploits were new or unknown. In the mid-1980s, he was part owner of two companies, Ellesmere Developments and Epicon. These companies were used to hide non-performing assets of the troubled Northlands Bank. Had Mr. Walker been dealt with appropriately at the time, he would not have been able to be reincarnated to abuse the public purse in the 1990s. One could say the same for the previously mentioned Larry Rollingher and his North West Trust adventure. He should never have been allowed to resurface either. This is the price the province pays when one party rules for a long period of time.

I confirmed that the former Acting Superintendent of the Alberta Treasury Branches, Mr. Elmer Leahy, acquired two pieces of Canmore property held by an Alberta company whose shares are held in trust by Mr. Leahy's personal lawyer, Mr. Norman Simons. If this was the conduct of the bureaucrats and politicians, what can we assume about the culture of corruption throughout the Alberta Treasury Branches and the Government of Alberta itself? Either Mr. Walker covered all his bases from the Premier to the Acting Superintendent of ATB or he was one of the luckiest men in Alberta history. From all over the world, tourists flock to the Canmore area for its justly famous panoramic vistas, but in the future, it may well be better known as a conservative theme park founded and dedicated to political corruption.

It is quite clear that Mr. Evans understood the writing on the wall. If the matter erupted into a massive scandal, the Attorney General would be questioned as to why a full investigation was not called for. If Mr. Evans elects to write his memoirs with Holmesian flourish, he might well term this non-investigation, the Case of the Missing Case. The fact that Mr. Evans decided not to seek re-election indicates that he could hold his head up high and say that he did not agree with the decisions of the Premier and his Cabinet. Retirement absolved himself from his role in the affair. If the matter remained covered-up, then he would resign as a successful politician and Attorney General of Alberta. It was the only logical decision that he could make. Brian Evans, private citizen, would not have to deal with the situation and could quietly ride into the Rocky Mountain sunset before spring returned and the frost made the cracks in his political career apparent.

This chapter opened by having you consider questions of logic. Think about what has just been described. How am I, lonely, outcast, and bankrupt without resources or a crack investigative staff, able to uncover the irregularities and improprieties rampant within the Alberta Treasury Branches and the Government of Alberta itself? Yet the Attorney General's department, on the opposite end of the resource scale, can find nothing in its self-investigation? Curious, is it not, Watson?

CHAPTER 19
DON'T VOTE--IT ONLY ENCOURAGES THEM
"Slip-Sliding Towards One-Person, One Vote"

For the quotation gracing the heading of this chapter, I must credit the Honourable Tom Thurber, the Minister for Municipal Affairs in the Cabinet of Ralph Klein. It comes from an article in the August 1, 1996, edition of The Edmonton Journal. Incredibly, Mr. Thurber believes that we in Alberta still are an agrarian society, a belief attributable, perhaps, to a mild version of Rip Van Winkle's disease: he has slept through the Industrial Revolution and the unbroken trend toward urbanization and now exists in a type of mental twilight.

The title for this chapter is a warning to people that if they vote under the current electoral boundaries, they only encourage Mr. Thurber's undemocratic behaviour, as he has demonstrated. The backbone of representational democracy is the equality of each individual's vote. Mr. Thurber, who supposedly is elected by representational democracy, believes that equality has been taken too far by Albertans. The following is a letter that was written to Mr. Thurber on August 1, 1996, the same day he allowed his Freudian slip to appear in print:

1 August 1996

Dear Mr. Thurber:

I don't know whether to laugh, cry, or just continue staring at your quote in the August 1 Edmonton Journal in total shock. You know the particular quote I mean, "I don't know how to stop this slip-sliding...towards one-person, one-vote". Astonishing. In fact it was so ridiculous, I had to check the name again to see if perhaps it was James Thurber not Tom Thurber who made the comment. Silly me, but I was always under the impression that is what true democracy meant and what we should strive for is balance and fairness in an electoral system.

It is obvious that Mr. Klein is well aware of these inequities i.e., we certainly don't have representative democracy in Alberta, not with the imbalance that currently exists with rural ridings being over-represented and urban ridings being under-represented. Even the proposed new electoral boundaries do not go nearly far enough and are designed to merely "improve the optics" of the situation before the next election. Let us also not drag out that tired argument about the rural ridings becoming too big to be adequately represented. I believe that Sir John A. MacDonald used that one. Surely, we could come up with something better after 129 years. That is merely a red herring to disguise the fact that the Tory power base is predominately in rural Alberta and obviously you and the other PC's want to make sure that power base remains secure (just ask Mr. Getty). Even the most arbitrary and tyrannical governments are compelled to have proper electoral boundaries in order to create the appearance of popular legitimacy, but apparently you are not willing to even concede that. The Alberta Government's recent legal challenge to the Canadian Wheat Board is further evidence that the Tory Government is pandering to the rural constituencies before the next election. Its not a very subtle strategy.

There are a few questions I have as well. <u>How does a man born in Herronton, Alberta, and whose life was spent in rural Alberta become a minister for Municipal Affairs</u>? I suppose that Mr. Klein took into account that you were the Vice Chairman of the Agricultural Farm Products Marketing Council. Oh, that's not it. It must be the fact that you were the Chairman of the Alberta Cattle Commission. No that's not it, either. It was because you were Director of the Alberta Farm Labour Pool. Now I realize why <u>Mr. Klein picked you; not because you had any knowledge about municipal affairs but because rather he needed a watchdog to protect the electoral boundaries and someone who would turn a deaf ear to the municipalities</u>. On second thought, my apologies to Mr. Klein - it was a good choice. Your background makes your comments, although ludicrous, hardly surprising. When is the Government going to test themselves against a truly representational electoral system? Yes, that's right, Tom - one-person, one vote. You should be embarrassed for yourself and the Progressive Conservatives. You should do the honourable thing and effect the political equivalent of the disgraced general falling on his sword; resign as Minister of Municipal Affairs because it is obvious you do not have the concerns of the major urban municipalities in mind. It is obvious that your handling of this portfolio leaves something to be desired in light of the problems that are currently facing Alberta's municipalities - especially the mess that Edmonton is in today, which mirrors the depression of the 1930's.

MONIER M. RAHALL

cc: **Honourable Ralph Klein**
    Premier of Alberta

The refreshing part about this story is that while it took nearly a month for Mr. Thurber to muster a reply, he did not shrink from his responsibilities, unlike several of his Cabinet colleagues. The following is a copy of the August 28, 1996, letter sent by Mr. Thurber in a brave attempt to defend his position, playing Tonto to Ralph Klein's Lone Ranger.

August 28, 1996

Dear Mr. Rahall:

Thank you for sharing with me your thoughts on my comments as represented in the article "Rural politicians fight for ridings" in the August 1, 1996 edition of the Edmonton Journal.

I believe that representation in our Legislature has to reflect the geography of the province as well as where Albertans choose to live. Democracies today work only when representation is by more than just counting votes--as important as that is. It is a fact that some constituencies are massive and that MLAs, regardless of the party they belong to, do not get to visit all the communities that they serve as often as they need to. If the distance disparity between urban and rural MLAs worsens then rural Albertans will lose representation in the Legislature. How can that be balanced and fair?

I am surprised that you have taken such a keen interest in my personal history that you would know of my humble birthplace. Let me assure you that I am proud to have been born in Herronton, proud to be from rural Alberta, and equally proud to be an Albertan. I am also extremely proud to have the privilege to be the MLA for all the people, both rural and urban, in the Constituency of Drayton Valley-Calmar. As the Minister of Alberta Municipal Affairs I am equally privileged to represent the interest of all Albertans, living in both rural and urban municipalities.

Furthermore, in your research you seem to have overlooked the fact that it was also my privilege to serve as Councillor and then Reeve of the County of Wetaskiwin #10 for a number of years.

Alberta's communities, and the people of Alberta, enjoy all the benefits of the "Alberta Advantage" not the least of which is the preservation of strong communities with affordable and responsive local government. I have called upon municipalities, both urban and rural, to consider doing as the provincial government has done and prepare a three-year business plan to determine where greater efficiencies and economies can be made. Various options, including restructuring and joint provision of services, are open to the people in local communities who must work together to ensure good local government.

In closing, I would like to share with you the thoughts of an editorial writer from the urban community of Fort McMurray. In his column "The Bottom Line" in the August 13th, 1996l edition of Fort McMurray Today, Randy Provincial writes: "Fair representation doesn't always mean equal representation. It makes sense in a utopia, but in real-world Alberta geography plays a big part in how the political map is drawn."

Yours sincerely,
Tom Thurber
Minister

cc: Premier Ralph Klein

What was incredible about his reply was his lack of knowledge surrounding the circumstances of the latest attempt to revise the electoral boundaries of the Province of Alberta. I am referring to the June 1996 "Proposed Electoral Division Areas, Boundaries and Names for Alberta," final report to the Speaker of the Legislative Assembly of Alberta. Catchy title, don't you agree? Even the Alberta Court of Appeal has called the current boundaries into question and said that ... "the disparities between the urban and rural ridings ... cannot be permitted to continue if Alberta wishes to call itself a democracy."

Mr. Thurber's letter created more questions and answered none. Described in boxing jargon, his letter had Mr. Thurber leading with his chin. Not one to take unfair advantage, I thought to myself, he at least answered the bell and everybody deserves a second chance. Perhaps I was not clear in my letter or he did not understand the questions. Therefore, I put them in point form and wrote him once again in the hope that Mr. Thurber would achieve electoral redemption. This letter of September 3 follows:

3 September 1996

Dear Mr. Thurber:

Re: Your Letter of 28 August 1996

Thank you for your response to my letter regarding your comments in the Edmonton Journal. I was pleased to see that it was Tom Thurber indeed and not James Thurber who penned the response. Unlike some of your cabinet colleagues, you, at least, have the moxie to attempt to answer my letter. While I am offended, the Athenians who coined the phrase "one man, one vote", surely would be as well only more so.

However, with all due respect, it is fairly apparent that you have a great deal of difficulty answering my questions when written in paragraph form, so I shall put them to you again as a series of points so there can be no misunderstanding.

1.   Allow me to quote from your letter. "I believe that representation in our Legislature has to reflect the geography of the province as well as where Albertans choose to live". Sir John A. MacDonald used the excuse of too much geography when Canada was a highly underpopulated predominately agrarian society and the population was scattered over a vast area. If the venerable Sir John A. were around today, with the ability of people to instantly communicate, I truly believe that our first Prime Minister would have weighed in on my side of the argument. The geographical argument has become less and less convincing with mass communication and transportation improvements. Would you not agree that technology has made this argument obsolete?

2.   I quote your argument again. "It is a fact that some constituencies are massive and the MLAs, regardless of the party they belong to, do not get to visit all the communities that they serve as often as they need to." Let me point something out to you here.   When Alberta's electoral boundaries were originally drawn up, Alberta was an agrarian society. This is not the case today. In reality, then, I am not asking for a new set of rules, but only an adjustment to the existing rules to reflect the reality of Alberta on the verge of the new millennium. I had always thought that the "rep by pop" argument was fought for and won in the 19th century. Do you or do you not believe that the current electoral boundaries violate the Canadian Bill of Rights and the Charter of Rights and Freedoms and that the increasing weakness of urban voting clout is challengeable constitutionally?

3.   You continue "If the distance disparity between urban and rural MLAs worsens then rural Albertans will loose representation in the legislature." Tom, if you can't keep them down on the farm once they have seen Edmonton or Calgary, then don't punish them then by weakening their vote. The Charter of Rights and Freedoms guarantees mobility rights. What you apparently are saying is that it is okay to move to the cities, but don't bring the full power of your vote with you. Would you agree that the status quo increasingly penalizes a growing majority of Albertans that choose to live in urban areas?

4.   "Let me assure you that I am proud to have been born in Herronton, proud to be from rural Alberta, and equally proud to be an Albertan." I never questioned your pride in being an Albertan. I am a proud born and bred Albertan as well. However, would you not agree that where a person was raised affects their perception of the world and that the story teller has his own agenda?

5.   Would you agree that what you really mean by the "Alberta Advantage" is the "Alberta Rural Advantage" especially when it comes to voting power and electoral boundaries?

6.   As Minister for Municipal Affairs, are you or are you not taking responsibility on behalf of the Government of Alberta for the serious economic state of decline in the City of Edmonton and in addition is it not true if Edmonton had proper electoral boundaries, the outcome of the last provincial election may well have been significantly different? As well, would you not agree that Edmonton may not have been economically victimized to the extent it has been, had it had proper representation in the Legislature?

7.   "In closing, I would like to share with you the thoughts of an editorial writer from the urban community of Fort McMurray." This statement of yours is a dead give-

away if you think that Fort McMurray is the centre of urban activity in Alberta and that the most urbane Albertans would gravitate to Fort McMurray is preposterous. I notice that you did not include any ringing endorsements from a couple of other municipalities, namely Edmonton and Calgary. Why didn't you use them as examples?

8.　　Although I am sure Mr. Provencal is a sterling fellow, I suspect he is not an expert on electoral boundaries or constitutional law. His statement is narrative only - it is not based on the study of constitutional law surrounding the Charter of Rights and Freedoms. Please comment on whether or not you have better, more studied constitutional examples or legal precedents that support your point of view of representational democracy.

9.　　Would you please comment on the fact that the original chairperson of the latest electoral boundaries commission resigned because he refused to rubber stamp the commissions report?

10.　　Would you also please comment on the fact that the Justice that stepped down felt that the Gini Index was a flawed formula to calculate representational variance?

MONIER M. RAHALL

P.S. I sincerely hope that you have a little of that moxie that I mentioned left to answer this letter.

cc: **Honourable Ralph Klein**
　　　Premier of Alberta

Well, you guessed it. Tom declined to seek his own electoral redemption, by escaping the damnation of democracy. I suspect he may have been busy discussing urban concerns with some of his former colleagues at the Agricultural Farm Products Marketing Council or the Alberta Cattle Commission--just a hunch. As a side note, the new chairperson of the Electoral Boundaries Commission was Ed Wachowich, brother of Associate Chief Justice Allan Wachowich. (It's probably not important.)

But, let me not leave you with the impression that the Honourable Mr. Thurber was striking out on his own. Obviously, Mr. Klein values loyalty above competence. His attitude is consistent with the Conservative Government's approach to the electoral boundaries issue. In fact, it is the electoral strategy that they have used for over a quarter of a century to ensure the renewal of their mandate. The following letters of July 30 and July 31, 1996, were written to the Premier, the Honourable Ralph Klein, discussing these very issues:

30 July 1996

Dear Mr. Klein:

One of the chapters of my book, Banksters and Prairie Boys deals with Alberta's electoral boundaries and how the representational imbalance between rural and urban ridings has violated the voting right of Albertans, while allowing the Progressive Conservative to exploit the political landscape.

Unbeknownst to you Mr. Klein, and to your band of Tory faithful, we in Alberta are no longer an agrarian society.

News flash - urbanization has occurred in the Province of Alberta but the Progressive Conservatives are in denial about this fact for the purpose of self presentation. A case in point is that in the 1989 election, it is this writer's opinion that if the electoral boundaries were based on the concept of one person, one vote, then the Tories would not have received a new mandate. Rare indeed is it that a Premier should lose his seat, yet his party retain power. This is a clear example of the urban vote being subject or at the mercy of the rural vote. Mr. Getty did not receive a mandate from the people, a prerequisite for supreme executive power. In order for Mr. Getty to retain control of his party, and the province, not to mention the Alberta Treasury Branches he was forced to run in a rural riding to ensure victory. This is because as we all know in Alberta, most farmers vote for the Conservative Party. Mr. Getty and the Progressive Conservatives understood this and in fact they exploited it. If it wasn't for the imbalance of the electoral boundaries, Mr. Getty may have found himself pruning the hedge at the Legislature, since he would have no other reason to be there.

The Province's demographics have greatly changed; now the rural areas are consistently over-represented while the urban population is under-represented. This leaves the political power of Alberta firmly in the hands of the minority and rural special interests. When is the Alberta government going to uphold the principle of one person, one vote? Would you please comment on when the Progressive Conservatives are prepared to fight an election based on proper representation? Was the electoral boundaries report authored by Hanna-Barbera for the cartoon version of democratic representation? Could it be that the report's true and best use would be to prop up the chair of the Speaker of the Legislative Assembly? It is a fact that the city of Edmonton has been the subject of political and economic neglect for years by the provincial government because of this electoral imbalance.

Would you please comment on whether or not the Premier of Alberta will try representational democracy in the next election?

MONIER M. RAHALL

cc: **Honourable James Dinning**
Provincial Treasurer

31 July 1996

Dear Mr. Klein:

As I mentioned yesterday, a chapter of my book **Banksters and Prairie Boys**, deals with the representational imbalance of Alberta's electoral boundaries favouring rural over urban voters. The Tories have consistently played to this imbalance, that is currying the favour of the rural elector to retain power, something that has been going on for nearly 25 years. Nothing illustrates this more blatantly than the Alberta Governments declaring legal war on the Canadian Wheat Board. The method by which you intend to test the matter several months ago amounted to commercial fraud. I can see that by your comments in a July 25 article in the Edmonton Sun, provincial lawyers have advised you of this fact. Apparently, you have a problem in distinguishing the legal from the illegal.

In an obvious ploy to appeal to the populist vote, the Government launched its legal missile supposedly on behalf of the farmers of Alberta. The more cynical among us recognize the move for its true purpose. It is strictly a self-preservation strategy on the part of the Alberta Tories when you take into consideration the upcoming election. A laissez-faire Premier such as yourself must see the merits in allowing the farmers to fight their own battle. I find your imitation of Tommy Douglas somewhat puzzling by having the government intervene. You and the party faithful are only too well aware that even under the proposed electoral boundary system, sparse rural constituencies have an influence far greater than their populations would dictate in relation to urban ridings. The newly released report to the Speaker of the Electoral Boundaries Commission does not go nearly far enough to redress the imbalance. It goes just far enough to "improve the optics" but not far enough to seriously threaten the Tories' power base in the rural ridings. For that reason, despite the public relations exercise of recalling the Legislature in August to deal with this report, it will be passed with virtually no debate and protect the Progressive Conservative Alberta Advantage for a few years more, possibly.

I find it strange that you would risk a felony conviction for the grain farmers of Alberta, yet when it comes to the City of Edmonton, where personal and business bankruptcies are at an all time high, and in commercial office space rates in the world Edmonton ranks 103 out of 103, it is this writer's opinion that you have already committed a crime against the people of Edmonton by subjecting them to Kleinonomics and depriving them of a fair electoral representation while creating a depression-like environment of the 1930s. You should also keep in mind that I am a capitalist - not a liberal or an apologist for socialism. I merely think that the Government of Alberta should repair the economic damage done to the capital of Alberta and do its job by creating an environment conducive to the growth of business. Would you please comment on whether the Government will take the initiative and ask the commission to go back and give us a report that ensures proper representational democracy in the next election? If the Government of Alberta and in particular the Tory caucus does not realign the electoral boundaries fairly and properly to ensure representational democracy, it would be like the Tory Cabinet shooting par hitting from the ladies tee.

MONIER M. RAHALL

P.S. I am an Albertan, born and raised, and I have been waiting patiently for replies to my letters which I feel I am entitled to. As you are a public official, I am entitled to a response.

cc: **Honourable James Dinning**
Provincial Treasurer

Mr. Klein has never favoured me with a reply to date on any of my letters, and, as you can see by the postscript, I attempted to elicit such a response. The pandering to the rural voter can be seen in the great Wheat Board Caper. From The Edmonton Sun, July 23, 1996, "The Alberta Government has proposed buying grain from provincial farmers for $1, having it trucked to Montana and selling it back to the farmer for the same price." And again, in the next day's edition, July 24, 1996, "Alberta farmers yesterday challenged Premier Ralph Klein to lead border-busting convoys to Montana to fight federal control of grain exports. 'The fact is, we don't want to break the law. What we're going to do instead is mount a court challenge relative to the constitutionality of the Canadian Wheat Board because we think it's absolutely wrong'." Months earlier, however, King Ralph was willing to commit commercial fraud to ensure the rural vote remained loyal to the Progressive Conservatives.

Mr. Klein frequently has a stroke of luck that leaves him feeling that he is invincible. Not only has he won a couple of substantial lottery prizes, but also an even larger prize was sent to him in the form of Grant Mitchell, leader of the Opposition. You see, Mr. Mitchell has a problem distinguishing the innocuous from the important, such as proper re-apportionment of the electoral boundaries. This political lightweight gave his blessing and supported the electoral boundaries report in question without taking into consideration the ramifications of his actions. First, if Mr. Mitchell was electable, an extremely optimistic conjecture, he should have recognized that rural Alberta has never voted Liberal and, therefore, with the majority of electoral clout, was not likely to install his party as the Government of Alberta. Second, if he had opposed the Electoral Boundaries Report, it would have given him credibility by highlighting the inequities within Alberta's electoral system. This type of strategic decision-making ensured Mr. Mitchell's permanent relegation to the backwaters of Alberta politics.

This issue is most certainly headed for another constitutional challenge, with or without Mr. Mitchell. The equality of rights that are entrenched in the Charter of Rights and Freedoms are clearly being violated, and the status quo is simply not acceptable. It is highly unlikely that the Alberta Conservatives would support any drastic changes to the electoral boundaries, as it will never serve their electoral purposes. The new electoral boundaries still disqualify Alberta from referring to itself as a representational democracy.

The logical extension of the effect of the current electoral boundaries on the relative power between urban and rural voters is that Alberta taxes should be proportioned to reflect that difference. This is best summed up by a slogan our American friends hold dear to their hearts. "No taxation without representation." Mr. Klein and his government cannot have it both ways. The tree of democracy must be constantly nourished, a truth that the Klein government refuses to recognize.

CHAPTER 20
NO VIABLE ALTERNATIVE

"An army of stags led by a lion is more formidable than an army of lions led by a stag."

- Plutarch

While the Liberals blew it on the electoral boundaries re-apportionment, the problem of the Official Opposition in Alberta ("opposition" is used generously) is that the leadership of the Liberal Party has financial skeletons in its own closet. Haunting their own conscience, their skeletons do not allow these leaders to act with moral authority as a proper critic of the government nor provide effective opposition in a system of checks and balances.

Take for example, Liberal MLA and former finance critic, Mike Percy. It is well-known among legislative insiders, although not the public at large, that Mr. Percy and the Provincial Treasurer, James Dinning, were good friends. Consequently, Mr. Percy's criticisms of the Provincial Treasurer and the policies of the Alberta Treasury Branches were somewhat muted. The point is, it is difficult to be highly critical of one's friends. The mutual respect was highlighted by the contrast with the way Mr. Dinning treated Mr. Percy's successor as Treasury critic, Muriel Abdurahman. Mr. Dinning let her have both verbal barrels over a relatively minor rookie mistake. Let Mr. Percy speak naively for himself, saying that Alberta's finances are the envy of the country, thanks to Dinning. "He's done a heck of a good job." (<u>The</u>

Edmonton Sun, Friday, September 20, 1996). I confirmed that Mr. Percy was wooed by Mr. Dinning in an attempt to get him to cross the floor of the Legislature, knowing that Mr. Percy was not enamoured (nor could anyone be) of his leader, Grant Mitchell. Mr. Percy, a blue Liberal, and Mr. Dinning, a red Tory, are virtually identical in ideological outlook. It becomes very difficult to criticize a Provincial Treasurer who has similar views.

The following is another example of Mr. Percy's scathing critique of the Alberta Treasury Branches, and I quote from the Friday, June 14, 1996, edition of The Edmonton Sun, "Liberal critic Mike Percy said it's great that ATB is in the black--but its results don't measure up in spite of its immunity from income tax and insurance costs. Their net income, related to assets and equity is still pretty low compared to the chartered banks." This statement clearly proves that Mr. Percy will never be classified as one of the eminent financial critics of our time, despite his credentials as an university economist. Instead of focusing on the mundane, if Mr. Percy wanted to get to the heart of the issue, he should have pressured the Provincial Treasurer, Mr. Dinning, and the Auditor General, Peter Valentine, to have financial statements of the Alberta Treasury Branches prepared by a firm outside the public sector to ensure the validity of those financial statements.

Mr. Percy has missed the mark on several occasions including the Stewart Green Properties, West Edmonton Mall, and the Pocklington connections. The questions he posed in the Legislature on these issues displayed his naiveté by not zeroing in on such things as the fraudulent refinancing of the West Edmonton Mall by the Alberta Treasury Branches and the Alberta Government.

Mr. Percy has now announced that he will depart politics and not seek re-election as a Liberal. Very soon after his announcement, Premier Klein named Mr. Percy to head the political task force in Edmonton designed to study how the Government can address the problem areas in health care which may need "reinvestment." Mr. Percy's leader, Grant Mitchell was cut off at the knees, a stature he could ill afford to lose.

Now, let me deal with this irony-man, Grant Mitchell. Appointing Mr. Percy, Mr. Dinning's friend, as finance critic gives new meaning to the concept of political strategy. He puts Mr. Percy in a compromising situation since the Principal Group skeleton still hangs in Mr. Mitchell's closet. Mr. Mitchell's career started as a Budget Analyst for the Treasury Department of the Government of Alberta throughout the 70s and early 80s. His real mark, however, was made with the Principal Group, rising to Vice President, Operations. You would think with his Treasury Department stint and his rapid rise to power within the Principal Group, he would have left him within his element, especially when it came to analytical criticism of financial institutions such as the Alberta Treasury Branches. Mr. Mitchell was ineffective in that any criticism he could raise would inevitably be countered by reference to his own track record at Principal. This neutralized any chance that Mr. Mitchell could be an effective leader of the

Opposition. When the Principal Group collapsed shortly after he left in 1986, Mr. Mitchell, during the public inquiry, said that he was unaware of any irregularities or improprieties. Call me Cupid, but not stupid. It begs credulity that a Vice-President of Operations for the Principal Group would be unaware of fiscal mismanagement.

Let's take Mr. Mitchell at face value. If he did not know, then he is incompetent and, therefore, unacceptable as leader of the Liberal Party of Alberta and Her Majesty's Loyal Opposition. If he did know, then he is corrupt and dishonest and must resign from the leadership. These factors make Mr. Mitchell unelectable. The hardest things in the world are diamonds, and knowing yourself. He is unlikely to ever be Premier. The constant turmoil within the Liberal caucus shows that it is not only I who holds this opinion of Mr. Mitchell's leadership qualifications. By resigning, he will give the people of Alberta a viable political alternative, create an environment in which the Progressive Conservatives' arrogance through electoral superiority would be eroded, and force them to focus on their accountability.

With an effective and viable Opposition, the Province of Alberta would not suffer the abuses of lengthy periods of one-party rule. This factor is critical when discussing the abuses at the Alberta Treasury Branches. When the Progressive Conservatives have no fear of being turfed out of office every three or four years, corruption becomes entrenched from administration to administration. The PCs were left to plunder Alberta unopposed.

God must have loved Ralph Klein by the very fact that He sent him an Opposition Leader in the form of Grant Mitchell. Recently, Mr. Mitchell, a runner and tri-athlete, challenged Mr. Klein to run a mountain road race of twenty-two kilometres after Mr. Klein had made some comments about the Premier's own personal fitness regime. I called this the irony-man competition. This challenge was not surprising, however, as Mr. Mitchell knew that this was the only race against Mr. Klein that he could win. Someone forgot to tell Mr. Mitchell that running the fastest and farthest, carrying the largest spear, no longer qualifies one to be Chief. It is more likely that we will have another Immaculate Conception before Mr. Mitchell becomes Premier of the Province of Alberta. Without a viable alternative, Mr. Klein has no fear; and I fear for our Province.

CHAPTER 21
DON'T DO ANYTHING YOU CAN'T TELL YOUR MOTHER ABOUT

"An ethical man is a Christian holding four aces."

- Mark Twain

The Office of the Information and Privacy Commissioner and the Office of the Ethics Commissioner (which by the way, are all one and the same--go figure) yield some interesting facts. One is that the office of the illustrious Robert Clark (and the Auditor General, Peter Valentine) is in the same building as the head office for the Alberta Treasury Branches, better known as ATB Plaza. You will remember Mr. Clark as the former leader of the Social Credit Party in the 1970s. Mr. Clark also has recently re-investigated the infamous Multi Corp connection with the Klein government. His office also deals with the Freedom of Information and Protection of Privacy Act. As I will show, Mr. Clark has difficulty in distinguishing one Act from another. He is somewhat like a surfer in that he goes where the political waves take him. So sit back and watch Bob hang ten!

Here's some background on Mr. Clark's precedent-setting decisions. Mr. Klein's wife, Colleen, owned stock in Multi Corp, stock she had not paid for. The wife of Rod Love (the Executive Director of the Office of the Premier) also had Multi Corp stock under the same payment terms. Mr. Clark found that Mr. Klein and his entourage had used *bad judgment*, but they had breached no ethical guidelines. However, the Ethics and Privacy Commission handed down the powerful decision that perhaps Mr. Klein and company themselves should use better judgment in the future. I am not sure exactly what that means, but maybe he thought they should be more circumspect in how they would cover up any future dealings.

By delving a little further, one sees more "coincidences" surrounding the relationship between Government of Alberta and Multi Corp, coincidences and connections that Robert Clark cannot seem to get a handle on. You will recall that Kenny the "K" Kowalski, known as the former minister of cake and circuses, was offered a plum Government position by Mr. Klein that was retracted because of the public outcry. Mr. Klein then enlisted the help of his three closest generals, Rod Love, Hugh Dunne, and the ubiquitous Peter Elzinga. These were likely the Three Stooges, in his own words, Mr. Kowalski hinted had engineered his fall from grace.[9]

The Klein Government's headhunters found Mr. Kowalski a posh post at Multi Corp in October 1994, the same month he was removed from Cabinet . Mr. Klein admitted to the press in April 1996 that it was likely that Rod Love made the employment offer public (as if he didn't know). Neither Mr. Elzinga nor Mr. Love would deny that they were involved in getting Mr. Kowalski a golden parachute. The question then became why would the

---

[9] The Edmonton Sun. "It's Our Business Now, Ralph." Thursday, April 11, 1996.

Government and Mr.Klein's closest advisors exert influence on, of all companies, Multi Corp to prepare a soft landing for Mr. Kowalski? Finally, why would they attempt it not only once, but twice? Mr. Kowalski was cocky about his potential political demise. As he said in the April 11, 1996, edition of The Edmonton Sun, "I have been a [key Tory player] longer than a lot of people and will be a lot longer than a lot of other people."[10] These are strong words indeed from someone who was kicked out of Cabinet. Mr. Kowalski was letting certain individuals know that he knew where the bodies were buried.

Sometimes it is enlightening to compare consecutive newspaper articles about the same story. Mr. Kowalski's Multi Corp job offer is a case in point. On April 9, 1996, in The Edmonton Sun[11], Mr. Kowalski said he was not aware of how much money he was offered because "he never studied any contract." However, Mr. Kowalski must have had a moment of epiphany overnight because on April 10 in the same newspaper, he recalled that a $200,000 a year contract was an accurate figure.[12] I somehow suspect that the contradiction was more revealing of Mr. Kowalski's character than his powers of recollection.

In my meeting with Mr. Kowalski in April 1996, he informed me that he was forced out of Cabinet because he was stealing the limelight from Mr. Klein. Alas, Kenny was being a little disingenuous. That's not what he was stealing. It apparently came

[10] The Edmonton Sun. "Ken's Hangin' in There." Thursday, April 11, 1996.
[11] The Edmonton Sun. "No to Multi-Corp." April 9, 1996.
[12] The Edmonton Sun. "How Deep is Love." April 10, 1996.

to Mr. Klein's and Mr. Love's attention that Mr. Kowalski had been receiving brown bags of money for the placement of Video Lottery Terminals, and it is no secret that there was no love lost between Rod Love and Ken Kowalski. Mr. Love saw this as an opportunity to remove Mr. Kowalski's hyper-kinetic mouth from Cabinet. It was indeed a compromise. Mr. Kowalski's quote tells the story. He has been a part of all three Conservative administrations and was well aware of the sundry Government dealings, including Multi Corp. My money, by the way, is on Mr. Kowalski to make a triumphant return, as he knows more about the inner workings of the Conservative Government than does Mr. Love.

In the case of Mr. Elzinga, he and Mr. Kowalski both were point men in the fraudulent refinancing of West Edmonton Mall. It really came down to honour among thieves. They were not able to get rid of Mr. Kowalski totally, even with a job offer from Multi Corp for $200,000 per year, nearly double his MLA's salary. The fact that Mr. Kowalski turned down this position is living testimony to the potency of the information he possessed. Keep in mind they were strong enough to remove him from Cabinet, but not strong enough to remove him from the Government. Mr. Clark (remember him?) should learn to recognize the truly important aspects and assimilate them into his investigation.

In conclusion, Mr. Klein couldn't get involved in the internal bloodletting because of public perception. Even though the government said they had no connection with Multi Corp, Peter Elzinga and Rod Love exercised powers of persuasion Anthony Robbins would be proud of. The two magicians managed to elicit a $200,000 per year job offer from Multi Corp for Mr. Kowalski. Relatively speaking, $200,000 was quite a cheap price to pay for Mr. Kowalski's silence. Alas, Kenny the "K" did not take the bait. It was a classic "Mexican Standoff" and nobody wanted to draw first.

Let's now deal with the ex-Transportation Minister, the lovable and affable Pavement Peter Trynchy. Mr. Trynchy had his very long driveway paved by companies contracted to the Alberta Government to do road repair and construction. Mr. Clark was once again called upon to bring his powerful investigative tools to bear. It was a brutal investigation, but Mr. Trynchy survived. Mr. Clark's decision was that Mr. Trynchy had shown *bad judgment*. What insight! What Solomon-like wisdom! The reason that it had been brought to Mr. Clark's attention in the first place was that Mr. Trynchy did use bad judgment (perhaps even unethical). Surely, it must be tiring for Mr. Clark to continue to sit on the fence-- perhaps he has been nailed there by some of his political friends. But, as Jesus said to his disciples, "Let us move on."

With the Office of the Information and Privacy Commission, my problem began as I inquired about what fees were being paid to the professionals working on my file funded by the Alberta Treasury Branches. The ATB declined to give me this information and denied me the right even though this information concerned me directly and violated no confidentiality, therefore, could not run afoul of the Act. Something very strange was happening. In a foreclosure or receivership proceeding, the first thing the professionals do is submit their fees; but in my case, these fees were kept a secret. Ruining somebody is a very expensive undertaking and the costs could not be justified should they be revealed to the people of Alberta. Once disclosed, these fees would certainly become part of this book. These professionals hired by the Alberta Treasury Branches frequently boasted they had an open cheque book to get the job done. Seeing this as an obstacle, I made a request under the Freedom of Information and Protection of Privacy Act. My logic was this: There could be no violation of confidentiality, as these were my files. Lo and behold, I went to mediation, then to public inquiry seeking this information. This was where Mr. Clark came in. He ruled against me and said that he would not commit the Alberta Treasury Branches to divulge that information. This once again proves my complaint that self-investigation is improper. Mr. Clark's letter was the usual bureaucratic baffle gab.

March 25, 1996

Dear Mr. Rahall:

Re: Request for Review # 1038

By copy of my letter dated January 8, 1996, I advised you that your request for review (#1038) under the

*Freedom of Information and Protection of Privacy Act had
been received. Attempts to mediate this matter have not
been successful. Therefore, please accept this letter as
notice that an inquiry will be held with regard to this file.*

*Pursuant to section 66 of the Act, the inquiry will be
in private and written representations will be accepted
from the public body and the applicant. If you wish to
make a further representation regarding your request, it
should be a my office no later than 12:00 noon on April 11,
1996. Please indicate the file number (#1038) on the
outside of the envelope and mark if CONFIDENTIAL.*

*As stated in section 67(1) of the Act, <u>the onus of
proof that the applicant has no right of access to the
records files with the public body, not the applicant.</u> It will
be my intention to have a decision available as soon as
possible after receiving the submissions.*

Thank you for your attention to this matter.

Yours truly,

*Robert C. Clark
Commissioner*

This scenario was part of the culture as created by this
Progressive Conservatives of Alberta. They were able to lend
money to the bagmen and political cronies and yet manage to
avoid public scrutiny by using the Alberta Treasury Branches. The
ATB allowed them to use the Freedom of Information and

Protection of Privacy Act as a protective cloak over their sundry examples of payoffs and dealings of their political friends.

Let's take, for example, the Canola Industries Canada, Inc. (CIC). This was one of many Government of Alberta ventures that lost money, in this case, a reported 74 million. Even after the huge loss, the Government still could not sell this corporation, so how could they be rid of it? Very easily. They had the Alberta Treasury Branches do a "soft" deal not only to sell it, but also to remove it from public scrutiny. The Alberta Treasury Branches became a waste management site for financial boondoggles. Now, two years later, in October of 1996, the problem oozed back to the surface. The deal was soft, but not soft enough. If one sat down and actually calculated the losses to include interest and professional fees, not to mention the acceptance of shares instead of a repayment of the loan, the figure is probably closer to over 100 million. (Mr. Doug Tkachuk, the lawyer representing the Alberta Treasury Branches, is also the Council for my Trustee. I confirmed that he was awarded this plum for the job he did following instruction on my file.) Anyone with initiative who attempts to uncover this trail of deception is quickly discouraged by the obfuscation inherent in the ironically named Freedom of Information and Protection of Privacy Act. In this instance, the only thing this Act did was to protect Albertans from the truth about its elected officials.

A gentleman by the name of Mr. Paul Spiller was transferred from First Edmonton Place to Main Branch, Edmonton (two of the most corrupt branches in the system) and then to the Millwoods Branch (in South Edmonton) as manager in order to deal specifically with politically sensitive files such as CIC. He was well versed in handling politically sensitive loans, as well as in the culture of corruption. He had been under the tutelage of the infamous Larry Leroux, and was sent to Millwoods branch as the "fixer" to put a lid on this particularly messy loan. These and other files of the Alberta Treasury Branches needed a safe, faithful, and dependable watchdog and at an ATB location that was out of the way of prying eyes so they could be quietly disposed of. Now they would not be subject to discovery by so many employees who were not in the know. A suburban branch out of the way of much of the city's professional clientele is a much better hiding place, you know, none of those embarrassing chance meetings that would likely occur downtown between lawyers, accountants, and bankers. A small branch should never have been allowed to handle a loan of this magnitude. Curiously, as soon as this and other deals had been fixed, Mr. Spiller was transferred out, since the "fixer" had done his job. He went in, cleared the area, defused the situation, and then moved on. This is a prime example of the kind of relationship the Alberta Government and the Alberta Treasury Branches have cultivated for over a quarter of a century.

The Government can forget about drafting a new Code of Ethics for its members in the Legislature and the civil service. Like the new Code for Alberta Treasury Branches, Mr. Clark won't act on them anyway. I have yet to hear a decision of his which went against the Government. Instead, there is a much simpler way to handle the situation. Mr. Clark should have signs made that he can place on the door of the Legislature, as well as all Alberta Treasury Branches' offices which reads, "Never do anything here you can't tell your mother about." As it stands now, I fear for those mothers.

Any attempt to have Mr. Clark look at this in a fair and orderly manner is unlikely, and it is just as unlikely that he would rule against the government in any case. Perhaps he was blinded by their goodness. He has now re-examined the Multi Corp fiasco. This is an absolute farce. What makes the people of Alberta think Mr. Clark has suddenly been cured of his wilful blindness? What did Mr. Clark hope to uncover that he did not uncover in the first place? All of Mr. Clark's investigations were exercises in futility. Mr. Clark should keep in mind that the politically sensitive decisions are a part of his mandate. Mr. Clark shares with Willie Loman the onerous realization of unethical decisions, "It comes with the territory." In my mind, Mr. Clark is living proof that loyalty can be overdone.

CHAPTER 22
TOOTHLESS TIGER

"Fair fa` your honest, sonsie face."

- Robert Burns, Address to a Haggis

The hope of the Government was that while the corruption of a quarter of a century was unraveling before their very eyes, a newly appointed Chairman and Board of Directors as well as a new Superintendent to purge their conscience could avoid public scrutiny. That was the strange part about the whole episode. Mr. Klein and Mr. Dinning were part of the May 6, 1992, meeting of Cabinet that agreed to establish a Board of Directors with certain responsibilities. The following letter is a memorandum from the Deputy-Secretary to the Cabinet:

May 7, 1992

FROM: David Steeves
*   Deputy Secretary to Cabinet*
TO: Honourable D. Johnston
*   Provincial Treasurer*
SUBJECT: TREASURY BRANCH - ADVISORY BOARD

At its meeting of May 6, 1992, Cabinet AGREED that a Treasury Branch Advisory Board should be established with responsibilities as follows:

• To assist the Superintendent of Alberta Treasury Branches relating to those issues that he may bring before the Advisory Board for either counsel or direction.

- *To bring to the attention of the Superintendent such business opportunities that a Board Member may become aware of, and which are deemed to be suitable for ATB investment.*
- *To assist the Superintendent, on an individual Member basis in most instances relative to business development promotions in various regions of the province.*
- *To meet with or report to the Provincial Treasurer, as called upon, in respect of ATB business strategies, operating procedures and financial results, as well as such other matters or issues that are seen by the Treasurer to require the Input of the Board.*
- *The Board will not be a credit granting committee.*

The Board will have up to 15 members from various regions of Alberta. Members are to be appointed by Cabinet, and the Provincial Treasurer was REQUESTED to seek recommendation for membership from government members.

David Steeves

The most stunning thing about this memorandum was that it was approved on May 6, 1992, and the Government did not implement the legislation until June of 1996. Why did it take the Klein Government over four years to accomplish the implementation of the Board of Directors? If a proper Board would have been implemented by the government immediately, it would have prevented the additional funding of West Edmonton Mall and the Pocklington connection among others. Surely a four-year implementation is not a part of the natural legislative process. As indicated by the memorandum, Board members are appointed by Cabinet. If a member of the Board disagrees with Cabinet, he or she could be easily replaced by the Government.

The Board as constituted seems to be window-dressing. Under the Public Service Act, the influence and the power of the Government have not diminished by the implementation of the Board. The final decisions in the appointment of the Superintendent still rests with the Provincial Treasurer and the Superintendent reports to the Provincial Treasurer, not the Board. That is the inspiration for the title of the chapter. The Board has only the power that the Provincial Treasurer and the Government deems it should have and, as a result, is a toothless tiger. When this whole fiasco comes to light, the Government is going to rely on the argument that it has implemented a new Board and Superintendent to clean up the huge mess that they have uncovered. They, however, were the architects of the problem. What the average Albertan does not know is that the Public Service Act ensures that the Government remains in absolute control of the Alberta Treasury Branches. This optical purity is nothing more than a staged deception of the people of Alberta.

Consider the appointees to the Board of Directors as well as the new Chairman of the Board, Mr. Marshall Williams. What made the 73 year old Mr. Williams the best candidate for the job? Was it his age? Will Mr. Williams bring a fresh, new approach to the Alberta Treasury Branches or banking, in general, for that matter? How is Mr. Williams, a professional engineer, going to implement and oversee business strategies and operating procedures of a bank like the ATB with any effectiveness? There is nothing in his résumé that qualifies him to restructure the Alberta Treasury Branches. The Board's banking experience is minimal. Yet when a district manager for the Royal Bank applied to be on the Board, he was passed over with a letter of rejection saying that the job required people with more experience.

Perhaps Mr. Williams came to be the Chairman of the Board of the Alberta Treasury Branches based on his past political affiliations rather than his banking acumen. Mr. Williams was the Chairman of the Board of Transalta Utilities, and for many years was a consistently major contributor to the PC Alberta Fund. Mr. Williams has had ties to the PC Party from the Lougheed era to date. This includes a stint as head of the Financial Review Commission of 1993, and he was appointed to this position by Provincial Treasurer James Dinning to study the state of Alberta's finances. He was not qualified to head this commission.

Being appointed to head the ATB Board was the second time, Williams had been called upon by Mr. Dinning. The supposedly independent board had a very old acquaintance of the Government to head it. In fact, the circle was completed: It was Mr. Williams and his Financial Review Commission that recommended the Board be set up in the first place. Effectively, Mr. Williams created his own job. A question arises out of Mr. Williams' 1993 recommendation: Why was the recommendation necessary since the government had already approved the formation of the Board in May 1992? It appeared that Mr. Williams was buying Mr.

Dinning some additional time to complete additional fundings. One must reflect on the candidates that were turned down for the new Chairman of the Board. Surely, of all the candidates who applied for the position, there were candidates with more banking experience than Mr. Williams. Compare Mr. Williams with a major bank chairmen such as Matthew Barrett of the Bank of Montreal, a career banker and qualified to be a chairman of his bank. Mr. Dinning hand-picked Mr. Williams to ensure continued control for the Government, not for his independent-minded approach.

As you will recall, the government used the same approach when it installed Gary Campbell as head of North West Trust Company. He had no prior banking experience either. Remember from Chapter 17, under the auspices of Mr. Campbell, deals to the government's friends continued at NWTC and assets hidden in private corporations to disguise their true value from the public. The appointment of Mr. Campbell, like Mr. Williams, was to ensure the continued control of government without public embarrassment. Both of these appointments were for optical purity and not for their banking acumen. The Government wanted to give the people of Alberta the impression that the Board was going to be powerful and would rectify the financial problems and inappropriate loans portfolio, an illusion for public consumption. They have been sadly and grossly misled to think that Mr. Williams will inspire a new era at the Alberta Treasury Branches.

Mr. Williams has already shown his true colours by beginning to protect his political friends. Mr. Williams made statements to the press in the fall of 1996, shortly after the appointment of the new Superintendent. He showed that he was understating the magnitude of the problem through his own wilful blindness. During the September 27, 1996, Edmonton A.M. radio program, he told Kathy Daley, the CBC interviewer, that the new Chief Inspector of the Alberta Treasury Branches, one Andrew Wingate, was investigating the irregularities and improprieties at ATB. Of course, what the public was not told was that Mr. Wingate was also the Acting Auditor General before Peter Valentine. How is it then that these irregularities came as a revelation to Mr. Wingate? What was it that Mr. Wingate saw in his role as Chief Inspector that he somehow could not see as the Acting Auditor General when he signed off on the Annual Report of the Alberta Treasury Branches? Could he do this in good conscience? The answer is, of course, he could not. Here another Government bureaucrat has been caught by an embarrassing Catch-22. If Mr. Wingate was aware of the problems, then he was guilty of aiding and abetting the unethical conduct and corruption by not calling it into question. If he was not aware of it, then he was incompetent. He should have resigned or been terminated, not appointed as Chief Inspector of the Alberta Treasury Branches.

Mr. Williams on September 28, 1996, told an Edmonton newspaper that Mr. Wingate could "not find even a suggestion that any lending decisions were made on political implications or perceptions of staff." That statement alone should call into question Mr. Wingate's investigative abilities or his memory. On June 14, 1996, in The Edmonton Sun he said, "They want us to meet their social and political purposes."[13] As Ben Jonson said, "I have betrayed myself with my own tongue. The case is altered." Mr. Williams in those few words, was at his dissembling best. Mr. Williams was a wise government Chairman of the Board of the ATB. Even at a mere mention of any impropriety involving either the Alberta Treasury Branches or the Government, he has shown his willingness to sacrifice his own integrity.

In the September 28 article, Mr. Williams says that the Alberta Treasury Branches has guaranteed payment of loans worth more than 25 million dollars despite the 8 million dollar loss on West Edmonton Mall two years ago. This displays a stunning naiveté on Mr. Williams' part, not to mention just plain bad math. Considering the facts in Phase III, the ATB were on the hook for the full amount of the loan and as far as to what he says are projected losses, Mr. Williams is way off. Statements like these reaffirm the position that Mr. Williams is not qualified to be Chairman of the Board of the Alberta Treasury Branches. The financial statements clearly show a massive increase in loan guarantees. He admitted that the ATB will not be privatized soon

---

[13] The Edmonton Sun. "Marshall Raises the Stakes." Friday, June 14, 1996.

because "...it simply isn't healthy enough."[14] How's that for an understatement?

I had the distinct pleasure of speaking with Mr. Williams when I called him on Friday, October 11. Jack Shields, former Conservative MP and connected to the Tory insiders, had called me at 8:00 p.m. the previous evening insisting that I had not exhausted all the avenues of resolutions and I should call the Chairman of the Board, Mr. Williams. I told him I did not see the point in such a call. Mr. Shields continued to urge me to do so since he related that he had talked with Mr. Elzinga who informed him that going to the Chairman was a way of resolving the issue. There was never any malice on Mr. Shields' part and his intentions were honourable. I agreed to call Marshall Williams and in my short conversation with him he informed me he was well aware of my situation and saw no point in discussing it "at this time." In addition to asking the questions contained in this chapter, I sent Mr. Williams a time line of the events that happened on my file so he could not make any naive statements. I understand that Mr. Williams will support a public inquiry on the unethical conduct at the Alberta Treasury Branches, but only if the tentative members of such an inquiry include our old friends Kenny the "K" Kowalski, "Pavement" Peter Trynchy, friend of Multi Corp, Rod Love, and the Chairman, the ubiquitous Peter Elzinga. They are finally taking this thing seriously!

---

[14] The Globe and Mail. "Paul Haggis Takes on the ATB." December 9, 1996. (Business West column - Mathew Ingram.)

Dismayed after my conversation with Mr. Williams, I wrote him a letter informing him that I had been prompted into calling him. I decided to call Mr. Elzinga myself to straighten things out. I asked Mr. Elzinga why he would prompt Mr. Shields to get me to call Mr. Williams who was unprepared to deal with the resolution of the situation. Mr. Elzinga side-stepped the issue and asked if I would send him a letter stating what had happened. I sent him the same timeline I had sent Mr. Williams. Mr. Elzinga informed me that he would get back to me in a couple of days. He phoned me back November 1, 1996, and told me he was unable to sit down and talk "eyeball to eyeball," as he put it, with anyone to discuss the matter. I informed him that I felt I was getting the run-around and I was not going to let anyone else stall me any longer. Two weeks later, Mr. Elzinga did have an initial meeting with Mr. Henning which I relate in the last chapter.

Since September 16, 1996, the Alberta Treasury Branches has had Mr. Paul Haggis as its new Superintendent. In the title of this book, I refer to "Prairie Boys", those home-grown individuals who have always run the ATB. Mr. Haggis, however, is an ersatz Prairie Boy in that he used to head the Metropolitan Trust Company in Edmonton. The Government has it both ways with the choice of Mr. Haggis. While not a true Prairie Boy, he has spent a substantial amount of time in the Edmonton area and is a known quantity. He is well-connected with some high profile members of the Progressive Conservative Party of Alberta, and as you will see, a perfect choice all around for a Government doing damage control. With all humility, I would like to think that the title of my book had something to do with the choice.

Mr. Haggis has already shown himself to be part of the culture of wilful blindness. First, he has sent some of the most politically-sensitive files to Calgary under the auspices of Don Roberts, General Manager of Credit in the Calgary General Office and now the head of one of Mr. Haggis' two credit teams, one for Edmonton, one for Calgary. Mr. Roberts gained his experience at the branches noted for the special or designated credits. Some of these files are the Pocklington connection, West Edmonton Mall, Princeton Developments and the Lauring Group. Mr. Roberts is a part of the old culture. He was Mr. Wally Peters' protegé. (You will, of course, remember Mr. Peters who lent his daughter 100 thousand dollars through a customer with an ATB guarantee and should have been criminally exposed by the Auditor General.) Mr. Roberts is no angel. If Mr. Haggis investigated how Mr. Roberts' landscaped and renovated his home, he would know that Mr. Roberts was the wrong choice, having lost his ethical virginity a long time ago.

Mr. Haggis' new credit teams, in short, have players from the old roster who are already burdened by the baggage of corruption. Other members include Mike Dombrova, Stu Laird, Dana Wanamaker, Gary Comber, and Brent Twoniak. All have had experience with branches that handle special credits. Ninety percent of Mr. Haggis' new credit team has been immersed in the old culture at the Alberta Treasury Branches. It's quite possible they may be investigating loans that they helped prepare or prepared. If these individuals did not recognize impropriety at the time, what makes Mr. Haggis think they will recognize it in the future? Despite my expectations and the expectations of others that Mr. Haggis was coming in as a white knight to drive out the scourge of corruption from the Alberta Treasury Branches, his armour and his actions are tarnished, and he has now become part of the cover up. In the land of wilful blindness, the one-eyed man is King. It is doubtful whether Mr. Haggis' new credit team will recover their lost vision unless Mr. Haggis, like Billy Sunday, has the power to heal.

To reinforce the claims in this last paragraph, the ATB has just authored a new Code of Conduct and Ethics dated December 20, 1996. The old document was a few pages, whereas the new Code of Ethics is nearly fifty pages if you include the message from the Chief Executive Officer. The employees were required to take a course pertaining to the new Code. After the course was complete, the employees were polled on their reaction to the new set of guidelines. Eighty percent of the Calgary attendees said it was the same old thing while their counterparts in Edmonton were a bit more charitable. In Edmonton, fifty percent believed nothing had changed.

This comedy of errors gets even more interesting. The individual in charge of distributing and implementing Mr. Haggis' new Code of Conduct and Ethics is none other than Mr. Max Callaghan, Esq., more familiarly known as "Easy Max." He got the name "Easy Max" for his liberal lending practices while deputy manager at Edmonton Main branch. It is a well known fact that Mr. Callaghan was Mr. Leahy's closest colleague. The first time I met Mr. Leahy and Mr. Callaghan was at an Edmonton Oiler's hockey game. Mr. Callaghan was famous for riding on Mr. Leahy's coattails up the ATB corporate ladder. When Mr. Leahy became Acting Superintendent, he immediately promoted Mr. Callaghan to Vice-Superintendent in Administration. Many believe Mr. Callaghan was over-employed, but more importantly, he was well aware of Mr. Leahy's history of unconscionable conduct and condoned it. I don't know, but he sounds like the perfect candidate to administer and to monitor ATB's ethical practices!

Mr. Haggis' methodology for implementing the new Code of Conduct and Ethics issued in December 1996 has already failed the smell test for credibility within the ATB. The ATB employees are well aware of Mr. Callaghan's baggage, further discrediting the new Code of Ethics. Ethics after the fact are not ethics; they are cosmetics, and Mr. Haggis has just confirmed the statement by enlisting the assistance of Mr. Callaghan. This assistance turned out to be short-lived. Within a month (at the end of January), Mr. Callaghan had also found the exit door at ATB. He was allowed to retire rather than be terminated another soft landing for a faithful friend. Curiously, this was shortly after I had asked several questions about the new Code of Conduct and Ethics and who was administering it. Once again, Mr. Haggis turned to the cosmetic solution. Perhaps the Code of Ethics would have had more credibility had it been implemented after Mr. Callaghan's departure.

Another example of Mr. Haggis having acquired the culture of willful blindness is the deal involving the West Edmonton Mall refinancing. The old corporation which owned West Edmonton Mall, formerly known as the Triple Five Corporation, was being petitioned into bankruptcy by Corey Developments, Inc. The petition date was October 1, 1996. On that day, both sides, the plaintiff as well as the defendant, agreed to adjourn the matter as negotiations had been initiated. I know--I was in the Courtroom that day. I confirmed that a lawyer, John Karvellas, and Vice Superintendent of ATB, Russ Douglas, had met with the creditor a short time before the petition offering to settle the matter and to stop the petition. This would once again buy their friends, the Ghermezians, some additional time. As of the writing of this book, the petition date has now been delayed over six months.

Let's look at the two gentlemen Mr. Haggis sent to the meeting. John Karvellas was the director and one of the shareholders of the North West Trust, a corporation set up to camouflage the non-performing assets of NWTC from public scrutiny. Cruikshank Karvellas, his firm, has been hiding Alberta Treasury Branch assets for years. Mr. Douglas, who arranged for loans for his girlfriend at the ATB Strathcona Branch, did not shy away from his responsibility in this case when she eventually declared bankruptcy. As court documents show, he was kind enough to pay for the Trustee. He eventually married her after she resolved her credit problems.

I confirmed that Mr. Douglas has been given a six-month leave of absence. Mr. Haggis told Mr. Douglas that if he kept his mouth shut about the irregularities and improprieties in the ATB loan portfolio, he would consider approving his pension after the six-month period. Conveniently, the six-month probation period takes us past the next provincial election. If Mr. Haggis was truly independent, the timing with respect to the provincial election would be irrelevant. I would say that Mr. Haggis sent the right men for the job.

The fact that Mr. Douglas has been pushed out of the job does not negate the fact that Mr. Haggis directed him to stall the creditors from petition, the old West Edmonton Mall corporation, into bankruptcy. Mr. Haggis had already assumed his role as the Superintendent of the Alberta Treasury Branches on September 16, before the petition date. The matter was adjourned until December 16. Another adjournment until the new year was consented to by both sides, and negotiations are still in progress as of this writing.

The important issue here is why would the Alberta Treasury Branches offer to purchase the creditor's position for a corporation that has no assets and of no benefit to the ATB? Quite simply, a petition in bankruptcy would confirm the Alberta Treasury Branches and the Government were a part of the arrangement that allowed the Ghermezian family to repurchase the West Edmonton Mall through a fraudulent conveyance in order to avoid creditors.

A petition into bankruptcy and a forensic audit would reveal that they were accessories. The Alberta Treasury Branches' willingness to purchase the creditor's position is an admission of guilt. If the new Superintendent were truly independent and not part of these fraudulent activities, he would have called for a full criminal investigation. Mr. Haggis has become an accomplice.

In the new ATB Code of Conduct and Ethics, one of the directives regarding the reporting of ethical concerns reads:

> that senior personnel who are approached by staff with regard to ethical concerns or inquiries are required to initiate action relative to the concern or inquiry within twenty-four hours and ensure that the matter proceeds to finalization in a reasonable manner; those failing to do so will be subject to disciplinary action.

I wonder what type of disciplinary action Mr. Haggis suffered at his own hands. Mr. Haggis' brilliant new Code also deals with the effect of breach. "A potential breach of honesty or trustworthiness not only negatively impacts your ability to perform your duties, it may also cause other employees or members of the public to question your ability to satisfactorily carry out your duties." Guess what, Mr. Haggis, I'm questioning!

I understand that Mr. Haggis' defense against him being influenced by the government is that he has a five-year contract that grants him his independence. This does not eliminate the chain of command. Upon taking the position of Superintendent, Mr. Haggis was well aware that he reported to the Provincial

Treasurer under the Public Service Act. What makes Mr. Haggis think he can avoid taking direction from his boss?

Another indication that Mr. Haggis has become part of the old culture is the group of so-called "CK Holdings" companies. These corporations were set up by the law firm of Cruikshank Karvellas (hence CK) to hide Alberta Treasury Branches' assets from the prying eyes of the public, while protecting the balance sheet of the ATB. Recently, the Links Clinic was transferred into one of these CK companies (CK 17, I believe.) under the auspices of Mr. Haggis. (There are well over 20 of these companies.) It looks like the same old stories by the same old Tories. Some ATB officials have told me this was a way to get a better price for the real estate. What a joke! Realtors know the story behind the property and this transference is not normal banking practice. The people may have changed, but their modus operandi is exactly the same.

I have met Mr. Haggis, and he struck me as a fairly decent guy, but his actions concerning Mr. Briscoe make me question that. (He also neglected to thank me for creating the opening for his new job. That's gratitude for you!) The ex-Executive Manager of Public Affairs showed up for work one morning recently only to find someone else sitting behind his desk. Mr. Briscoe lied to me on a few occasions and while he should be terminated, surely someone should have had enough class to tell him directly. Mr. Briscoe has accepted the same fate as his former colleagues.

Mr. Haggis has created new regions within the Alberta Treasury Branches which he refers to as his new organization. The problem being his new vice presidents in these regions are somewhat suspect. The first individual I will deal with is Jay Hamblin who has been promoted as one of Mr. Haggis' new vice presidents. In reflection, this is not a wise choice for Mr. Haggis. Mr. Hamblin has had lengthy stints at many of the most corrupt branches in the system: Edmonton Main, Edmonton Strathcona and First Edmonton Place. At these branches Mr. Hamblin is in charge of some of the most politically sensitive files such as the Brick Warehouse, the Pocklington loans, Whitehall Square, and the Credit Union Equalization Fund (a 100 million dollar guarantee that the ATB provided in order to ensure confidence among the customers of the credit unions). Mr. Hamblin is known as a "fixer" and puts patches on loans that won't float anymore, never really dealing with the problem, but merely keeping the facts buried.

Another new regional vice president is Mike Ryan. Mr. Ryan learned his banking trade at First Edmonton Place under the infamous Larry Leroux. Mr. Ryan has handled his share of politically sensitive loans and special credits. An example of this would be Milcorp Industries whose principles had very close ties to the Progressive Conservatives Party and major contributors to the PC Alberta Fund. This file had a special note attached to it that no actions could be taken against Milcorp without the knowledge of the Vice Superintendent, Les Bellan. It was sent to Mr. Ryan's branch for that very reason. Mr. Ryan was also an entrepreneur having businesses on the side that directly competed with his customers and well as the ATB. I had written several letters about Mr. Ryan's sundry activities and Mr. Ryan had confessed to several people that he felt his days were numbered at the Alberta Treasury Branches. Instead of being fired as even Mr. Ryan believed he deserved, he has been promoted. Mr. Haggis' promise to clean up the Alberta Treasury Branches is as cosmetic as his Code of Ethics. Mr. Haggis changes their titles but keeps the same individuals creating the illusion of reorganization for political and public consumption.

Mr. Haggis makes a point of spouting off that he is totally independent yet the firm hired to review all loans over 1 million dollars by the ATB is none other than the Citibank Group, conveniently, Mr. Haggis' former employers. It appears that Mr. Independence is depending on some very old friends to review the ATB loan portfolio. It's probably not relevant.

The arrival of Mr. Haggis as the Superintendent of ATB reminds me of my grade school teacher who gave everyone an A at the beginning of the school year with the warning that it was now our job to maintain the grade. Mr. Haggis started his term with an A as well. but I fear he has not applied himself and has slipped to a C, or perhaps even D, in effort and an F in independence. He will need to work much harder and stop talking (to the government).

In November 1996 for an entire weekend, Mr. Haggis held meetings with all ATB managers. In those meetings, he informed them that the Alberta Treasury Branches were moving towards making the ATB a Crown Corporation. This is an admission by

Mr. Haggis that under the current Public Service Act, the ATB is not independent. By that admission, he confirmed that the new Chairman and Board of Directors were for optical purity and nothing more.

The political aspect has always been part of the Alberta Treasury Branches operation. Ask some of its employees. They will tell you that branches are built in some towns, not because they are needed, but because the local MLA is running for re-election. Or, how a cabinet minister will make a phone call to a branch loans officer requesting that they talk to one of the members of the constituency about a loan. If the new management wanted to get to the truth, an offer of immunity or partial immunity from prosecution to employees and ex-employees would find individuals yapping like sled dogs. This in turn will reveal who was really behind these unconscionable actions.

The ATB intends to write off over 300 million dollars in loans in the next financial statement, and this figure could rise to as much as half a billion dollars. Bear in mind that a write-off and a loss are not the same thing. The new Superintendent will make sure that any cancerous loans will be written off immediately to ensure that these can be blamed on his predecessors for two reasons. First, Mr. Haggis, for example, will write a loan down to ten cents on the dollar yet this loan is probably worth two to three times that. The reason is that two to three years hence Mr. Haggis can move the excess funds back into profits just in time for the next provincial election while collecting a personal bonus for himself based on ATB's profitable performance. The second reason is that Mr. Haggis ensures ATB's future profitability without really earning it.

Mr. Haggis will probably go overboard as he will receive no accolades for any borderline loans that may come back to haunt him in the future. Because of the financial nightmare that he is dealing with, his ruthlessness is unlikely to be checked. Of course, this ruthlessness will be directed at relatively small loans, as the big problems such as West Edmonton Mall and Peter Pocklington's loans will spill too much political blood.

The interesting part is the timing. The Alberta Treasury Branches' year end is March 31, but the actual financial statements will not be available until June 1997. The news of the financial disasters should not arrive before the spring 1997 election expected to be called by the Government. This will be done to avoid any pre-election embarrassment, plus it will give Mr. Haggis and the Government four years to erase it from the minds of Albertans.

The process that sought out Board members was a very delicate one. Many bankers and ex-bankers who applied to be Board Members were turned down and rejected in favour of individuals who had no banking experience. Many prominent Albertans who were offered the positions were prepared to become Board Members on a condition that the ATB financial statements be done externally by an independent accounting firm. Their request was denied so they rejected the offer. The shoddy process of choosing the Board and the reluctance of the Government to relinquish control points to their involvement in the misappropriation of loans at ATB. The greatest gesture that Mr. Haggis and the Board could take to ensure Albertans that indeed a new regime was in place would be order external and quarterly audits of the financial statements. By not doing so proves that the ATB could not withstand an outside audit and the resulting political fall-out.

The Board, the Superintendent and the Chairman of the Board will have a great deal of explaining to do by not calling for a criminal investigation. By not saying anything, they condone what has taken place. If things do come to the surface, and these individuals say they did not know, they are admitting incompetence, rendering themselves ineffectual. If they did know, then they have become party to the cover up. This so-called near bank, the ATB, has the potential to undermine the integrity of the entire Canadian banking system.

CHAPTER 23
HE KEPT HIS WORD

"The probability that we may fail in the struggle ought not to deter us from the cause we believe to be just."

- Abraham Lincoln

A positive influence such as listening to a well-played symphony by Beethoven or Mozart has an uplifting, sustaining effect. In contrast, a negative influence such as corruption can eat away internally at an organization like the ATB. It becomes self-destructive so that trust and morale become early casualties. The ATB has been in a terminal phase if the reports on staff morale are accurate. Many believe that after the next provincial election the government could sell the ATB totally to the Canadian Western Bank based on a full government guarantee, of course. Or, the commercial portfolio could be sold so the ATB exists similar to a credit union or perhaps become part of a credit union.

For many reasons, I know that some of my prose in the previous pages has dripped with sarcasm, irony, and some self-deprecating humour. First, it has been necessary to sustain myself through some trying times as a recovering entrepreneur. In yet another paraphrase of a political leader, only when you have been in the deepest valley can you appreciate being on the highest mountain. Second, many of the players in this outlandish episode were really like the Keystone Cops. I want to assure readers that I have not lost sight of the gravity of these issues.

In a way, the culture of corruption at the Alberta Treasury Branches specifically, but to some degree at the Government as well, can be likened to a classic biology experiment. In the experiment, one gradually raises the temperature of a container of water with a frog immersed in it. At first, the frog's system adjusts to the temperature change. As the temperature climbs, however, rather than escape the water, the frog keeps trying to adapt until it finally self-destructs. The ATB adapted itself to increasingly corrupt practices of its senior management and employees until it could no longer contain or sustain it. The ATB is nearing the self-destruction phase.

We in Alberta need to discern the truly important from the innocuous. A sound health care system and sound financial statements are not the same thing. As a person who is fiscally conservative analyzing the Progressive Conservatives if the PCs had run a better ship when it came to loan guarantees and the Alberta Treasury Branches, perhaps the health care system would not be suffering the consequences it has today.

The average Albertan does not have enough time in the day to consider the conduct of their government or how it affects their lives. As one of my associates has pointed out, I looked down and beaten. Let me assure you, however, that the battle certainly is not over. It may appear that I am a lion caught in a net, but I can also assure you I remain a lion. I did not choose this fight. If it could have been resolved any other way, I would have preferred it. I was continually thwarted in my attempts to seek a resolution while the

ATB and the government continued to do damage control. In many ways, this has become one of the most unproductive periods in my life. Van Gogh cut off his ear to be heard. I hoped I would not have to be that drastic.

The absolute lesson that I have learned here is that a small dispute can turn into a mammoth one and the more one struggles against the quagmire, the deeper one sinks into it. I made every effort possible to try to resolve this in a business-like manner, because it doesn't matter whether you win or lose at the Courthouse. As soon as you walk through the doors, you've lost and it becomes an unproductive process for all parties. The Government of Alberta may benefit from a study of Confucianism. Many people are probably not aware that Confucius' philosophy is based on human morality and on the principle of a government that served its people and government by moral example. A secular philosopher, Confucius, was interested in only human and political morality and the conduct of those individuals. It was his belief that government exists for the well-being and enhancement of the people and not vice-versa. He continually stressed that a leader must govern by a predominantly moral example. The Confucian ideals remain entrenched for more than 2000 years for the following reasons: Confucius' own sincerity and integrity remain unquestionable. Next, he was moderate in his thinking, and his philosophy applied to real world situations, not theoretical constructs. Codes of personal behaviour were defined within reasonable limits; he did not demand sainthood of others when all he asked was honour.

I do not want the people of Alberta to think that I want Mr. Klein and his government to be saintly; but I do believe it is their fundamental obligation to be honourable with their public trust. In order to show my goodwill, I wrote the following letter to Premier Ralph Klein, and I believed it was an olive branch offered in an effort to reach a solution and uncover the truth.

August 20, 1996

Dear Mr. Klein:

It seems that my letters have caused a certain degree of consternation at the Legislature Building. I must assure you that the whole point of my labours is to get to the bottom of the rampant corruption throughout the Alberta Treasury Branches and the Government of Alberta, which I was swept up in for daring to question its unethical operation. By exposing this corruption, my abuse at the hands of the legal, political, and banking systems in this province will also be highlighted. I am fully prepared to return to the legal arena to continue my fight against the Alberta Treasury Branches.

I was petitioned into bankruptcy by the Alberta Treasury Branches to take away my rights to due process and to also eliminate my lawsuits against ATB by subsequently asking for security for costs. If you believe in the legal concept of "clean hands", the Alberta Treasury Branches should not have indulged in impropriety in relation to the transactions on which they sought relief. Obviously, they could not risk going before the Courts violating this legal principle in spades. Taking away my rights to due process before the law was much more expedient without the necessity of answering inconvenient questions. They ensured that I had no resources to battle them fully in the Courts. The ATB did this knowingly and maliciously, totally outside the bounds of what one would consider fair treatment in the adversarial system. This is why I have battled so strenuously and relentlessly. The Alberta Treasury Branches, with their monetary influence over the financial landscape of this province cannot be allowed the means to get away with this while their own misdeeds and, in fact, criminal actions are swept under the bureaucratic carpet. If the heavy-handed tactics are further pursued, they will surely be exposed.

I will not be made into the Alberta Treasury Branches' whipping boy while government friends are bailed out of and propped up in serious financial boondoggles. Quite frankly, because of their actions, the freedom of speech is all I had left and therefore the need to write my book, Banksters and Prairie Boys. This stated, however let me make the following proposal as a demonstration of my true intent and my good faith in this matter.

My proposal is simply this. If you agree to have the Attorney General and the Auditor General from another province properly and fully investigate the conduct of the Alberta Treasury Branches and the Government of Alberta I shall agree, in return, to abandon the publishing of my book. I shall also agree to abide by whatever the findings of such a full criminal investigation uncover about the Alberta Treasury Branches and the Alberta Government. In addition I want a full investigation of my file and the abuse I have been subject to for exposing the corruption at the ATB. If my accusations are found to be groundless, so be it. This, in turn, I believe will validate my lawsuits. If I do not hear from you forthwith, then I shall presume that you have chosen not to accept my offer. However, please be aware that until such time as I do hear from you, I shall continue writing my letters seeking validation of the information that my research for my book Banksters and Prairie Boys has uncovered. I look forward to receiving your decision and response as soon as possible.

MONIER M. RAHALL

cc: **Honourable James Dinning** Peter Valentine
Provincial Treasurer Auditor General
Honourable Brian Evans **Jack Briscoe**
Attorney General Alberta Treasury Branches

This letter was also sent at a later date to Mr. Paul Haggis, the new Superintendent of the Alberta Treasury Branches, and to Mr. Marshall Williams, the Chairman of the Board. That the Premier did not grasp the olive branch only validates the issues raised in this book. If he had had the will to resolve this properly, he should have accepted my offer. Perhaps what I hadn't uncovered was far worse than what I did uncover. Ralph Klein's slogan in the recent election campaign was "He kept his Word." The book you are now holding in your hands is proof that I kept mine.

Now I will deal with the legal concept known as "clean hands." If the Alberta Treasury Branches had clean hands, then my lawsuits against them would have been frivolous and vexatious. The reason they petitioned me was that by asking for security for costs for my lawsuits, they ensured that my resources to fight those lawsuits were non-existant. In a court of conscience, if the issue was allowed to go to trial, the court would have seen that their hands were not clean; the risk was too great and they sought ways to deliberately undermine my rights.

341

The most important part of my letter to Mr. Klein was my offer not to publish the book with one simple condition: That self-investigation is improper. Like a children's game, it appears that merely stating something as fact renders it so, without the need for any independent examination. If the Premier and his Cabinet have clean hands and are innocent of corruption, they should have welcomed an Attorney General or Auditor General from another province to clear the air once and for all. That was the only condition that I asked for. Instead, they opted for a game of Russian roulette, spinning the chamber of strategies with the new Board of Directors and Chairman. Logic must now dictate their actions. I must point out once again that I do not have the resources as would be available to the Attorney General to investigate these and other matters.

While this book does expose corruption, it is quite obviously only the tip of the iceberg. In essence, the investigation by an Attorney General from another Province will be able to uncover a far worse scenario than my story describes here. The greatest travesty of all is that while the Klein Government is well aware of this book, it has been confirmed that in a meeting on November 15, 1996, between Roy Henning and Mr. Elzinga in the home of Jack Shields, their plan is to call a public inquiry as a remedy to the publication. It was a last ditch attempt to resolve the situation. One of the terms the participants in the negotiations used was that the Government was not going to resolve the outstanding issues, and that if I were going to print this book, then I had better take my best shot. It is my opinion that what you will see in response to the publication will be a well-planned public relations exercise in damage control that will attempt to discredit me by whatever means possible, including moral and ethical grounds

The consummate chess player never makes the move his opponent expects him to make. This is true of Mr. Klein and his government. I had hoped to have this book completed before the end of the provincial election. Unfortunately, the Progressive Conservatives realized that if they called the election early, they would be able to whitewash several of their problems over the next four years. The fact that my book was soon to be completed, the fact that the former Triple Five Corporation was to be petitioned into bankruptcy March 19, 1997, that the ATB's year end is March 31, plus several other problems that could surface over the next few months led Mr. Klein's government to call the earliest spring election in Alberta's history. Mr. Dinning's mini-budget was to be presented on February 20, but in their haste, the PCs instead presented it on February 11. I caution voters that there are many decent and ethical people within the Conservative and Liberal Parties. Unfortunately, they are not in the leadership of those parties.

I admit to making mistakes, and I have already been subject to a lengthy character assassination by many of the individuals involved. Many already consider me a marked man. Perhaps suffering is a necessary part of redemption. This present narrative, unlike the Horatio Alger stories, has no happy, formulaic ending.

What might become the greatest tragedy here is a campaign to discredit me in an effort to disguise the truth.

Parts of this book may seem harsh, but to have written it any other way would have sacrificed my convictions on the entire subject. In fact, the scenario was posed to me that if I would soft-pedal the part of the government, the new Board of Directors, the new Chairman, and the new Superintendent, a resolution may be more easily arrived at. The quest for affection is unlikely to reveal the truth. Not only did I not trust them but, in my opinion, the information was too powerful to bury. In the alternative, maybe they thought I was bluffing; then they are incompetent. Anyone who seeks to change or expose corruption must realize that he will alienate those who profit from the status quo. The morals of individuals become blurred and hazy when money is involved. In the words of Franklin Roosevelt, "Judge me by the enemies I've made." I have done all I can do with the resources available to me. If Albertans decide that this is not important and are willing to accept a public inquiry, it is beyond my control. A public inquiry is nothing more than a government controlled investigation, an improper course in this case considering the far-reaching ramifications within the ATB and the government itself. Many years ago I was watching a documentary on India and saw how the Swamis threw a rope in the air and as it fell, they gave the illusion that they were climbing the rope. A public inquiry is just such an illusion. The depth of the corruption can only be addressed through a criminal investigation by the Attorney General of another province or the Solicitor General of Canada. Self investigation, never seen as proper, will reflect poorly on our Alberta society as a whole. Eventually, all of us must face and live with the truth about ourselves.

—A—

—B—

—C—

Coopers & Lybrand, 25, 28, 30, 31, 32, 33, 34, 35, 36, 37, 38, 39, 40, 42, 51, 52, 57, 62, 63, 93, 101, 153, 220, 223, 237, 248, 259, 262
Crozier, Mike 146
CWB, 143

—D—

Dallas Stars, 216, 217, 218
Darrow, Clarence, 107
Dickie, Bill 279
Dinning, James (Jim), 133, 140, 141, 164, 165, 173, 179, 206, 207, 218, 228, 237, 238, 252, 262, 263, 265, 268, 273, 281, 295, 300, 301, 315, 318, 341
Diogenes, 83
Disney Corporation, 197
Dollar Rent-A-Car, 40, 43, 51, 52, 53, 63, 81, 89, 91
Dombrova, Mike, 324
Ducky's, 45
Dumont, Maurice, 91
Dunne, Hugh, 306

—E—

Edwards, Richard, 99, 100
Elzinga, Peter, 157, 175, 180, 209, 210, 306, 308, 322, 323, 342
Ericksen Nissan, 43
Evans, 238, 269, 271, 272, 281, 283

—F—

Fidelity Trust, 132, 133, 134
Fidelity Trustco, 132
First Boston, 164, 167, 169
Forest, Ric, 262, 263
Fossen, M. D., 42, 88, 93
Fraser, Keith, 188, 189, 191

—G—

Gainers, 30, 137, 138, 143, 174, 205
Galileo, 264
Gentra, 160, 162, 165, 167, 169, 170, 172, 180, 183, 184, 186, 190, 191, 196, 211
Gepetto, 174
Getty, Donald, 22, 137, 147, 150, 151, 207, 263, 285, 294
Ghermezian Family, 85, 147, 158, 176, 179, 181, 182, 183, 186, 258, 328
Ghermezians, 147, 158, 159, 161, 164, 166, 169, 172, 176, 179, 180, 181, 184, 185, 187, 188, 192, 194, 197, 327
Ghermezian, Eskandar, 158
Ghermezian, Nadar, 158, 168, 169, 180, 188, 194
Goebel, Doug, 36, 41, 42, 46, 51, 52, 53, 56, 57, 62, 160, 169, 174

Green, Norm, 216
Green, Robert, 221
Gronberg, Rory, 62
Gulliver's Travels, 81
Gunderson, Mark, 46, 47, 48, 49, 50, 51, 52, 54, 57, 58, 65, 147, 160, 174, 215

—H—

Haggis, Paul, 89, 224, 239, 244, 252, 315, 322, 323, 324, 325, 326, 327, 328, 329, 330,
    331, 332, 333, 334, 335
Hamblin, Jay, 331
Henning, Roy, 34, 35, 56, 57, 58, 67, 70, 86, 87, 88, 96
Hill, Janice, 48
Hilton, Conrad, 205
Hogan's Heroes, 96
Horne, Dennis, 260
Howell, Barbara, 193
Hurlburt, Katherine, 101

—I—

—J—

Johnston, Dick, 138, 315
Jones, Brian, 51, 217
Jonson, Ben, 321
Joudrie, Dorothy, 83

—K—

Karvellas, Cruikshank, 32, 327
Karvellas, John, 327
Kennedy, Blaine, 40, 41, 51, 52, 53, 56, 62
Kenny, William (Bill), 70, 71, 100, 101, 106, 143, 168, 174, 176, 178, 182, 195, 219, 220,
    221, 307, 309, 318, 319, 320, 321, 322, 323
Keystone Cops, 336
Kipnes, Irving, 202, 203, 204
Klaray, Thomas, 38, 39
Klein, Premier Ralph, 20, 21, 22, 23, 24, 164, 165, 166, 167, 168, 169, 170, 171, 173, 224,
    226, 228, 238, 239, 267, 269, 270, 276, 277, 278, 279, 280, 282, 283, 284, 285, 286,
    287, 288, 292, 293, 294, 295, 296, 297, 298, 299, 302, 304, 305, 306, 307, 308
Kowalski, Ken, 168, 170, 171, 172, 173, 180, 209, 210, 306, 307, 308, 309
Kunciak, Ron, 47, 48

—L—

—M—

—N—

Novatel, 140
NWTC, 202, 203, 207, 255, 256, 257, 258, 259, 260, 261, 319, 327

—O—

Oilers, The Edmonton, 131, 134, 135, 136, 153, 241, 242
Oswald, Lee Harvey, 172

—P—

Partow Park Holdings, 182, 220
Peacock, Fred, 254
Peat, Jack, 236, 261
Penmore Investments, 46, 47, 48, 49, 50
People's Trust, 47
Percy, Mike, 300, 301, 302
Perkins, Geoff, 212, 236
Peters, Wally, 217, 249, 250, 253, 324
Peterson, Wayne, 217, 249, 253
Pinocchio, 174
Piquette, Maurice, 42
Pitcher, Detective Terry, 272, 273, 274
Pocklington, Peter, 30, 131, 132, 133, 134, 135, 136, 137, 138, 140, 142, 143, 205, 241
Progressive Conservative Party, 22, 59, 133, 175, 254, 293
Proppe, Eric, 250

—R—

R&S Autobody, 40, 52
Rahall, Monier, 85, 86, 87, 88, 90, 93, 101, 103, 104, 105, 111, 113, 121, 123, 127, 228,
    233, 239, 244, 245, 265, 267, 273, 276, 281, 286, 287, 292, 295, 310, 341
Ramsey, Gil, 62
Rasmussen, G., 214, 215
Rasputin, x
Readman, Darcy, 229
Revenue Canada, 37, 38, 185
Reynolds, Ian, 112
Reynolds Mirth, 178, 195, 220
Roberts, Don, 324
Rolingher, Sol, 230
Rollingher, Larry, 66, 67, 202, 203, 204, 206, 206, 207, 208, 230
Roosevelt, President Franklin, 344
Royal Bank, 44, 53, 178, 220, 318
Royal Trust, 53, 59, 170
Russell, Charles, 32, 34, 36, 52, 63, 91, 92, 93, 101
Ryckman, Larry, 153, 154, 155, 156, 157, 207, 248

—S—

—T—

—U—

—V—

—W—

—Y—

—Z—